YOUR GUIDE
TO
GREAT
SEX

YOUR GUIDE
TO
GREAT
SEX

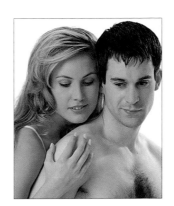

Created and produced by
CARROLL & BROWN LIMITED
20 Lonsdale Road
London NW6 6RD

Book club edition published for Doubleday Direct, Inc.,
Garden City, New York

ISBN 0-7394-0636-1

Reproduced by Colourscan, Singapore
Printed by Tien Wah Press, Singapore

Foreword

Your Guide to Great Sex deals simply and frankly with the day-to-day questions, problems and mysteries surrounding our sexuality, sexual health and relationships.

The need for clear and practical information about sex is great in today's society—a time when men and women are interested in getting the most out of their sex lives in terms of fulfillment and freedom of expression, while taking on board the serious safety and health implications of a sexually active existence.

A knowledge of the sexual body, the principles of sexual attraction and the best sexual techniques empowers us as lovers, allowing us to please our partners and enjoy sex to the full ourselves. Your Guide to Great Sex answers all our questions about finding a sexual partner and making sex a bonding and fulfilling experience, providing a fascinating overview of the sexual being.

Our changing bodies and changing needs demand an ability to adapt our sex lives as our lives progress and for this we need to be aware. Your Guide to Great Sex provides us with the information and advice we need to ensure that our sex lives are always exciting, unpredictable and fulfilling.

Practicing safe sex is more than just contraception. Every aspect of sexual health is considered lucidly and comprehensively. Sexual health worries, such as prostate or testicular cancer, cervical or ovarian cancer are discussed in a reassuring and all-encompassing manner and there is up-to-date, informative discussion about symptoms and signs, as well as available tests and treatments.

Your Guide to Great Sex contains a wealth of carefully illustrated, authoritative information, written to be comprehensive and accessible. The aim of the book is to provide us with the knowledge and confidence we need to make sure that our sex lives are the best they can be, and the safest.

Contents

Introduction 8

Sexual Attraction 11

Theories of Attraction 12

The Language of Attraction 39

The Physiology of Attraction 43

Finding a Partner 46

Homosexual Love 49

The Physical Expression of Love 33

Sex and Gender 34

Masturbation 38

Foreplay 40

The Role of Erotica 47

Sexual Intercourse 52

Prolonging Sexual Intercourse 56

Oral Sex 64

Anal Sex 66

Love and Sex Throughout Life 67

Sexual Statistics 68

Adulthood 70

Middle Age 76

Advanced Age 80

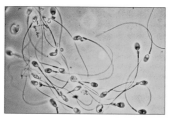

Sexual Anatomy and Physiology 85

The Sexual Body 86

Puberty 88

Male Sex Organs 91

The Sperm Cell 94

Female Sex Organs 96

The Ovum 100

The Breasts 102

The Sexual Response Cycle 104

Maintaining Sexual Health 111

Sexual Health **112**

Contraception **116**

Safer Sex **128**

HIV and AIDS **130**

Other STDs **134**

Female Disorders **140**

Male Disorders **149**

Abnormal Sex Organs **154**

Overcoming Problems in Love and Sex 155

Causes of Sexual Problems **156**

Male Problems **161**

Female Problems **165**

Treating Sexual Problems **169**

Glossary 174

Index 186

Acknowledgments 192

Introduction

Over the past few decades, great improvements have developed in the way that sexual matters are treated by society as a whole. Gradually, a more open environment has lessened the stigma and secrecy that were once attached to topics of a sexual nature. Issues such as the use of Viagra to prolong sexual potency and the rise in cases of HIV and teenage pregnancy have highlighted the necessity for a sexually informed public. Although still in its infancy, this openness offers huge and rewarding advances—a greater satisfaction with one's sexual abilities and sensual experiences; more widespread awareness of sexual health issues and the need for safer sexual practices; less guilt, repression and anxiety about sexual feelings; and better communication between sexual partners.

Relating to the opposite sex
Sexual experimentation usually begins in the form of flirting. Chapter 1 addresses the roles of flirtation and body language as indicators of attraction.

EXPRESSING SEXUALITY

Sexuality is how we express ourselves as desirable beings, through dress, flirtation, body language, solitary sexual behavior, our fantasies and desires, and ultimately through sex with a partner.

People are born as sexual beings, and we know that babies derive comfort and sensual pleasure from breast-feeding and being cuddled. The desire to touch and be touched is one of many basic human needs. Studies have shown that touch deprivation can have profound effects on a person's basic sense of well-being. As we develop sexually, we need to satisfy that need for human touch and express it in different ways. Repressing such feelings as they grow and change can be harmful to our development as rounded human beings.

Achieving a sense of ease with our bodies and with the way we use our bodies to express desire and love is important when it comes to satisfying our sensual needs. The more we learn about our bodies, the better we can enjoy our sexual lives.

Safe lovers
Discussing safe sex with a new partner can be daunting, but can actually bring you closer together and help you to relax into your lovemaking.

Love match
Keeping the flame of that first passion alight requires commitment and energy. The two of you need to adapt to each other's needs as your sexual life progresses.

FINDING A SEXUAL PARTNER

To find a partner, you need to be able to "read" the signs and respond to them. Chapter 1 *Attracting a Partner*, deals with the whys and wherefores of physical attraction—be it conscious or subconscious. It tells you how to recognize when someone is attracted to you and also when you are attracted to someone—even if you don't think you are! The chapter also gives you some great tips on how to meet your ideal partner—which can be a tall order in today's busy world.

MAKING SEX MORE EXCITING

Men and women often find different things sexually stimulating—a fantasy of yours may do nothing for your partner, and his or her favorite sexual position may not be so enjoyable for you. It is often said that, when it comes to sex, men are visually stimulated while women are mentally stimulated. This may be true to a certain extent, but it is foolish to generalize completely. The key to achieving a sex life that is great for both you and your partner is experimentation—learning to push each other's buttons in the bedroom (or elsewhere)! Chapter 2 introduces tips for spicing up foreplay, invites you to try out a variety of exciting sexual positions to suit your needs and offers advice on how to prolong your lovemaking to promote mutual sexual fulfillment.

DIFFERENT STAGES OF LIFE

Sexuality changes throughout life. A young man making love for the first time is likely to have ideas about sex that differ from those of a man of 65. The former is apt to be eager and curious about sex, perhaps prone to hyperarousal and premature ejaculation. The latter may desire sex as much as ever but find that it takes longer to have an erection and to ejaculate. Older men may also place more emphasis on nonsexual factors, such as companionship and understanding, than younger men. These stereotypes demonstrate that age and life situation—such as pregnancy and menopause for women—can have profound effects on sexual needs and responses. Chapter 3 *Sex Throughout Life* details the major factors that can influence sexuality at each life stage, whether these are related to an individual's age, physical health, life situation or relationship. Understanding and recognizing changes when they happen, such as a middle-aged man's sudden preoccupation with his appearance, can be the first step toward coping with them.

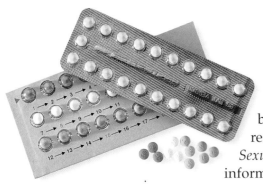

Birth control
The pros and cons of different contraceptives, from the pill (shown here) to the condom, are discussed in detail in Chapter 5 (Maintaining Sexual Health).

THE SEXUAL BODY

A knowledge of the sexual system allows you to understand why the sexual body behaves the way it does and why sexual responses change over the years. Chapter 4 *Sexual Anatomy and Physiology* gives you that information, taking you inside the sexual body and showing you why your body reacts the way it does during sex. It tells you why you become sexually aroused, how hormonal activity produces a reaction in your body and how orgasm is reached. Diagrams illustrate what happens to your body when you reach orgasm.

It is important for the sexually active individual to have an awareness of sexual health issues. Chapter 5 *Maintaining Sexual Health* informs the reader about sexual hygiene (why obsessive cleanliness can be counterproductive for example), sexually transmitted diseases, how to recognize symptoms that may need investigating and how to practice safer sex.

SEXUAL TROUBLESHOOTING

When individuals or couples become overly anxious about sex, problems can start to emerge. Sexual anxiety can be caused by many factors: inexperience, worries about performance, relationship problems, stress, past sexual trauma or general hang-ups. Chapter 6 *Overcoming Sexual Problems* outlines the different types of sexual difficulties that men and women of all ages can face, including problems that can have a physiological origin. The causes and symptoms of different problems are discussed, together with treatment options that enable individuals to overcome inhibitions and express their sexuality in the most enjoyable way.

Your Guide to Great Sex will leave you enlightened and encouraged—it dispels the myths about sex and gives you the facts, arming you with the knowledge to fulfill your sexual potential through all the stages of your life.

Positive self-image
Staying fit, promoting health and maintaining a positive attitude during midlife can counter the negative effects of aging. The physical changes that accompany menopause are described in Chapter 3 (Sex Throughout Life).

SEXUAL ATTRACTION

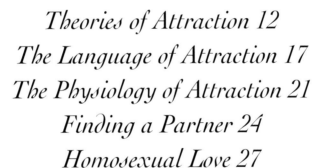

Theories of Attraction 12
The Language of Attraction 17
The Physiology of Attraction 21
Finding a Partner 24
Homosexual Love 27

Theories of Attraction

There is a wide range of theories about what attracts one person to another. Some people argue that physical beauty is a primary factor, while others point to similarities or differences between partners as the basis of compatibility.

From childhood onward, attractive people are often given the benefit of the doubt; they tend to be given credit for their positive factors, while their negative factors are attributed to bad luck, other people or circumstances that are "beyond their control." This typically creates a self-fulfilling prophecy, because being consistently seen as good, desirable and successful tends to encourage self-confidence, which in turn encourages success.

Exceptional good looks, however, can be a handicap, distorting others' perception of a person and his or her own sense of self. Popular stereotypes often equate glamorous good looks with shallowness, lack of intellect or arrogance. Some people who are thought of as beautiful may have deep-seated insecurities, feeling that others relate to them on the basis of how they look rather than who they are.

In the West, opinions on ideal physical attractiveness remain surprisingly consistent and are learned from an early age. Young children see book illustrations, television programs and movies featuring images of beautiful princesses and ugly witches, handsome heroes and deformed villains. Most people have a sense of how attractive they appear to others and how they compare to the ideal notion of beauty. This self-rating can be a powerful factor in determining choice of partner. Studies have shown that couples whose attractiveness ratings are similar have longer-lasting relationships than those whose attractiveness ratings are dissimilar.

WHICH FEATURES ARE ATTRACTIVE?

For both sexes, facial features rank high, with the eyes, the "windows of the soul," attracting attention first. Large, bright, receptive eyes are held to be the ideal, and certain types of eye contact are understood to initiate flirting. Western societies find an oval face, prominent cheekbones, a small straight nose, a medium-size mouth and ears that do not stick out attractive. A clear complexion, wrinkle-free skin and even, white teeth are desirable because they are signs of healthiness and youthfulness. The expression "long in the tooth" refers to the natural receding of gums that occurs with age. Any indication of aging, especially in women, is considered to be less attractive, reflecting the relationship between increasing age and the onset of female infertility. Average features tend to be more attractive than extremes: enormous or very small breasts, for example, or excessively muscular or thin bodies are generally not considered to be attractive.

Sexual self-perception Sexual attractiveness is often a self-fulfilling prophecy: if someone believes himself or herself to be attractive, others also find that to be true.

Child is told that he or she is "pretty" or "handsome."

Child comes to perceive himself or herself as attractive.

Child associates being attractive with receiving praise.

Child grows up expecting positive response from people.

Self-confidence is found attractive by person's peer group.

Person is treated positively by others.

Self-esteem is fueled.

Person perceives himself or herself as physically, sexually and socially attractive.

ATTRACTION AND GENDER DIFFERENCES

Men are reputed to respond to a woman's looks more quickly and powerfully than women do to a man's physical attributes. Men admire the particular physical qualities in women that distinguish them from men: fuller lips; thinner eyebrows; softer, smoother skin; and a lack of facial hair. Traditionally, men seek younger women, with their potentially higher fertility.

Men generally consider large, firm breasts, which symbolize fertility and reproduction, to be desirable. The ideal breast is pert rather than pendulous, again reflecting the preference for youth over age (the density of breast tissue declines as a woman grows older, and her breasts become more inclined to sag). Men are also attracted by slim but curvy body shapes with a narrow waistline and long, slim legs. These are all, however, generalizations. Many men have preferences that do not match the stereotypical image of feminine beauty.

Studies suggest that women may be more likely to be attracted by a man's status than his looks. A woman may make a detailed assessment of a partner's personality, dependability and material assets from a very early stage of a relationship. A woman may even reject a potential partner on the basis of his job, wealth and perceived social standing. Traditionally, women also tend to seek slightly older men, with their potentially greater status, wealth and ability to provide for and protect future children. This kind of selection often operates on a subconscious rather than a deliberate level.

The physical characteristics that many women favor include a large, square jaw; a strong chin; a slim, muscular build with a flat stomach; and small, well-formed buttocks. Biologically, these attributes may be symbolic of physical prowess: hunting, fighting and survival skills. In gay and lesbian relationships, considerably less emphasis tends to be placed on both potential fertility and financial resources.

Long and sleek

Long and natural

THE SEXUAL SIGNIFICANCE OF HAIR

For both sexes, thick, healthy hair is considered attractive. In men, plenty of hair symbolizes power and masculinity, as in the Old Testament story of Samson. Shaved heads often connote religious celibacy, old age or pursuit of a particular lifestyle (skinheads, for example). In women, long, thick, shiny hair traditionally symbolizes female sexuality and availability—one of the reasons why strict Orthodox Jewish and Muslim women keep their hair hidden in public. In some cultures, however, long hair can symbolize virginity, which has its own erotic implications. Paradoxically, in the 1920s, women with short, bobbed hair were considered sexually independent. Today short, androgynous haircuts are seen as sexy or fashionable in certain circles because they subvert gender boundaries. Women sometimes perceive balding men as sexually attractive, perhaps because they are reputed to have high levels of the male sex hormone testosterone.

Shaved head

Sexual signals projected by different hairstyles
Some hairstyles have specific sexual connotations.
Cropped or messy hair is androgynous; long,
groomed hair is feminine; stylized hair may be
associated with glamour and vampish sexuality.

Wispy bob

LIKE ATTRACTS LIKE

There is a popular theory that "like attracts like." It could be that a person recognizes sexual compatibility when he or she identifies someone as being similar. Many people are attracted to a partner with a similar background. In such cases couples may share a similar education and religion and similar interests, attitudes and aspirations.

Being attracted to a partner with a similar background may include the subconscious perception of safety and continuity of leaving the childhood home but still remaining connected to it. Paradoxically, this is true even for couples from similar negative backgrounds; people from broken homes, for example, tend to attract one another. Positive similarities, such as wealth, status, religion, political affiliation or education, may be obvious to two people from the start. Negative or more obscure similarities, such as being adopted, the death of a sibling or a family history of depression, may emerge only at a later stage.

Subconscious recognition of similarity

A family's emotional dynamics are in part expressed by its members through body language: posture, facial expression, gesture and way of moving. People from emotionally similar families recognize these nonverbal signals and feel at ease with them, long before any conversation occurs. Individuals from families with secrets or scandals such as illegitimacy or suicide, for example, tend to attract each other, although it may take years for the secrets to be revealed. And people whose emotional development was stopped at a certain stage—so that they struggle with the low self-worth resulting from a lack of parental love or with gaining independence from possessive parents—are commonly drawn to each other.

The more self-confident a person is, the more selective he or she tends to be when choosing a partner. People who are "centered"—self-accepting and nondefensive—tend to choose others with a similar level of stability. No one likes rejection, so someone who lacks self-confidence is likely to choose a partner who is similarly lacking, though one or both of them may have a veneer of self-confidence. Men with low self-esteem tend to choose traditional, dependent and nonthreatening women, while men with a high sense of self-worth feel confident about choosing more assertive and independent women—for example Julius Caesar and Cleopatra.

COMPLEMENTARY PERSONALITIES

Although relationships between matching personalities can be successful, some similar couples lack vitality in their relationship and share a fear of difference. Complementary personalities may function very

Attraction in motion
When two people meet for the first time, they will consciously and subconsciously make assessments of each other. How attractive is this person? Are they like me? In what ways are they different from me? How are we getting along? This couple's body language indicates a growing sense of mutual attraction.

On first meeting, a couple's body language may indicate reserve or even mild hostility. Here, both have their legs crossed away from each other, although mutual interest is signaled by eye contact.

As a conversation evolves, body language becomes less defensive and more open. The couple turn their bodies toward each other, and expressive hand gestures become more frequent.

well together: a dominant character may suit someone who is submissive, a dependent person may deal well with a nurturing person, and an assertive individual can combine well with a passive one.

The Language of Love

The "other half" is used to describe a partner, highlighting the idea of the two halves of the relationship making the whole.

HOW IMPORTANT IS IQ?

Very different levels of intelligence can be detrimental to a long-term relationship. A highly intelligent person's inclinations to protect, rescue, parent or "improve" a much less intelligent partner, or to make himself or herself feel better by comparison, may later backfire in a relationship. Intelligence and level of education are not synonymous, however. In addition, different, complementary types of intelligence exist: for example, one partner might have the ability to solve practical problems in a direct, logical and rational way, while the other looks at problems from many different angles and seeks creative solutions.

DO OPPOSITES ATTRACT?

Psychologists have long noted the powerful attraction of opposites. Being attracted to someone from a different race, religion or class may reflect the need to express independence from parents and the values they represent, especially around the teenage years and in tightly knit families or communities. Such a choice may also arise from a feeling of isolation from one's family or express a need for constant reassurance of separateness. Someone who has a fragile sense of identity, who has never felt able to have feelings of his or her own, may choose a partner who is as seemingly different as possible, and even move to another culture to reinforce that sense of separateness.

Individuals sometimes create a marriage or partnership of opposites to compensate for the qualities lacking, or perceived to be lacking, in themselves—in short, to gain a sense of completeness. It can also be a way for a person to offload onto the partner the qualities or characteristics that he or she considers unacceptable or dangerous in himself or herself. This type of reasoning is rarely conscious, but it often explains why a shy person selects a socially assertive or dominant partner, why a cautious person selects a risk taker and a repressed person selects an uninhibited one.

WAIST-TO-HIP RATIO

Biologists argue that men find a slim waist and full hips attractive in women for evolutionary reasons. The waist-to-hip "ratio" reflects a high level of estrogen and a low level of testosterone, a combination generally linked to high fertility.

The heavy, Rubenesque female body shape considered beautiful in other periods of history and cultures may also have biological origins. For example, in cultures in which food is scarce, plumpness indicates health, wealth, social status, and the potential to sustain pregnancy and nursing.

Mutual attraction becomes obvious as a couple relax into a conversation. Smiling, eye contact and increasing physical proximity demonstrate a desire for greater intimacy.

Each partner has recognized the other's body language and given tacit permission for things to progress further. The man touches the woman's knee and their postures are roughly symmetrical.

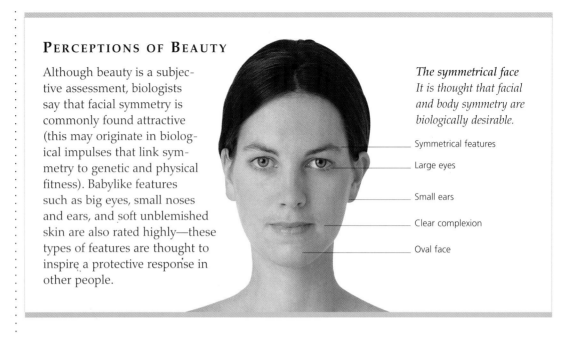

PERCEPTIONS OF BEAUTY

Although beauty is a subjective assessment, biologists say that facial symmetry is commonly found attractive (this may originate in biological impulses that link symmetry to genetic and physical fitness). Babylike features such as big eyes, small noses and ears, and soft unblemished skin are also rated highly—these types of features are thought to inspire a protective response in other people.

The symmetrical face
It is thought that facial and body symmetry are biologically desirable.

Symmetrical features

Large eyes

Small ears

Clear complexion

Oval face

PARTNERS WHO RESEMBLE PARENTS

According to Freud, part of a young child's normal psychological development is the wish to seduce or even marry the parent of the opposite sex. While in most cultures incest is taboo, this unfulfilled attraction affects the adult's notion of the idealized partner, who tends to resemble childhood memories of the opposite-sex parent.

The conscious search may well be for a partner with the opposite-sex parent's positive qualities. An individual's desire to re-create the dynamics of childhood relationships, however, and to correct any dysfunc-

tions that occurred then, is so strong that the selected partner will almost inevitably have the opposite-sex parent's negative qualities as well.

ATTRACTIVENESS AND CULTURE

What is considered attractive in one culture may be repellent in another. In some non-Western cultures, ritual disfigurations such as an elongated neck, ears, lips, vulva or penis; filed and stained teeth; and scarred face or breasts are considered attractive.

Attractiveness in a multicultural society can be complex. Minority, nonwhite races in predominantly white cultures have, until recently, been presented with white standards of beauty as the only ideal. In countries such as South Africa and India, in which minority whites had political control, the white standards prevailed as well.

In white-dominated cultures, nonwhite skin, hair and body characteristics were often considered inherently inferior to their white correlatives. Attempts to compensate for this sometimes led to mixed messages. For example, black dolls had dark skin but European features. Meanwhile, minority efforts to mimic the "ideal" white appearance ranged from hair straighteners and skin lighteners to cosmetic surgery. Marriage between a member of a nonwhite race and a white spouse symbolized status. Interestingly, the first white settlers and explorers in Africa were considered hideous albinos by the indigenous population.

SIGNS OF COMPATIBILITY

OBVIOUS SIMILARITIES IN	HIDDEN SIMILARITIES IN
Appearance/attractiveness	Emotional dynamics of family
Sense of humor	Experiences of loss in family
Race, religion and social class	Position in family (eldest, only, middle child and so on)
Leisure pursuits and friends	Relationship with opposite-sex parent
Education, intelligence and ambitions	Secrets or scandals in the family
Attitudes toward money, having children and parenting	Sense of self-worth

The Language of Attraction

A person can express sexual attraction in various nonverbal ways, including modifying appearance—particularly dress— flirtatious body language, fragrance and body adornment using jewelry or makeup.

The language in which a person signals his or her initial attraction for another person is usually nonverbal. Some signals are instinctive, probably cross-cultural and made unconsciously. Others are overt and intentional gestures made to increase attractiveness. These tend to be culturally specific—what is considered acceptable and attractive in one culture may be thought repellent or indecent in another.

DRESS

Dress can powerfully express sexuality and give strong clues about sexual interest. What makes clothing attractive, however, is often a matter of taste. Many people find ethnic or exotic clothing erotic, reflecting a common fantasy that foreign cultures are more highly sexed than Western culture. This can be true as well for clothing worn by other social or economic classes in one's own culture, based on a similar fantasy. For some people, sexually ambiguous dress that creates a moment's uncertainty as to the wearer's gender is sexy. Others find uniforms of any sort or cross-dressing—wearing clothes obviously meant for the opposite sex—sexy.

Among some people, loose or disorderly dress suggests that the wearer could easily discard his or her clothes. Similarly, a top that slips off a woman's shoulder or a partly undone garment worn by either sex hints at the possibility of total nudity. Tight, short or otherwise revealing garments that emphasize the breasts, belly, buttocks and/or groin also tend to be erotic—for example, skin-tight jeans, miniskirts or nipple-revealing T-shirts.

The wearing of animal skins in the form of leather, suede or fur has always had strong sexual overtones, although conservation issues have altered the connotations somewhat. In primitive times, someone wearing a fierce animal's skin was thought to absorb its qualities; thus a modern woman wearing fox may be seen as desirable and wily—a "foxy" lady. Black leather, belted, zipped and studded clothing has sadomasochistic overtones. Lizard, crocodile or snakeskin convey wealth and cold-bloodedness.

Sexual dress Certain dress styles send sexual signals. Tight or revealing clothes and spandex or fur all have sexual connotations.

Unbuttoned shirt

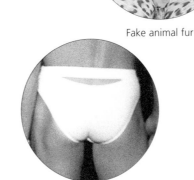
Fake animal fur

Tight trunks

Hipster skirt and crop top

Body Language

Although each courtship seems unique to the couple involved, it usually follows a ritualized pattern. In the initial, "attention-getting" phase, territory is established—a space in a room, for example. Exaggerated body movements announce presence and intent. For example, males swagger and laugh heartily and females stretch. As well as announcing desirability and availability, these actions also give the signal that it is safe for a potential partner to approach. Although it may seem as if the male initiates courtship, very often it is the female who actually makes the first move.

During the "recognition" phase, eye contact occurs, followed by "grooming" small talk. What is said is often less important than the intonation.

"Intention cues," such as leaning toward, or moving an arm or leg closer to, the other person, culminate in brief physical contact. Often initiated by the woman, this slight, gentle touch of a non-erogenous zone such as the shoulder is responded to with a smile or return touch that is equally subtle. Eventually, "body synchrony" occurs. The couple moves into a face-to-face position with the shoulders aligned, and their actions—for example, crossing or uncrossing legs, lifting a drink, or laughing—increasingly mirror each other.

Synchrony is a common feature of courtship and a way of expressing sexual intent. Dancing is a form of overt sexual synchrony, or even a prelude to sex itself. Sharing a meal or a drink is another example. Couples may eat in unison and pause to talk simultaneously. Eating is recognized as a sensual activity.

Mistakes or rebuffs during flirtation, such as avoiding eye contact, speaking sharply, saying too much or too little, flinching when touched or responding too hastily or slowly, can hamper the potential courtship.

Female flirtation signals
A woman may send signals of attraction with a range of facial expressions: widening the eyes, raising the eyebrows or drawing attention to her face in general. She may also signal attraction toward someone by smiling and touching her hair.

Signs of intimacy
Close body contact, gazing into the eyes and smiling to expose both top and bottom teeth indicate attraction and the desire to be intimate. Nervous gestures ("displacement activities"), such as rearranging clothes or hair, are unconscious attempts to dispel sexual tension.

Male flirtation signals
Men tend to signal attraction by a change in stance that draws attention to their height or stature. For example, common gestures of flirtation include thrusting the chest outward or pulling the body up to its full height to indicate dominance and physical strength.

FLIRTING AND BODY LANGUAGE

Flirtatious expressions transcend cultural boundaries. A woman smiling at her admirer swiftly lifts her eyebrows, opens her eyes wide, drops her eyelids, tilts her head down and to the side, and then gazes away, possibly touching her face with her hands. Similarly, the "eyebrow flash"—rapidly raising and lowering the eyebrows—is a universal sign of flirtation.

Both sexes employ the so-called copulatory gaze, gazing intently into the eyes of a potential mate. The pupils dilate, then the eyelids drop and the face is turned away. This is often followed by a "displacement activity," a nervous gesture such as touching the hair or straightening clothing, which is an unconscious way of dispelling the sexual tension.

FRAGRANCE

Smells are transmitted, via the olfactory nerve, directly to the brain's limbic system, which is involved in the control of sexual desire and long-term memory. Unlike other senses, the sense of smell is alert even during sleep. Certain smells can evoke intensely erotic feelings, and through smell people often relive events long after they occurred.

The body's own scent is a powerful perfume. Each person's scent is unique; glands in the armpits, around the nipples and in the groin become active at puberty and release a special scent that is retained by the body hair. This scent contains pheromones, powerful chemical sexual signals that may work on an unconscious level (see page 22).

Some contemporary cultures, such as those of the U.S., Britain and Japan, find sweat and other body odors offensive and, ironically, use manufactured fragrances to conceal the natural ones that originally served as sexual signals. However, some people find the smell of fresh sweat appealing and arousing.

The word "perfume" derives from the Latin for "through smoke" and originally referred to the scents released during burnt offerings. The same perfume smells different on each person. People generally apply scent to the neck, chest or wrist, where body warmth increases the rate of evaporation.

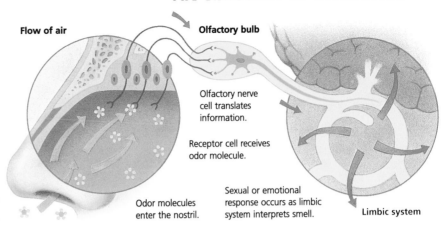

Flow of air

Olfactory bulb

Olfactory nerve cell translates information.

Receptor cell receives odor molecule.

Odor molecules enter the nostril.

Sexual or emotional response occurs as limbic system interprets smell.

Limbic system

The importance of fragrance Many people underestimate the importance of smell, but specific fragrances can evoke powerful feelings. Smell particles enter the nose and are translated into nervous impulses that travel straight to the limbic system—the part of the brain that controls emotional and sexual responses.

DECORATING THE BODY

Jewelry
Ornamenting the body with jewelry often draws attention to delicate or fragile body parts.

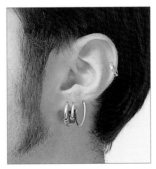

Piercing
Rings and studs that penetrate the skin are often worn on the body's erogenous zones.

Nail painting
Decorated nails symbolize leisure and wealth and may act as a signal of predatory sexuality.

Tattooing
This permanent form of body adornment suggests toughness and machismo.

Expressing new ▶
love New or young
lovers often display
unique body language
in public, effectively
creating their own
space while oblivious
to what is happening
around them. This
couple also show
postural echo.

ADORNING THE BODY

Long fingernails on a woman suggest that she does not do manual work and, by extension, symbolize leisure and affluence. Polished nails, which need frequent attention, reinforce this symbolism. Red nails hint at untamed sexuality, perhaps because they suggest the bloody claws of predatory animals.

In agricultural economies, where most people work outdoors, tanned skin is often considered lower-class and ugly, while pale skin tends to symbolize wealth and leisure. In more industrialized societies, where most people work indoors in office environments, a suntan, especially in winter, is considered alluring. Its desirability may also derive from the Western myth that darker-skinned races are more highly sexed. Current concerns over skin cancer and premature wrinkling, however, have led to a revised attitude toward sunbathing.

In the West, tattoos were traditionally an affectation of working-class men, particularly sailors. Today tattoos, especially small, discreet ones, are fashionable among women as well.

Jewelry

Traditionally, jewelry has carried connotations of social status, wealth and power, even though fake designer and costume jewelry can easily mislead.

People can convey their religious, political or sexual preferences simply by their choice and positioning of jewelry on the body or limbs. A woman's jewelry may also indicate her romantic history and act as a warning (or challenge) to potential admirers.

Jewelry can emphasize parts of the body with sexual connotations: delicate bracelets on slender ankles or wrists, for example; chains, necklaces or pendants against the skin of the chest; and chokers around the throat. For both sexes, earrings call attention to a common erogenous zone—the earlobes. Armlets or "slave bracelets" have connotations of submissiveness.

Pierced body parts hint at pain and sado-masochism, which some people find erotic. Because navel and nose piercing has become much more common than it used to be, it tends to be read as a fashion gesture rather than a serious erotic signal.

Makeup

A woman's style of makeup may indicate conformity to fashion—for example, the bee-stung mouths of the 1920s or the ghostly pale lips of the 1960s. Makeup can also be used as a statement of individual rebellion. However, the goal of most makeup remains to conceal imperfections and signs of aging and to emphasize and enhance attractive facial features.

Many cultures view large eyes as beautiful, and cosmetics are often used to draw attention to them and make them look bigger. Lipstick makes the mouth darker and fuller, possibly mimicking the vaginal lips. Blusher helps create an impression of flushed cheeks and smooth skin.

In the past, makeup was not produced exclusively for women, and today male skin-care products have once again become popular. They are marketed to suggest virility and physical prowess.

Feeding each other
Literally feeding
one's partner is a
courtship ritual that
may precede sex.

COURTSHIP FEEDING

Throughout the animal kingdom, a male animal will feed a female in return for anticipated sexual favors. For example, gorillas offer pieces of fruit to prospective mates. In Western culture, the "dinner date," for which the male traditionally pays, has primitive origins: the male is demonstrating his abilities as a provider to the female. When a man buys a woman an expensive meal as part of a date, there may be an assumption that sex will follow later. The relatively recent custom of sharing expenses reflects the evolving emphasis on equality between the sexes and the rejection of the gender division into provider and receiver.

The Physiology of Attraction

When someone feels strongly attracted to or infatuated with another person, he or she may experience a number of physical symptoms. Anxiety, excitability, sleeplessness, loss of appetite, lack of concentration and mood swings are all common.

The chemistry of the brain plays a key role in both the physical symptoms and the emotions of love. The limbic system (see page 87)—and especially the *HYPO-THALAMUS*, one of the earliest parts of this organ to evolve—is thought to be involved in controlling emotions and the capacity to love. When a person is infatuated, a chemical called phenylethylamine (PEA) floods the brain. For both men and women, this amphetamine-related compound triggers feelings of high energy, pleasure, excitement, giddiness and optimism. PEA also raises the metabolism and curbs the appetite. Levels of another neurotransmitter, dopamine, increase during periods of infatuation, and this results in intensified sexual desire. Levels of oxytocin, the so-called cuddle chemical, also increase.

The decline of infatuation influences brain chemicals as well. Usually within two years of the start of an infatuation, a group of opiate-like chemicals called endorphins are released by the brain to counteract high levels of PEA. Calming and anxiety-reducing, endorphins make a person feel relaxed and secure. Some people respond to this by craving the former levels of PEA to such an extent that they become "love addicts." To ensure that the elation of a PEA high is constantly repeated, love addicts tend to choose consistently unsuitable partners.

With counseling or therapy, the love addict may be able to understand the roots of his or her addiction—frequently traced to

dynamics between the family members during childhood—and gradually to form healthier relationships.

PEA is found in certain natural substances, such as cocoa and rose water, which may explain why chocolates are a traditional romantic gift in the West, and Turkish delight, which is made using rose water, has a similar appeal in the East. PEA is also an ingredient of some diet drinks.

THE NERVOUS SYSTEM

The sympathetic nervous system is responsible for the reactions experienced by a person who is afraid or feels threatened: called the "fight or flight" response. This causes the heart and breathing rates to increase, which enables the person to run faster, exercise more muscle power and generally cope better with the threat, either through acts of aggression or by running away.

A similar thing happens when an individual experiences a strong physical attraction toward another. This results in symptoms similar to those associated with fear: a dry mouth, fluttering heart, clammy hands and butterflies in the stomach. The chemicals mostly responsible for these sensations are epinephrine and norepinephrine. These are released from the *ADRENAL GLANDS* and

◄ Oxytocin This light micrograph shows crystals of oxytocin, a hormone released by the pituitary gland in the brain. Oxytocin levels increase when a person is infatuated.

Sources of PEA The infatuation chemical — PEA—that floods the brain during the initial stages of a romance is also found in cocoa, rose water and rose petals.

Kissing During a ▶ *kiss, the heart rate increases, saliva is exchanged via the mouth and the first signs of sexual arousal in the genitals occur.*

nervous system and they act on specific body parts.

Lovesickness

At some point in their lives, most people suffer from feelings of deep or lingering sadness as a result of unobtainable, unrequited or terminated relationships. As with initial attraction and infatuation, there is probably a biological basis for this, such as chemical imbalances in the brain.

In some instances, unrequited infatuation can be so severe that doctors treat it as an obsessional disorder. The person cannot accept that his or her feelings are not reciprocated or that a relationship is over. In some such cases, doctors might prescribe an antidepressant drug that causes the levels of 5-hydroxytryptamine—a chemical naturally found in the brain—to increase, and this has been found to be helpful.

PHEROMONES

Before the physical symptoms of love can occur, one or both individuals must become attracted to the other. Sexual and emotional attraction involve a whole barrage of sig-nals. These are primarily visual (the other person's appearance), auditory (the sound of his or her voice) and tactile (the feel of his or her body). But there are other, subtler forms of communication that are in operation at a primitive level: pheromones, or scent signals.

The role of human pheromones (from the Greek word "phero," meaning "to convey") in courtship has stimulated much debate, but at least some evidence exists for their occurrence in women. It has long been noticed that when females of childbearing age are in close proximity for several months at a time—for example, women soldiers in barracks or nurses living in a dormitory—the timing of their individual menstrual cycles slowly alters until they coincide. This may be due to pheromones.

In bygone eras, the ability to have synchronized menstrual cycles would have been highly advantageous, particularly for nomadic tribes. It would increase the likelihood that pregnancy and childbirth would also occur at the same time, and ensure that the youngest (and most vulnerable) off-

THE BODY'S RESPONSE TO ATTRACTION

Many of the sensations associated with attraction can be attributed to a network of nerve pathways called the sympathetic branch of the autonomic nervous system. This network of nerves is linked to the brain and hormone-releasing glands throughout the body, and is involved in some powerful emotional states. Messages about physical attraction passed via the nervous system cause the adrenal glands to produce epinephrine—this raises the heart and breathing rate, and blood pressure.

The sympathetic autonomic nervous system
This system prepares the body for stress or excitement. A chain of ganglia alongside the spinal cord relays messages to specific organs.

Pupils dilate and mouth becomes dry as salivation is inhibited.

The heart rate speeds up—blood is pumped faster around the body.

The production of gastric juices in the stomach is inhibited.

Arousal occurs—the uterus rises and the vagina expands and lubricates.

Epinephrine
These are magnified crystals of epinephrine, a hormone that makes people feel excited or "high."

spring would be at the same stage of development when it was time to move on. Because women cannot consciously alter their menstrual cycles, a plausible explanation for the change is that they are responding to pheromones. If so, humans may produce other smell signals, perhaps involved in sexual attraction.

Pheromone production in humans

Humans give off a highly individual odor that enables tracker dogs to follow the scent of one person and not be misled by the scent from others (apart from identical twins, who have exactly the same smell). This scent may also contain unique pheromones that people respond to unconsciously.

Human scent is produced by the apocrine glands. These glands are widely distributed in the fetus, but shortly before birth most are lost, with the exception of those found in the armpits, genital and anal areas, and the areolae around the nipples. The apocrine glands do not develop further until puberty, when they start to produce scent.

The secreted scent is milky and viscous and must be diluted before effective dispersal, mainly by sweat. An increase in sweating, which is a common reaction to sexual and emotional arousal, could well have evolved as a way of transmitting pheromones. The male sex hormones (see page 123) androsterone and androsterol have both been found in the underarm scent glands and may act as sexual attractors.

Pheromones may also be transferred by direct physical contact. During kissing, for example, an oily secretion from the mouth and lips called sebum may be exchanged. It is thought that sebum may have pheromonal properties.

Interpreting pheromones

How pheromones could influence the brain and make one person attractive to another is still unknown. Even if research proves that they do, they will almost certainly be only one facet of attraction, with auditory, visual and tactile signals playing a more important role in courtship.

LOVING FEELINGS

PHYSICAL SENSATION	CAUSES
Dry mouth	Hormonal and nervous stimulation inhibits the salivary glands.
Fluttering heart	The heart is stimulated by the sympathetic nervous system.
Unsettled stomach and loss of appetite	Blood flow is diverted away from the digestive organs, and gut motility is reduced.
Sweating	Epinephrine increases perspiration from the palms, the soles of the feet and the groin.
Trembling	Epinephrine produces a rush of blood to the brain and muscles, causing muscle tremors.

Perhaps a combination of all of these signals is necessary to bring about the physiological response we call sexual attraction, possibly switching on special courtship genes. Each person may respond to a combination of stimuli that is unique to him or her, explaining why one individual appears highly attractive to one person but not necessarily to another.

Artificial pheromones

The role of pheromones has been widely examined in animals and insects. Moths, for example, have the ability to detect pheromone signals from a potential mate from many miles away. For hundreds of years, natural pheromones, extracted from animals' scent glands, have been added to perfumes in the hope that they will act as aphrodisiacs. It is now possible to buy pure, artificial pheromones, which are marketed as "mimicking naturally produced chemicals that make us attractive to the opposite sex." These can be added to commercially produced fragrances, but until more research has established the role of natural pheromones, the use of synthetic versions would seem to be an expensive hit-or-miss experiment.

◀ *Identical twins*
Everyone's pheromone scent is unique, except in the case of identical twins, who share the same smell.

Moths
Moths are able to detect pheromone signals from a mate from many miles away.

Finding a Partner

Much thought, discussion and business focuses on the ways in which individuals may meet compatible sexual partners. Many people meet their partners through peer groups or jobs. Others find partners through dating services or personal ads.

Older people As ▶ people age, they may find it difficult to meet prospective partners. Specially organized vacations have provided a good way for many older people to meet others.

Searching for a partner A few people go to dating services to meet a partner, but the majority of people meet others through contact in a social, religious, professional or educational environment.

- In a work environment
- At high school or college
- Common ways to meet potential partners
- Through friends or family
- At an association, club, church or religious activity
- Chance meetings at a bar or other public place

Searching for a special person with whom to share the emotional side of life can be a compelling impulse, regardless of age or culture. The ways in which people set about finding a suitable partner vary tremendously.

MEETING PEOPLE THROUGH FRIENDS

Relationships often begin with an introduction through friends. Since friends tend to have the same values and interests, their acquaintances are likely to share a common outlook. Friends may also have a good understanding of each other's expectations of a partner and be able to assess possible candidates from among relatives, colleagues, neighbors or friends.

Introductions through friends can happen in a number of ways. Sometimes they occur purely by chance or through a joint invitation to a social event, such as a dinner party or concert. Alternatively, they may occur more formally through a blind date. Each arrangement has its own advantages and disadvantages. Meeting a potential partner in the presence of friends can make both people feel safe or it can make them feel under scrutiny.

A blind date that goes wrong can feel like a failure, but it has the advantage of having no observers.

Introductions by friends or relatives are associated with their own unique problems. The partners may be tempted to use the mutual friend as a source of information about the other's past history and character. This can place stress on the friendship and give rise to a difficult dynamic among all three people. If only one person wants to pursue a relationship, the rejected partner may hold the mutual friend responsible, which also produces tension.

CASUAL MEETINGS

Potential partners may meet for the first time in a highly selective situation. College alumni groups, professional associations, gyms or clubs, for example, bring together people with common interests. Meeting regularly in such an environment opens opportunities for friendships and relationships to develop naturally. In semi-selective situations, such as libraries, bookstores, museums, galleries and religious services, people may also meet through a shared interest.

Potential partners may meet casually on public transportation or in supermarkets, laundromats, bars or nightclubs—places that have little, if any, selective context. Such meetings may seem romantic, but they often develop into short-term sexual liaisons rather than long-lasting relationships. People may also meet on vacation. While such romances can seem appealing, meeting someone in an alluring setting a long way from home, without all the usual constraints, can make the relationship seem more attractive than it actually is and carry it further than good sense would dictate.

With new acquaintances, striking a balance between approachability and personal safety is important. Women may prefer to meet a new date for the first time in a public place, have transportation home already arranged and give a work rather than a home telephone number.

Private party/
social club/gym

Work

School

Elsewhere

Bar/personal
ad/vacation

Church

MEETING AT WORK

The workplace is a well-established venue for meeting potential partners. Long-term, close contact and a common purpose allow friendships to develop gradually. Working with a colleague with whom a good relationship is developing can even enhance professional performance.

Conversely, having to continue working with a colleague when the relationship is stormy or has ended can be embarrassing or depressing and can adversely affect work performance. Because of this, some companies are reluctant to employ two people who are in a sexual relationship, and many companies in the U.S. and Canada have rules against dating coworkers.

A romance between people on different rungs of the professional ladder—for example, boss and secretary, or doctor and nurse—can put the job of the junior employee (often the woman) at risk if the relationship ends. Problems are easier to avoid if the relationship exists between colleagues

from different departments, if one partner works on a part-time basis or if the couple manage to maintain a strictly nonsexual relationship at work.

Some professions, such as construction, are predominantly male, while others, such as elementary school teaching, tend to be female. Although stereotypes are changing and gender biases are called more into question, such imbalances still exist and can reduce the chances of heterosexuals meeting a potential partner.

SINGLES EVENINGS AND EVENTS

Social occasions for single people range from the highly selective, such as those run by an educational organization, to the relatively nonselective—for example, singles evenings in a bar. The less selective the group, the less likely a person is to find potential partners with similar backgrounds, attitudes and goals.

Some singles events, such as sightseeing tours or concerts, are open to all unattached adults; others are intended for particular age groups or for specific religious or ethnic groups. While many events are advertised, others may require an invitation. Events range from intimate gatherings to large crowds. They may last less than an hour or, in the case of vacations, days or weeks. While some events are free, others are very expensive, meaning that the high cost acts as a selective factor.

Where do people meet partners? The most frequent ways for couples to meet in the U.S. and Canada are through school or work or at a social occasion such as a party or a club function. A sizable percentage of people, however, meet outside the categories listed above.

◀ *Lunch dates First dates—whether blind dates, introductions through dating services or meetings with a new acquaintance—are invariably loaded occasions. The rising popularity of lunchtime meetings may be due to the relative informality of this kind of date.*

Graduation day

Graduating from school may mean leaving education behind, but many people sustain the relationships that they form in high school or college. Educational environments are highly selective, meaning that there is a high chance of meeting compatible partners.

Internet dating ▶

This couple met and fell in love as a result of communicating on the Internet, a worldwide system of interconnected computers. As more people gain access to the Internet, the number of couples meeting in this way will increase.

Events that simply showcase potential partners can feel artificial or even desperate, especially when the women outnumber the men. In cases like these, attending with a supportive friend or avoiding events that do not have an easy escape route (such as singles vacations) can offset awkwardness. Singles events that have an additional purpose, such as conservation work or gourmet dining, may be more comfortable.

DATING SERVICES

The growth of dating services reflects the increasing tendency of people to move away from their place of origin, to relocate frequently, to spend more time at work and less time at leisure, and to postpone marriage until well into their twenties or later. It also reflects the high proportion of unattached women compared with unattached men—an imbalance that increases with age.

Dating services may be local or nationwide, and some deal only with specific groups. Agencies usually match people based on information provided by detailed questionnaires or in-depth personal interviews. Some also make videos of their clients. Agencies usually guarantee to arrange a specific number of dates.

Lunch-dating services, which organize a set number of business-lunch blind dates, are a relatively new but successful phenomenon. Because such arrangements provide short, daytime contacts, they allow the diners to meet in an informal way and either disengage gracefully or agree to meet again.

The services of marriage brokers, matrimonial specialists or human-relationship specialists cost more. Staffed by trained psychologists or social workers with national or even international contacts, these services help clients improve their social skills, self-confidence and appearance before arranging introductions.

IN THE PAST

In Western cultures today, people have many avenues to meet partners. Until recent decades, however, people tended to settle close to their families and places of birth and to meet and marry those who lived nearby—often people within a mile of home. Limited opportunities for educational and professional advancement meant that people tended to continue in their parents' lifestyles and occupations and to marry partners from similar backgrounds.

Religion played a more important role than it typically does today, and many couples who later married first met at their shared place of worship. Because cultural, ethnic and racial boundaries were more clearly delineated, few people chose a partner beyond these boundaries. The opinion of parents and family carried more weight than personal attraction, and relatives would take an active role in matchmaking, arranged marriages being an extreme example. Placing an advertisement for a partner was almost unheard of.

Homosexual Love

Homosexuality is sexual attraction between people of the same sex. The word derives from the Greek "homos"—same—and the Latin "sexualis"—sexual. The words "gay" and "lesbian" are more widely used today.

Experimentation with same-sex play is a normal part of the sexual development of most boys and girls both before and during puberty. By the time they reach adulthood, most individuals have developed a clear idea of their sexual orientation, with the majority becoming heterosexual. Sometimes homosexual activity occurs in situations in which otherwise heterosexual individuals are deprived of regular contact with members of the opposite sex, most commonly among long-term prisoners. This form of behavior also occurs, but usually less widely, in institutions such as boys' schools and in the armed forces, where single-sex groups are in close confinement for long periods of time.

GAY SOCIETY

As a result of legal restrictions and the widespread social disapproval that still exists toward public displays of affection between members of the same sex, many homosexuals have formed their own separate social network from which heterosexuals are largely excluded. Information on the gay community travels by word of mouth, through the gay press and on the Internet.

Most cities and large towns have formal or informal places for gay men and women to meet, either for purely social contact or specifically to pursue potential sexual relationships. Gay bars and clubs, parks, beaches, restaurants, public baths, and gyms all serve as gathering spots.

Many homosexuals will readily admit their sexual orientation and the full and open part they play in the gay community. Sometimes they will also express defiance of the heterosexual world. Not everyone is vocal: some people, particularly those in the public eye, present a heterosexual persona in public (some may be married with children) but have homosexual relationships in secret. Their reticence is often due to a fear of social disapproval, job loss and violence.

Gays and their supporters have made a concerted effort in recent years to encourage society to develop a more tolerant attitude toward homosexuality. They have worked to eliminate discriminatory legislation against gay people and also to remove laws that criminalize homosexual activities between two consenting adult men or women.

As part of this process, gay rights activists encourage secretive homosexuals to openly acknowledge their sexual orientation, or "come out of the closet." In a process which is known as "outing," some of the more militant activists have taken to publicizing the

◀ Homosexuality in the past Ancient artifacts depicting homosexuality suggest that it may have been widely accepted in some cultures.

San Francisco This city is renowned for its established gay community and liberal attitudes toward homosexuality.

THE GAY GENE

Dean H. Hamer's research into the genetic cause of homosexuality discovered that a small area known as Xq28 at the tip of the X chromosome, inherited from the mother, was shared by 33 out of 40 pairs of gay brothers. A random sample of 314 other pairs of brothers, with about 2 percent assumed to be homosexual, did not show the same link. This would seem to suggest that the chromosomal region Xq28 contains a gene that influences male sexual orientation.

Dean H. Hamer
One of the pioneer researchers into the biological roots of homosexuality, Hamer has also researched the role of genes in complex medical conditions, including the progression of HIV and Kaposi's sarcoma.

thought homosexuality was a disease, they could "cure" it in a matter of weeks. Attempts to change the sexual orientation of homosexual men in this way have consistently failed to work and have been widely criticized on ethical grounds.

The Canadian Psychiatric Association never listed homosexuality as a disorder, but many professionals were influenced by U.S. attitudes. It was not until 1974 that homosexuality was deleted from the American Psychiatric Association's list of psychiatric conditions, and only in the late 1980s did the World Health Organization follow suit. This perception of homosexuality as a disorder has led to medical research for underlying causes for homosexuality.

Brain differences

In 1994 Dr. Simon LeVay, the American scientist who founded the Institute of Gay and Lesbian Education, published research that claimed to show that there might be a provable biological basis for homosexuality. LeVay studied a group of cells, known as INAH3, that are found near the front of the *HYPOTHALAMUS* in the brain. It has already been established that this group of cells is twice as large in men as in women, but LeVay produced evidence to show that there also may be a size difference in INAH3 between straight and gay men.

LeVay studied the brains of 19 gay men who had died of AIDS and 16 heterosexual men, 6 of whom had also died of AIDS. INAH3 turned out to be between two and three times as large in heterosexual men as it was in gay men, regardless of the cause of death. Statistical analysis of LeVay's results suggests that the probability of this happening by chance was about one in a thousand.

Inheriting sexuality

Other studies, which appear to back up the work of both Dean H. Hamer (see box) and LeVay as to physiological and genetic factors that may influence sexual orientation, have examined the family trees of gay men and lesbians. The combined results of these studies show that 50 percent of the women who were identical twins shared their sister's sexual orientation; among male twins the figure was

The role of the fruit ▶ fly Experiments using this species have resulted in important genetic discoveries, including the isolation of a gene that may affect sexuality.

homosexuality of celebrities and people in the public eye whom they believe to be falsely claiming to be heterosexual. Many homosexual people feel that this highly controversial move only intensifies the social climate of fear and hostility that homosexuals have traditionally had to face. Moderate gays believe that each individual should make their own personal decision about whether or not to live openly as a homosexual.

WHAT MAKES SOMEONE GAY?

Modern society used to take the view that homosexuality is a psychological disorder and that homosexuals cannot lead as satisfactory lives as heterosexuals. As a result, attempts have been made to change or modify homosexual behavior with a range of psychological techniques. Among these techniques are psychoanalysis, aversion therapy, desensitization and group therapy. Even sex therapists Masters and Johnson wrote in the 1970s that, although they no longer

57 percent. Among siblings, the percentage of gay people who had a gay brother or sister was 16 percent. The fact that identical twins—who have the same genetic makeup—more often share the same sexual orientation than nonidentical siblings lends some weight to the genetic arguments. It is important to bear in mind, however, that if sexual orientation were determined solely by a person's genes, identical twins would always share the same sexuality—something that has been shown to be untrue.

Can hormones cause homosexuality?

Since the discovery of hormones and their influence on human sexual characteristics, researchers have explored the possibility of a hormonal basis for homosexuality. The first theory proposed by experts was that the level of male and female hormones in adulthood determined sexuality, but this has since been rejected.

More recent theories suggest that fetal exposure to hormones may be important. Exposure to high levels of androgens (male hormones) before birth may lead to heterosexuality in men and homosexuality in women. Conversely, low fetal androgen levels may lead to homosexuality in men and heterosexuality in women. Researchers in this field have drawn the majority of their conclusions from observing the mating behavior of laboratory rats which have been exposed to various levels of sex hormones before birth.

Some studies seem to indicate that the level of hormones present in homosexuals differs from the levels present in heterosexuals. However, while it is well known that physical sexual characteristics such as body hair and fat distribution can be changed by the injection of sex hormones, little evidence shows that sexual orientation can be altered in this way.

Although there are large sections of the scientific community who find the arguments for a biological basis for homosexuality compelling, there remains relatively little consensus about what causes homosexual behavior.

Social conditioning toward a particular sexuality

Possible factors affecting sexuality

Genetic predisposition

Style of parenting

Exposure to hormones as a fetus

Specific experiences in an individual's life

The cause of homosexuality There is little consensus on what factors contribute to sexuality, and many gay and lesbian people feel no need to find a "cause" for their sexual preferences, but the range of possibilities has been the subject of much research.

WHY RESEARCH HOMOSEXUALITY?

Opinions in the lesbian and gay community are sharply divided about the benefits of proving a biological basis for sexual orientation. Early gay activists in the U.S., Canada and the U.K. asked why lesbians and gay men should have the causes of their sexual orientation explored in a way that heterosexuals never would. They argued that if a gene exists for homosexuality, comparable, say, to that for cystic fibrosis, it is theoretically possible to eradicate that gay gene just as scientists believe they will be able to eliminate genes that cause disease.

Another argument against research into biological causes is that parents who discover that their unborn child carries a gene

THE GAY BRAIN

Simon LeVay's research into the anatomy of the brain has revealed that there may be a difference between the brains of heterosexual men and the brains of homosexual men. An area known as INAH3 near the front of the hypothalamus may be significantly smaller in gay men.

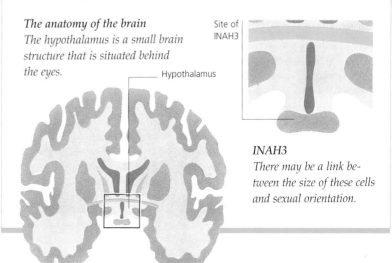

The anatomy of the brain
The hypothalamus is a small brain structure that is situated behind the eyes.

Site of INAH3

Hypothalamus

INAH3
There may be a link between the size of these cells and sexual orientation.

marker that would predispose him or her to homosexuality could, in theory, use this information to justify abortion of the fetus.

The opposing argument suggests that if sexual orientation is inborn, just as are skin color and other physical traits, lesbians and gay men indisputably deserve equal treatment under the law. It also undermines the assumption that homosexuality is a matter of individual choice and therefore can be treated or reversed.

Psychosocial theories

During the early part of the 20th century, sexual orientation was viewed as clear-cut: a person was either heterosexual or homosexual. Sigmund Freud (1856–1939), the Austrian founder of psychoanalysis, theorized that homosexuality is "a variation of the sexual function, produced by a certain arrest of sexual development."

Freud believed that human nature was fundamentally bisexual and that although most people exhibit heterosexual behavior, they repress homosexual desires that exist in their subconscious. Similarly, the "germs

of heterosexuality" are present in every homosexual person. He proposed that sexual orientation develops as a result of an individual's life experiences, so that family and social factors ultimately determine whether an individual's "latent homosexuality" becomes evident or remains hidden.

Another theory of homosexuality concentrates on styles of parenting. The "overbearing mother/absent father" theory suggests that boys grow up to be homosexual if their relationship with their mother is too close, if they grow up without a father or if the father does not provide a strong enough heterosexual role model. The highly controversial German psychiatrist Richard von Krafft-Ebing claimed that boys who prefer "girls' games" or dress in "girls' clothing" will grow up to be homosexual. This idea is now almost completely discredited.

Theories such as these assume that certain characteristics and social behaviors are gender-specific and that children must be taught to follow these as rules. These theories also depend on the stereotypes of the effeminate gay man and the masculine or "butch" lesbian, ignoring the wide range of characteristics and identities found within the lesbian and gay community.

LESBIANISM

Derived from the name of the Greek island Lesbos, which was legendary in the ancient world for its female homosexuality, the word "lesbianism" refers to sexual relations between women. This activity has long been one of society's ultimate taboos, more so than male homosexuality, but in recent years social attitudes toward lesbianism have shifted. The so-called lipstick lesbian—young, usually white, fashionably dressed and well groomed—has replaced the masculine-looking gym teacher as the image of female homosexuality in the popular imagination.

Feminism may have allowed more women to explore their sexual options, but, ironically, it is in the era of post-feminism that large numbers of young women have "come out" as lesbians. An examination of the mass media during the 1990s might lead to the conclusion that there are more lesbians than ever before. Some famous actresses and musicians have publicly affirmed that they are lesbians, and glossy magazines now realize that lesbianism sells.

Can We Talk About It?

DISCUSSING SEXUALITY

For parents, accepting that a son or daughter is homosexual may seem like an impossible request. As a result, a gay child may put off telling their parents because they fear a negative reaction or rejection. Many people believe that homosexuality is a psychological problem, possibly brought about by a failure in their parenting. They may feel guilty, have strong moral or religious objections or simply fear for a child living with society's prejudices. They may also resent the fact that their child is less likely to produce grandchildren. A gay child may have to educate parents about what being gay or lesbian means, but attempting to communicate can be fruitful in the end.

But it remains impossible to obtain an accurate figure for the percentage of women who identify themselves as lesbian. As with male homosexuality, sexual activity and identity are not always the same thing, and not all women who have sex with women are exclusively homosexual.

Theories of lesbianism

In comparison with the burgeoning field of research into male homosexuality, little scientific interest has been shown in the potential causes of lesbianism. Some women are never interested in men as sexual partners, while others experiment with heterosexual sex before settling into a pattern of lesbian relationships. Social expectations can make it difficult for women to resist marriage and motherhood, and some women with lesbian inclinations do not begin to form sexual relationships with other women until their thirties, forties or later.

In the 1970s a commitment to political lesbianism led some women to enter sexual relationships with other women. Rather than being motivated by sexual preference, this may have been an extension of a feminist rejection of men and patriarchal values.

One psychosocial theory of lesbianism states that traumatic experiences with men, such as rape or sexual abuse, can cause women to "turn into lesbians" as a way of avoiding men. Most lesbians would say, however, that men are irrelevant in their choice of sexual partner: they don't hate men; they simply prefer women.

HOW MANY PEOPLE ARE GAY?

No consensus exists about how many adults have had some kind of homosexual experience. Alfred Kinsey's surveys, *Sexual Behavior in the Human Male and Female*, conducted in the 1940s and 1950s in the U.S., revolutionized attitudes toward sexual orientation by suggesting a 7-point scale ranging from 0 (solely heterosexual) to 6 (solely homosexual) with 3—the midpoint—representing bisexuality (sexual relationships with both genders). According to Kinsey, 75 percent of men and 85 percent of women are solely heterosexual; 2 percent of men and 1 percent of women are solely homosexual; and 23 percent of men and 14 percent of women have had a combination of heterosexual and homosexual experiences.

In their study *Evidence for a Biological Influence in Male Homosexuality*, Simon LeVay and Dean H. Hamer state that current estimates for homosexuality range between 1 and 5 percent of the population. They point out, however, that these figures represent only those who are exclusively attracted to members of their own sex.

All these figures can be manipulated for the purposes of those who are quoting them; certainly the number of adults who have had some kind of homosexual experience is greater than the number of adults

Behavior only

Self-identification only

Desire and behavior

Desire and self-identification

Desire, behavior and self-identification

Behavior and self-identification

Desire only

Defining gay feelings
Among those who express gay sexual feelings, the majority desire same-gender sex but do not act on it ('desire'), others act on this desire ('behavior'), and some openly identify themselves as gay ('self-identification'). There is also overlap between these groups.

HOMOSEXUALITY IN OTHER CULTURES

In non-Western societies, particularly Islamic ones, men can have sex with other men without being perceived as gay. Homosexual sex is simply a pleasurable pastime that does not reflect upon an individual's sexuality (in fact, it may have more to do with the inaccessibility of women). The practice of young boys—known as pleasure boys—working as male prostitutes is widespread in countries such as Pakistan.

Homosexuality in Pakistan
Cinemas showing pornography are also popular places for men to pick up other men. These men would be unlikely to define themselves as gay.

Gay festivals ▶
Carnivals, marches, parades and festivals form part of the annual gay calendar in many Western countries. Some of these events are highly politicized; others, such as this one, are fun events that are celebrations of camp exhibitionism.

Gay weddings *Long-term gay lovers may wish to show their commitment formally, although homosexual marriages are still not legally recognized in many countries.*

who would identify themselves as gay, lesbian or even as bisexual.

While not every country openly accepts homosexuality, many do recognize that it exists. For example, some tribes in rural Africa recognize female "husbands"—women who provide other women with the economic support traditionally associated with men. In societies that are intolerant of homosexuality, people may have sex with same-sex partners yet also bow to cultural expectations and marry and have children.

Some bisexuals claim that they are doubly discriminated against: by heterosexual society for having gay relationships, and by lesbian and gay society for being uncommitted, undecided or just too cowardly to come out. Many bisexuals, however, say that their sexual orientation is simply due to a need for greater variety in their sexual relationships.

TRANSVESTISM

A transvestite is someone who takes erotic pleasure in wearing clothes that are associated with the opposite sex (cross-dressing). Because it is more socially acceptable for women to adopt male-style clothing, the term is generally applied to men only. Many transvestites are heterosexual men who enjoy conventional sexual relations with women. Sometimes they are married men whose partners cooperate with their cross-dressing.

For some people, however, cross-dressing is more than just a sexual fetish. Living and dressing as a member of the opposite sex is a fundamental part of their sexual identity and may precede gender reassignment surgery (sex-change operations).

Among gay men, cross-dressing is known as dressing in "drag" and may have nothing to do with transvestism or transsexualism. It has been a popular form of entertainment for centuries. In the U.K., especially, the character of the pantomime "dame," played by a man (not necessarily a homosexual) in a woman's dress and wearing garish makeup, is an enduring part of traditional entertainment.

TRANSSEXUALS

Some people grow up with an overwhelming sensation that they are trapped in a body of the wrong gender and feel that they can live a satisfactory life only if they "change sex." The most radical way to achieve this is to have gender reassignment surgery. In order to qualify for this surgery, an individual must convince a psychiatrist that personal dissatisfaction with the gender they were born with is genuine. The individual is required to dress, live and work assuming the new gender role for a period of two years.

For female-to-male transsexuals, gender reassignment surgery can include removal of the breasts and the female reproductive organs and, in some cases, construction of a penis from vaginal and clitoral skin, and muscle and skin from the forearm. People who have undergone this type of surgery must take male hormones for the rest of their lives in order to maintain muscle bulk, facial and body hair, and deeper voices.

For male-to-female transsexuals, surgery can include *CASTRATION*, construction of a vagina using tissue from the penis, and breast implants. Female hormones inhibit the growth of facial and body hair and allow the voice to rise in pitch and sound more feminine.

Once gender reassignment surgery has taken place, the individual may receive documents identifying him or her by a chosen new name, although such documents do not include a gender-specific title such as Miss, Ms., Mrs. or Mr.

THE PHYSICAL
EXPRESSION
OF LOVE

Sex and Gender 34

Masturbation 38

Foreplay 40

The Role of Erotica 47

Sexual Intercourse 52

Prolonging Sexual Intercourse 56

Oral Sex 64

Anal Sex 66

Sex and Gender

Significant differences exist between male and female sexual behavior and responses. Among other things, men and women often need differing levels of stimulation before they reach orgasm, and they may attach different meanings to sex.

Many differences between male and female sexual behavior can be attributed to social and cultural influences. For example, society has long portrayed the typical male as thinking constantly about sex, being easily aroused and regularly requiring sexual release. Women, on the other hand, have been characterized as sexually more passive and requiring sexual satisfaction less frequently. These kinds of stereotypes can have a direct impact on the way that individual men and women think and feel about their own sexuality.

FEMALE SEXUALITY

Sex researcher Alfred Kinsey highlighted the practical implications of cultural beliefs about sex when he reported that most married women surveyed had never experienced orgasm. Furthermore, a significant number did not even know it was possible for a woman to experience the same degree of sexual satisfaction as her husband. This meant that many women obtained little or no pleasure from sex and even tried to find ways to avoid it. This in turn led to the euphemistic "I've got a headache" response from wives to any sexual overture by their husbands.

Assumptions about female orgasm and sexuality have often originated from social conditioning rather than from knowledge about physiological differences between the sexes. Many women in the past were brought up to believe that they were immoral and unnatural if they enjoyed sex. No one thought it appropriate to teach women about sex, and thus many women entered marriage in a state of total ignorance about intercourse. While society exercised no such scruples about making sexual knowledge available to men, husbands were nonetheless typically as ignorant as their wives about sexual matters. As a result, many women played no active part in sexual intercourse and never discovered how best to achieve sexual stimulation for their own satisfaction.

DO MEN NEED SEX MORE THAN WOMEN DO?

There is a misconception that men have a greater need for sex than women do. In fact, both sexes can survive without sexual intercourse, and many women perceive their "need" or desire for sex as equal to or greater than that of their male partner. Once men and women reach a high level of arousal, both sexes may experience sexual frustration or discomfort if they do not reach orgasm.

Sexual desire and gender
The misconception that men need sex more than women do may have arisen because men ejaculate and women do not. A man does not need to ejaculate through sexual intercourse or masturbation; his sperm can be reabsorbed or released during nocturnal emissions.

Today, society's views about female sexuality and the woman's role in sexual intercourse have changed, and it is widely recognized that a woman has a natural sexual drive that can match or even exceed that of her partner. Now that it is deemed normal—and in fact desirable—for women to take an active role in sex, the differences that exist between male and female sexual behavior have become less marked.

REACHING ORGASM

Cultural factors can have a direct bearing on women's experience of sex, but physiological differences also exist between the genders. For example, men experience a stage after orgasm during which they are unable to achieve erection or ejaculation (see page 110). For most women, the equivalent period is very short or nonexistent, giving them the potential to achieve several orgasms in a short period of time (known as multiple or sequential orgasms). While women typically seem able to have more orgasms than men, emotional factors, distractions and anxiety affect their sex drive more easily.

Both sexes may become excited in the presence of someone whom they find attractive, but men are more likely to become aroused by objects or situations that they associate with sex (in extreme cases this is called a fetish).

Men and women reach their sexual peaks at different ages. Many men in their teens report having five orgasms a week—this falls to two or three by their forties. Women experience a much steadier pattern. In a survey by Kinsey (1979), women ranging between ages 20 and 60 who reported masturbating said that they experienced orgasm on average once or twice a week.

Variations and extremes of sexual activity and responses exist in both sexes, so that someone of either sex may become aroused and reach orgasm through intercourse or masturbation several times a day, while another person may remain unexcited and sexually inactive for long periods of time.

fact or fiction?

Women do not need to masturbate.

Fact. Neither sex needs to masturbate for health reasons, but masturbation is a way of releasing sexual tension and learning about sexual responses. Until recently it was accepted that men masturbated but not that women did. Now masturbation is considered acceptable in both sexes.

IMPORTANCE OF RELATIONSHIPS

While it's clear that everyone responds differently to the experience of sex in a relationship, certain gender-specific differences appear to exist in attitudes toward the need for emotional bonding. In particular, many women consider it much more important for lovemaking to occur as part of a permanent and meaningful relationship than do their male partners.

In *The Hite Report on Love, Passion & Emotional Violence* (1991), the overwhelming majority of women questioned (83 percent) said that they preferred sex in the context of an emotional involvement—in other words "sex with commitment"—to a purely casual sexual encounter.

Although the majority of women surveyed said they had often had sex on a first date (76 percent), most said that they would have much rather waited until the relationship had reached a more established footing, no matter how physically aroused they were. For many men, however, sexual intercourse is seen as a sufficient goal in itself,

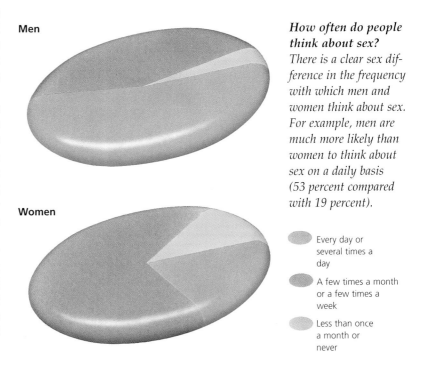

Men

Women

How often do people think about sex?
There is a clear sex difference in the frequency with which men and women think about sex. For example, men are much more likely than women to think about sex on a daily basis (53 percent compared with 19 percent).

Every day or several times a day

A few times a month or a few times a week

Less than once a month or never

and they will commonly find it easy to separate the purely physical aspect of lovemaking from any emotional feelings.

This gender difference is often reflected in sexual encounters occurring outside of a steady relationship. Men are more likely than women to have casual sexual affairs, and more men than women say that such encounters are for sex alone, resulting from a purely physical attraction, and have no emotional significance.

Women who have affairs, on the other hand, more often say that they were attracted to a man for emotional reasons and that sex is a secondary factor. A woman might be attracted to a man because he shows a more considerate or caring attitude than her regular partner or because he shares many of her ideas and interests. Such encounters are frequently an indication that a woman is unhappy with her present partner and lead to her breaking up the relationship, whereas men who have affairs usually return to their existing partner.

According to Shere Hite's report, most women are motivated primarily by the desire to form a permanent bond when seeking a sexual partner. The majority of women in her survey (84 percent) said they believed that having loving relationships is one of the first priorities in life but did not believe men had the same priorities. In fact, 85 percent of women in their teens and twenties, when questioned, said they thought most men "see sex as a sport" and "try to get a girl just to increase their score."

PREMARITAL SEX

Someone who has a greater than average number of sexual partners is often termed promiscuous. What that average number is varies from culture to culture, and even for people of similar backgrounds it is largely a matter of individual perception. Cultures that regard virginity as an important sign of personal morality frown on premarital sex for both sexes, but especially for young women. In the West, however, premarital sexual activity is becoming more prevalent and less stigmatized.

In a U.K. survey conducted in 1994, *Sexual Behaviour in Britain*, men consistently reported greater numbers of partners than did women. In the 16 to 24 age group (this is usually the most sexually active group), 11.2 percent of men, compared with 2.5 per-

BODY IMAGE AND SEX

There is a clear gender difference in the way that body image affects men's and women's perceptions of their sexuality. Women who are overweight or perceive themselves as physically imperfect may extrapolate from this and label themselves sexually undesirable. Conversely, it is thought that some women may overeat and put on weight in an attempt to "desexualize" themselves. Men are far less likely to jump to conclusions about their sexual desirability based on their appearance, although this is something that may change as the media places increasing emphasis on the erotic nature of the male body.

The Language of Sex

"Nymphomania" is a word that was invented in the 18th century, combining "nymph" (a beautiful maiden in Greek mythology) and "mania," a word used to describe a mental abnormality or obsession. In the past the term was used to describe any woman with a sexual appetite, since it was considered wrong for a woman to enjoy sex for its own sake. The pressure for women to conform to society's expectations was once so strong that what people would now regard as normal sexual expression was then seen as a disease. Today the term "nymphomania" has become largely obsolete except in cases of sexual obsession, usually arising from mental illness.

cent of women, reported 10 or more partners in the previous five years.

The latest figures in the U.S. and Canada tend to support these findings. Of those currently aged 16 to 24 years, 73 percent of American men and 56 percent of women experienced first intercourse before the age of 18. This compares with only 55 percent of men and 35 percent of women in the early 1970s. A Canadian survey conducted in 1994–95, *The Canadian Health Monitors*, reported 27 percent of 15-year-old men engaging in sexual intercourse compared to only 7 percent of 15-year-old women. In the 15 to 19 age group, 12 percent of men reported 6 or more partners (no women did).

Men and, especially, women are having sex at a younger age, and this may result in their having more sexual partners during their life than previous generations had.

FANTASY AND EROTICA

One area of sexual behavior in which men and women are becoming more alike is in their attitude toward erotic literature and even pornography. Traditionally men have found a greater number of sources to feed their sexual fantasies, particularly in terms of images of women as sexual objects, in newspapers, magazines, advertising, and in erotic films or books.

Today, however, many more women admit that viewing sexually explicit material increases their interest in sex. As a result, publishers are aiming an increasing number of erotic magazines and books primarily at women. The work of Nancy Friday (see page 172) shows that women can be aroused by a wide range of stimuli and that erotic images help them to achieve sexual arousal.

For women, as for men, erotic material can provide the raw material for sexual fantasies. Sex researchers now know that fantasies play as important a part in a woman's sexual behavior as they do in a man's. Just like men, women use fantasies to enhance their sexual arousal and to aid masturbation. But important gender differences exist in the types of sexual fantasies experienced by men and women.

For most women, romance plays a much greater part in their fantasies than for men. Many women fantasize about a man who is well known to them, usually their current sexual partner or a former lover. Women often prepare themselves for a sexual meeting by fantasizing about the evening ahead.

On the other hand, men typically fantasize about a woman other than their current partner, such as a complete stranger, celebrity, friend or neighbor.

As a rule, more men have fantasies in which they are the dominant partner, while more women imagine situations in which they play a submissive role. With fantasies, however, as with most other aspects of sexual behavior, numerous exceptions exist to such rules. In fact, a significant number of women report having fantasies in which they have a male sex slave, while some men fantasize about being forced to have sex by a woman. A woman brought up in an environment in which it was considered wrong to have strong sexual feelings may imagine being forced to have sex as a way to free herself of any feelings of guilt associated with sexual intercourse. In effect, the woman is creating a scenario in which she has no control over the sex act and so cannot be blamed for taking part and enjoying it. For similar reasons, some women experience arousal only during bondage sex— being tied up before sex.

CHANGING SOCIAL ATTITUDES TOWARD FEMALE SEXUALITY

Shere Hite
Social historian Shere Hite produced some of the most pioneering studies of sexuality in the 20th century. Her book The Hite Report is a collection of first-person accounts of female sexual experience.

Strip shows for women ▲
In the past, strip shows were performed by women for the benefit of men. Today shows in which men strip and dance naked or semi-naked for women are common.

Provocative fashion ▶
Exposing the body is no longer taboo. Fashion designers often create clothes that emphasize the female form— less exaggerated forms of these clothes filter down onto the street.

Masturbation

Taboos surrounding masturbation have lessened in recent decades. Experts have dispelled long-held beliefs that self-stimulation can lead to blindness, weakness, madness or loss of virginity.

It used to be assumed that only boys and men masturbated, but it is now widely acknowledged that women of all ages masturbate too. In a 1966 survey, 46 percent of women admitted to having masturbated by the age of 20. The same survey, when repeated in 1981, indicated that this figure had increased to 73 percent. The work of Nancy Friday (see page 172) offers ample evidence of the rich fantasy and masturbatory lives of women.

Although babies and children gain sensual pleasure from genital touching, true adult masturbation begins around adolescence. Adult masturbation usually involves stimulating oneself to orgasm, often employing fantasies or erotic thoughts.

WHAT HAPPENS DURING MASTURBATION?

People masturbate in different ways. Boys and men usually stroke the penis repeatedly with the hand until they ejaculate. The penis also can be stimulated in other ways, such as being rubbed against a towel or mattress. To reduce friction and increase sensation, men sometimes apply a lubricant such as massage oil or saliva to the penis when they masturbate.

Girls and women usually masturbate by rubbing or stroking the clitoris with one or more fingers, but *The Hite Report* (1976) revealed a great variety of different methods—some women insert their fingers or a dildo into the vagina and rub the clitoris at the same time;

The instinct to masturbate Young children and infants of both sexes handle their genitals for comfort, pleasure and out of curiosity. Childhood masturbation is both normal and natural.

some hold a vibrator or a jet of water from a shower against the clitoris; others move themselves against a soft object such as a pillow or a bed; others cross their legs and squeeze them together rhythmically. Some women stimulate or caress other areas of their bodies, such as the breasts or the anus, while they masturbate.

Both men and women commonly have sexual fantasies during masturbation. Some people look at erotic material—reading a sexy story or watching a film in which people make love—and as they become sexually aroused, stimulation of the genitals tends to increase arousal and erotic thoughts, which results in more genital stimulation and so on, until this cycle of pleasure culminates in orgasm.

The physical changes that accompany masturbation are the same as those that accompany intercourse. A man's penis becomes erect and a clear secretion may appear at the opening. When sexual arousal reaches its peak, he ejaculates semen. A woman's vagina produces lubrication, and the labia and clitoris become engorged with blood. With sufficient clitoral stimulation, the woman reaches orgasm.

In years past, people believed that masturbation could damage an individual's capacity for sexual enjoyment during intercourse. In other words, a man or a woman would become so dependent on masturbation for sexual pleasure that he or she would be unable to enjoy stimulation from a partner. Today most sex therapists agree that masturbation serves an important function in helping people to learn about their own sexual potential. When a person has first explored and come to fully understand his or her own body in private, he or she may find it easier to communicate their sexual needs to a partner and therefore derive greater sexual satisfaction.

MASTURBATION WITH A PARTNER

Couples often engage in masturbation as part of foreplay or as an alternative to sex. One partner stimulates the other's genitals to orgasm, or both partners stimulate each other simultaneously. Mutual masturbation is commonly a feature of heavy petting in couples who, for whatever reason, do not want to have penetrative sex.

Stimulation may be with fingers, vibrators, dildos or other sex aids. Partners can show each other how they like to be touched, or each can learn what the other wants by watching his or her partner masturbate. Many people feel self-conscious and inhibited when discussing masturbation and what they require for sexual satisfaction. Women are embarrassed about showing a partner how to give clitoral stimulation. If reservations and inhibitions can be overcome, many people find masturbation a very useful and enjoyable accompaniment to lovemaking.

Masturbation during intercourse

Apart from mutual masturbation as foreplay or as an alternative to sex, women can masturbate during sex when the penis is inside the vagina. A sex therapist may recommend this for women who do not reach orgasm from penile thrusting alone or for women who wish to reach orgasm more quickly than penile thrusting allows.

Some sexual positions make masturbation during intercourse easier than others. The missionary position gives limited access to the clitoris, whereas woman-on-top or rear-entry positions provide easy access. A man can also use his hand to stimulate his partner's clitoris in any sexual position that allows this.

Masturbation may also enhance a sexual encounter after sexual intercourse, if either partner (more often the woman) did not reach orgasm or wants to have more orgasms. If a man is suffering from premature ejaculation, postcoital masturbation provides a good way for a woman to reach

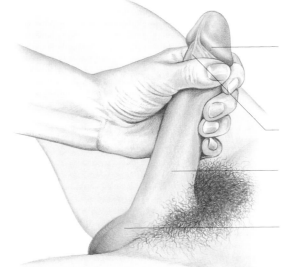

The glans, or head, is the most sensitive part of the penis.

The frenulum (the fold of skin that joins the foreskin to the glans) responds to friction during masturbation.

The shaft is rhythmically stroked in masturbation.

Some men enjoy having their testicles cupped or stroked during masturbation.

orgasm (although in severe cases of premature ejaculation, the sufferer may require proper treatment—see page 163).

Some people think that masturbation has no place in the context of lovemaking. They feel that it violates the spirit of lovemaking, which is about the giving and receiving of sexual stimulation by a partner—not by oneself. Others enjoy masturbation during lovemaking, and argue that any technique that increases arousal is not a failure.

Stimulating the penis
Everyone has their own masturbation technique. Women can talk to their partners about how they like to be touched and then ask for feedback.

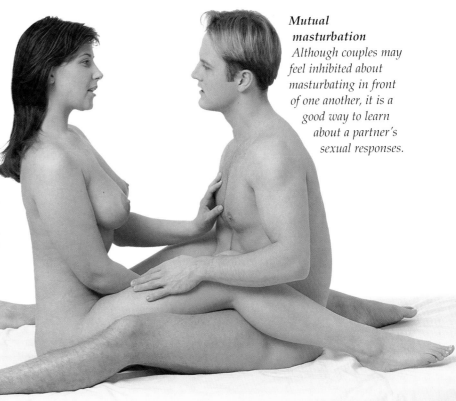

Mutual masturbation
Although couples may feel inhibited about masturbating in front of one another, it is a good way to learn about a partner's sexual responses.

Foreplay

The arousing behavior that a couple enjoy before sexual intercourse is called foreplay. It can include kissing, cuddling, gentle biting, stroking each other's bodies, caressing the breasts and genitals, sensual massage, oral sex, and using sex toys.

Foreplay allows the body to become ready for sexual intercourse. As a couple kiss, cuddle and stroke each other's bodies they become sexually aroused, and their bodies prepare for penetrative sex (although foreplay does not always have to lead to intercourse). The man's penis becomes erect, and the woman's vagina lengthens and produces lubrication that will allow penetration to occur comfortably. The *LABIA* around the vagina swell and open, making the vagina more readily accessible. Since women, in general, reach arousal more slowly, foreplay is usually more important for them than for men, especially if they want to become sufficiently aroused to reach orgasm.

Foreplay also helps a couple to relax, enjoy each other's proximity and feel close emotionally as well as physically. Sexual intercourse requires openness, trust and mutual acceptance. Foreplay allows people to reach this necessary level of intimacy.

CREATING AN INTIMATE ATMOSPHERE

The right setting is important for any sexual intimacy. Privacy is essential—both partners should be equally committed to not answering the door, the telephone or the pager. The importance of personal hygiene can vary among couples (and cultures), but the generally accepted standard and unspoken consideration between partners includes clean teeth, hair and skin—especially armpits, feet and genitals. Many couples find that sharing a bath or a shower helps them to unwind together. Aromatherapy oils added to bath water can have relaxing or energizing properties, and washing each other's hair or massaging each other with scented lotions or oils encourages feelings of closeness (see page 44). The bathroom can also be an exciting place in which to make love.

Preparing a room for sexual intimacy can enhance pleasure. The right temperature, soft music, soft lighting (candles) and even seductive scents (heated essential oils, scented candles, incense or fresh flowers) can all be used to set the scene.

The buildup to intercourse

Individuals vary greatly in the amount of foreplay they enjoy. Sometimes couples like to take their time and engage in a variety of activities until they feel unable to postpone penetration any longer. In this case, foreplay ensures a slow buildup to the consuming excitement of intercourse. Other times a couple may become aroused very quickly and may indulge in little or no foreplay before they have intercourse. Some couples have intercourse several times with foreplay that lasts as long as the man's *REFRACTORY PERIODS*; in this case, foreplay may be as important as intercourse itself.

THE POWER OF SUGGESTION

In sexual matters, subtlety can be very arousing—a glimpse is often more erotic than complete exposure. A wide range of moods are possible—ripping each other's clothes off in the height of passion can be

Undressing Foreplay can begin before a couple get into bed. Many couples enjoy a bath together or undressing each other.

very exciting on occasions, but sometimes it may be more seductive to reveal one's body very slowly, bit by bit. Many people find it extremely arousing when their partner concentrates on touching subtler erogenous zones such as the thighs, buttocks or feet rather than immediate stimulation of the breasts or genitals.

Suggestion can be used in many other ways to heighten sexual arousal. Simply creating a mood or an awareness of sexual intimacy is a type of foreplay. A telephone call or a letter hinting at sensations to come can kindle desire even at a distance. A romantic dinner or a country walk may serve as a preamble to sex no matter how long a couple have been together. Devoting plenty of time to kissing, caressing and touching before sexual intercourse may also build excitement. The power of suggestion can even be applied to genital touching: one partner gently circles the other's genitals without directly stimulating them.

EROGENOUS ZONES

Specific areas on the body, known as erogenous zones, often produce a high level of sensual and sexual pleasure when touched. While the breasts and genitals are the two most obvious erogenous zones, there are many other parts of the body that respond to stimulation as well. By exploring these parts, partners can make sex an experience involving the whole body, rather than one concerned just with genital stimulation.

Starting at the top of the body, many people enjoy their hair being stroked, brushed, kissed or even gently pulled. Many also respond to having their ears and earlobes nibbled, caressed with the tongue or gently blown or whispered into. Stroking, licking and kissing the back of the neck, lips and mouth and the area around the breasts, such as the inner arm, chest and armpits, gives great sexual pleasure to many men and women. Men's nipples vary in sensitivity—some men enjoy having them nibbled or sucked; others do not.

The buttocks and the inner thighs are also erogenous zones that respond to caressing, gentle biting and even playful slapping. Lower down the legs, the backs of the knees, calves and ankles are sensitive, as anyone who has ever played "footsie" under a dinner table knows. Finally, the feet and toes are well-known erogenous zones—many people enjoy having them massaged, licked and sucked. Most people have their

ALL-OVER TOUCHING

Kissing, licking, nibbling and stroking the erogenous zones can be highly erotic for both giver and recipient. The toes, backs of the knees, fingers and eyelids are areas that are often neglected during foreplay. Giving this sort of sensual pleasure provides a slow, luxurious buildup to sex, and can be a novel experience for many couples.

Touch the lips and cheeks with the fingertips.

Stimulating the erogenous zones
Prolonged caressing of the erogenous zones can set the scene for sex or can be a type of sexual play in its own right—sex need not involve penetration.

Brush the fingertips against the backs of the knees.

Stroke and caress the breasts and belly.

Kiss the soles of the feet and suck and nibble the toes.

Massage the muscles of the calves and thighs.

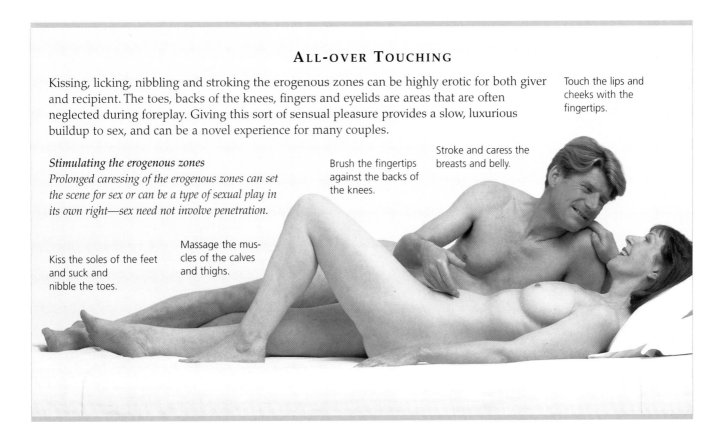

own personal preferences about how and where they like to be touched, and a perceptive lover will discover these and use them to give pleasure during foreplay.

KISSING

The lips, among the most sensitive areas of the body, contain a rich supply of nerve endings. Kissing is a deeply erotic and intimate act. The great number of works of art that depict the kiss in all media—painting, sculpture, literature and film—testify to its erotic power. The meaning of a kiss can range from the urgent passion of a new relationship to the everyday currency of affection in a long-standing one. Kissing often initiates the first intimate physical exchange between people who are going to become lovers. It is also said to be the first activity to stop (even before intercourse) when a relationship is under strain.

As many lovers know, kissing is not the same activity over and over again but a mutual and varied exploration of the lips, tongue and mouth. Some people find deep penetration with the tongue very arousing, but so too subtler kisses, licks and nibbles. In fact, it is the variety that many people enjoy, from light kisses to deep ones and back to light ones again.

Passionate kissing
Kissing can be one of the most intimate and erotic ways for lovers to express their feelings. Passionate kissing is often the sign of a new love, and something that longer-term couples may neglect.

CARESSING

Touching and stroking are important parts of foreplay. A caress eloquently expresses love, affection and sensuality. Lovers may begin foreplay by kissing and touching the face, neck and hair and move on slowly to other areas, such as the shoulders, back and belly. Movements can be light strokes in which the flat of the hand barely touches the skin, gentle scratching along the back using the fingernails or massage strokes (see page 45).

THE *KAMA SUTRA* ON KISSING

Along with a wealth of other advice on lovemaking, the *Kama Sutra* lists many different types of kissing techniques, among them the straight kiss, the bent kiss, the turned kiss and the pressed kiss. In the straight kiss, the two lovers bring their lips into direct contact; for the bent kiss, lovers bend their heads toward each other; for the turned kiss, one partner "turns up the face of the other by holding the head and the chin"; and for the pressed kiss, the lower lip is pressed with "much force."

The book's author, Vatsyayana, described French kissing as "fighting of the tongue." He considered it to be an extension of the clasping kiss, which is where one partner takes the lips of the other between his or her own. The parts of the body that Vatsyayana recommended for kissing included "the forehead, the eyes, the cheeks, the throat, the bosom, the breasts, the lips and the interior of the mouth."

Caressing often leads to more focused genital stimulation and possibly sexual intercourse, but it can also be very relaxing and rewarding in itself. By definition, caresses are not rushed, painful or ticklish, especially when concentrated around the sensitive genital areas. Partners can show each other how they like to be caressed and take turns massaging each other.

NONPENETRATIVE SEX

Foreplay does not necessarily conclude with sexual intercourse. Many couples enjoy foreplay on its own, and sex therapists say this type of lovemaking, which takes place without the penis entering the vagina, can be as satisfying as penetrative

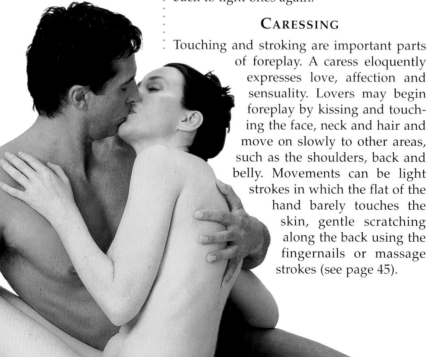

sex: both partners can reach orgasm in their own time, under less performance pressure and with a strong emphasis on the sensual enjoyment of sex.

Many people practice both penetrative sex and nonpenetrative sex, adding variation to their sex life, but there are many reasons why couples may choose nonpenetrative sex, other than the sheer enjoyment of foreplay in its own right.

If one partner has a sexually transmitted disease, foreplay provides a sexual outlet that avoids the danger of infecting the healthy partner. Nonpenetrative sex in this case still requires safer sex practices (see page 128). Some people avoid penetration with a new partner because they do not know enough about that person's sexual history, or because they want to wait until they feel sure that their relationship has a stable basis. Others avoid penetration for personal or religious reasons, usually in the belief that intercourse is appropriate only in the context of marriage. Advanced pregnancy and certain medical conditions or disabilities may preclude full intercourse, and other circumstances such as menstruation may make nonpenetrative sex desirable.

During adolescence many teenagers, especially girls, explore their sexuality through nonpenetrative sex because they do not feel ready to engage in sexual intercourse or fear the risk of pregnancy. Experimenting with kissing and cuddling provides an outlet for sexual feelings without having to make the major emotional decision to have sexual intercourse for the first time. An adolescent should not feel pushed into having sex either by their partner or by peer pressure. Many people who have first sex at a young age later wish that they had waited until a time of greater maturity or until they had found a partner to whom they felt total commitment.

Some adolescents simply have little or no interest in sex, and this is perfectly natural too; there is no obligation for anyone to be sexually active if they do not want to be.

SENSUAL MASSAGE

Whether or not it leads to lovemaking, massage provides a good way for partners to explore each other's bodies and become intimate in a sensual, relaxed setting. The rules for foreplay apply to massage as well. Complete privacy and a warm and comfort-

able room create the best atmosphere. Massage oils, which can be bought commercially or mixed at home, increase the pleasure by eliminating friction. Aromatherapists recommend adding specific essential oils that are thought to have relaxant properties to a base oil (see page 44).

Can We Talk About It?

FOREPLAY THAT DOES NOT LEAD TO SEX

Foreplay focuses on fun, affection and becoming aroused. It can lead to sexual intercourse, but it does not have to. Couples may feel just as fulfilled by massage, masturbation and stroking as by penetrative sex. If, however, sexual encounters begin and end with foreplay when you desire intercourse, or if your partner is pressuring you to have intercourse when you do not want to, you should discuss the situation.

If you are frustrated that foreplay does not progress to intercourse, gently and sympathetically question your partner and encourage him or her to talk about their feelings. Is your partner inexperienced sexually? Have you had intercourse with your partner before? If not, would intercourse with this person have traumatic consequences or lead to overwhelming guilt? Have you ever asked your partner what sort of foreplay he or she likes or does not like? Is there tension in your relationship? Is your partner anxious, depressed or fearful of pregnancy? Has your partner ever suffered from a sexual problem such as vaginismus or premature ejaculation? Has your partner had a disastrous or traumatic sexual encounter in the past? Does your partner simply not feel interested in or ready for intercourse?

If, on the other hand, you feel that your partner is pressuring you to go further sexually than you want to go, try to explain your reasons for resisting this. Say what you do and do not feel comfortable doing. If you do not want sexual intercourse, but are happy stimulating your partner to orgasm then say so. It is fine to say that things are moving too fast for you, that you do not feel ready to have sex or that you would like your partner to do different things during foreplay. Open discussion may enable you to work out how your sex life should progress.

Sensual Massage

Massage can be a blissfully relaxing or sexually stimulating event. You and your partner can use it to lie back and enjoy each other's bodies without having sex or you can use it to build up sexual intimacy as a prelude to sex—you choose.

No particular skills are needed to give a massage, but knowledge of some simple guidelines and the basic massage strokes can help. The person receiving the massage should lie flat on the floor. The person giving the massage can sit astride the buttocks, between the legs or at the head of the partner. The hands should be coated in oil so that they glide smoothly over the skin, and once the hands have made contact with the skin, they should be removed as little as possible for the duration of the massage. Bear in mind that massage oil damages condoms, so make sure to wash before intercourse.

CREATING THE RIGHT ATMOSPHERE

Bathing before intimacy can really improve your mental and physical state and thus enhance any sensual experience. A hot bath will open the pores, allowing toxins to be expelled, and soothe tired, aching muscles.

Incense, particularly sweet scents such as jasmine, rose, ylang-ylang, sandalwood, rosemary, lavender, amber, mandarin, and patchouli have the capacity to soothe and stimulate both body and spirit. You can mix essential oils with water and spray the mixture into the room or onto the sheets and pillows. You could also use candles to provide a soft, romantic light.

Towels can be rough on the skin, so spread out old sheets (they may become stained by the oils), which will be much softer and drape fabric over any hard edges. Have plenty of soft pillows or cushions handy to support your bodies in different positions and make sure the room is warm enough to be naked in.

MASSAGE OILS

Using massage oil allows your hands to glide easily over your partner's body with smooth, clean strokes. Use a ready-made

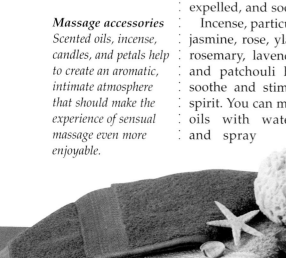

Massage accessories
Scented oils, incense, candles, and petals help to create an aromatic, intimate atmosphere that should make the experience of sensual massage even more enjoyable.

EFFLEURAGE

This is a long gliding or sweeping stroke in which the flat palms travel across a large expanse of skin such as the back. If different parts of the body are being massaged—the buttocks and the shoulders, for example—effleurage strokes can be used to move the hands from one place to another.

PETRISSAGE

This stroke involves kneading movements. The person giving the massage gently squeezes, twists and rolls the flesh between the hands and the fingers and thumbs. Petrissage aims at getting rid of tension spots in muscles that have built up through stress, anxiety or bad posture.

FRICTION

A variation of petrissage, friction involves constant pressure or small circular movements applied to a small area. The pads of the thumbs or the knuckles are used to apply pressure. Like petrissage, friction helps to ease knotted muscles.

HACKING

The person giving the massage forms the hands into loose cup shapes and chops or hacks the skin. As an alternative, hacking can be performed with the hands held straight. Hacking is designed to invigorate and energize rather than relax.

massage oil or create your own by blending three drops of an essential oil into a tablespoon of base oil, such as a vegetable oil, almond oil, or sweet oil.

Gently warm the oil before use by standing the bottle in a bowl of warm water or rubbing it between your hands before applying it. Pour about a teaspoonful of oil into your hands at a time and rub your hands together to spread the oil over. Then use your hands to spread this oil evenly over the area of your partner's skin that you are going to massage.

MASSAGE TECHNIQUES

When giving the massage, you should keep one or both hands touching your partner's body from the moment the massage begins until it ends. Experiment with different speeds and pressures, and find a rhythm that enables you to make the strokes flow from one movement to another. Use your common sense to guide you when choosing which strokes to use on different parts of your partner's body—notice his or her reactions and adapt the type, speed, and pressure of your strokes accordingly.

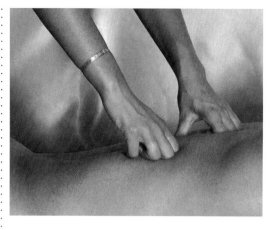

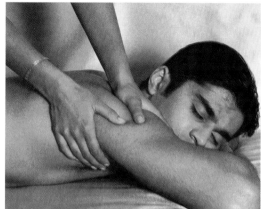

Fleshier parts *of the body such as the buttocks respond well to firm strokes such as knuckling, where you apply a gentle pressure with the bony parts of your fingers.*

The arms *should be massaged from the top of the shoulders downward, so that you end by manipulating the wrist, the hands and the fingers.*

Massage sequence
You should first massage the whole of the torso several times from the shoulders down to the buttocks and back up again before concentrating on individual areas such as the shoulderblades. Ask your partner to roll over and massage the shoulders and neck before working down each arm and then the front of the torso. Then massage the front of the legs and finish by massaging the scalp and face.

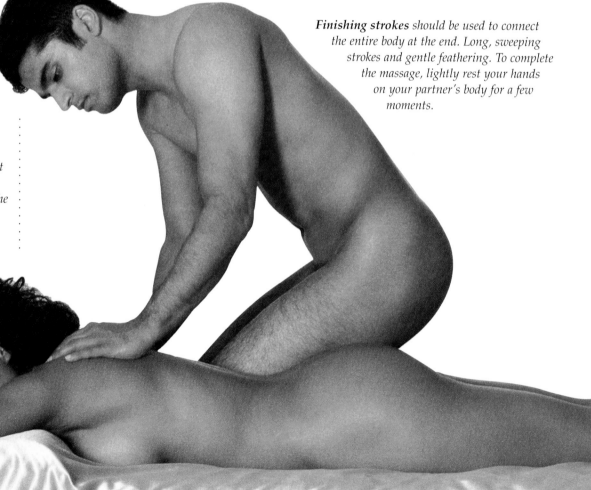

Finishing strokes *should be used to connect the entire body at the end. Long, sweeping strokes and gentle feathering. To complete the massage, lightly rest your hands on your partner's body for a few moments.*

The Role of Erotica

Erotica, in varying degrees, plays an important role in the sex lives of many people. It is used to trigger or increase sexual desire, intensify physical pleasure and make the art of lovemaking more exciting.

Many individuals and couples use books, magazines, pictures or videos describing or depicting sexual activities to stimulate their sexual appetites and imaginations before making love. Couples who enjoy using such material do so because it arouses and entertains them, often reduces their sexual inhibitions, and broadens their knowledge of sexual activities and techniques.

Contrary to popular belief, most women can enjoy erotica as much as men do; but they are less likely to be aroused by material that presents sex from a purely male point of view, and they usually prefer women to be depicted as equal sexual partners rather than providers of male pleasure. Many people—male and female—find the explicit depiction of sex distasteful in any form. No one should be forced to view explicit sexual material.

Sexually arousing material is often divided into two broad groups—erotica and pornography—but these categories are sometimes difficult to distinguish. In general, erotica portrays sexual activity in a subtle and sensitive manner and has, or aspires to, some artistic or literary merit. "Pornography" is a term used to describe material that objectifies and degrades a person (usually a woman) with the sole aim of titillating the audience. Psychologists argue that objectifying potential sexual partners dehumanizes them and robs sex of any emotional intimacy. Highly explicit pornography is referred to as hard-core; less explicit pornography is referred to as soft-core.

Erotic literature and art have a long history, and examples of sexual imagery can be found in the cultures of most of the ancient civilizations, including those of China,

India, Egypt, Greece and Rome. The Chinese "pillow books," for example, were illustrated books of sexual instruction and advice, one of the most famous being the *Su Nue Ching* (*The Classic of the Plain Girl*), which dates back to about 200 B.C.

Today the range of sexually explicit material available is wide. It extends from mainstream books and movies that include erotic scenes of conventional lovemaking, through soft porn magazines and books, to the kind of extremely hard-core pornography, usually cheaply produced and expensive to buy, that most people would find disturbing. Any couple wanting to use erotica to enhance their sex life should have no

Indian erotic paintings There is a wealth of erotic paintings depicting 18th- to 19th-century Indian princes and their lovers engaged in exotic or athletic sex positions.

trouble finding suit-able material, but when deciding what to choose, partners should take account of each other's likes and dislikes.

EROTIC CLOTHING

Clothes can exert a powerful erotic in-fluence, and dress-ing in a way that a partner finds allur-ing may stimulate his or her sexual desire as a form of foreplay, a prelude to making love. Clothing that draws atten-tion to or emphasizes certain body parts, particularly the breasts or chest and the hips, buttocks and crotch, is overtly sexual, and most people respond to it. Individual preferences can vary greatly, though.

Underwear
Seductive underwear and nightwear are the most common forms of erotic clothing. Most underwear is inherently sexy because it is worn next to the skin, normally hidden from view and revealed and removed when couples undress for lovemaking. The choice

Sexual stereotypes
There are popular stereotypes about what is sexy in men and what is sexy in women. Black garter belts and stockings or white silk or lacy underwear fea-ture heavily in erotic images of women, whereas men are depicted in clothes or states of undress that emphasize their muscularity.

The Language of Sex
The term "erotica" comes from the Greek word "erotikos," itself derived from the Greek word for love, "eros," while "pornography" is derived from "pornographos," which is a Greek word meaning "writing about prostitutes." Usually simpler and more explicit than erotica, pornography often makes little effort to create a credible storyline or context for its graphic depictions of sex.

of underwear and nightwear for men is limited. Women enjoy far more var-ied and imaginative choices—intimate wear that shapes, conceals and rev-eals. For example, push-up and peep-hole bras emphasize the sexual nature of the female breasts; corsets make the waist look slimmer, which enhances the rounded shapes of the breasts and but-tocks; and stockings and garter belts create a visual framework for the crotch and buttocks.

The visual impact of erotic clothing can be enhanced if it also has a sensual texture, which is why silk and satin are generally preferable to nylon and why some couples prefer more exotic materials such as leather, plastic and rubber. Erotic clothing made from these materials is usually smooth, shiny and tight-fitting, molding itself to the contours of the body like a second skin and hinting at the dark and mysterious aspects of human sexuality.

APHRODISIACS
Any food, drink, drug or other substance that is thought to stimulate sexual desire is termed an "aphrodisiac." Throughout histo-ry, countless foods have been associated with aphrodisiac properties. Some can sim-ply be eaten in a suggestive manner. Sometimes a food's shape, texture, taste or smell is suggestive of genitals, semen or vaginal fluids—for example, asparagus, cel-ery, eels, oysters, mussels, caviar, freshly picked tomatoes, fresh figs, bananas, pota-toes, and roots such as carrots, ginseng, gin-ger and eryngo (the testicle-shaped root of sea holly). Whether or not there is any sci-entific basis for the action of these and other reputed aphrodisiacs, the claims made for them tend to be self-fulfilling—they work for people who believe in them.

Hot spices also have a reputation as aphrodisiacs, partly because they cause an apparent rise in body temperature and a flushing of the skin, both of which are asso-

ciated with sexual arousal. They also mildly irritate the bowels and bladder in a way that can actually encourage sexual arousal, and this is the principle behind one of the most notorious of all the aphrodisiacs: cantharides.

This substance, also called Spanish fly, is made from the dried and crushed bodies of a bright green beetle that produces a secretion that can blister the skin. Cantharides works by irritating the urethra, the tube through which the bladder empties. Although it may be an effective aphrodisiac, Spanish fly is also a dangerous poison, and its use can be fatal.

The only other substance that has been shown to have a definite and repeatable aphrodisiac effect is yohimbine. Obtained from the bark of a central African tree of the same name, it causes erections in men and physical arousal in women by dilating the blood vessels of the genitals. Yohimbine is not widely available as an aphrodisiac because it can cause a potentially fatal drop in blood pressure. The drug amyl nitrate ("poppers") can also have the same effect and may be extremely dangerous.

The placebo effect

Apart from cantharides and yohimbine, almost all of the other aphrodisiacs work only if the user believes that they will; their effects are psychological rather than physical (which is known as the placebo effect). The exceptions, including

certain narcotics, generally cannot be used safely owing to highly dangerous side effects. Food, however, can help to enhance sexual arousal—a meal for two in intimate, softly lit surroundings can be a sensual prelude to lovemaking, especially if it includes foods that can be eaten suggestively, such as asparagus, oysters, ice cream and soft, juicy fruit.

Sex and scent

Animals signal their readiness to mate by secreting substances called pheromones that are related to hormones. The smell of these substances triggers an instinctive sexual response in potential mates. The extent to which pheromones trigger arousal in humans is far less important. Pheromone preparations advertised to make men irresistible to women have no proven effect—

◀ *The Orgy* This painting by Cézanne (from the late 1860s) depicts naked figures after a feast. Orgies and bacchanalia were featured frequently in the painting and literature of this time.

Sensual foods
Although it is rare for a food to have provable aphrodisiac properties, many foods have erotic or sensual associations. Figs, champagne and oysters are just three examples.

Champagne

Figs

Oysters

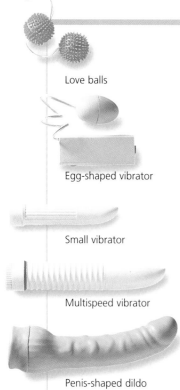

Love balls

Egg-shaped vibrator

Small vibrator

Multispeed vibrator

Penis-shaped dildo

SEXUAL AIDS

Some sex toys are designed to closely resemble a man's penis in texture and shape, while others are designed solely with function and discretion in mind. Love balls differ from vibrators and dildos in that they are intended to be inserted into the vagina for a sustained period of time. Once inserted, the covered metal balls are designed to produce pleasurable sensations by moving against each other. Vibrators are probably the most popular type of sex toy—when such a device is moved against a woman's clitoral area, the high-speed vibrations can provide a reliable way of reaching orgasm for many women.

Using sex toys
Sex toys should not be used on swollen or inflamed body parts or skin eruptions. Shared sex toys, such as vibrators, must be covered with a condom.

not because they have no detectable smell but because human sexuality is far more complicated than that of other animals.

Smell does, of course, play an important role in getting people into the right mood for lovemaking. Some aromatherapy oils, such as rose oil, are said to have an aphrodisiac effect. Two other aromatic substances, musk and civet, have been used since ancient times as the basis of perfumes. Musk is obtained from a gland near the penis of the male Himalayan musk deer and civet from the anal scent glands of male and female civet cats. These two substances play a part in triggering sexual activity in the animals that produce them.

SEX TOYS

Vibrators and dildos are the most popular sex toys, and both provide a very direct and reliable form of sexual enhancement. Sex toys can be used by individuals during masturbation or by couples during lovemaking.

Vibrators

The typical vibrator is a penis-shaped sex toy containing a small, battery- or electricity-powered motor that makes it vibrate. When it is held lightly against a woman's

clitoris, labia, nipples, PERINEUM or anus, or inserted into her vagina, its vibrations arouse her by stimulating the abundant nerve endings in these places. This arousal can be sufficiently intense to trigger orgasm, even in women who do not normally climax during intercourse. This has made the vibrator a popular aid to masturbation, but it can be equally effective in lovemaking.

During foreplay, a woman or her partner can use a vibrator to heighten her enjoyment and arousal, perhaps even bringing her to orgasm before intercourse begins. Vibrators can also be used on a man's penis, scrotum, perineum or anus to increase his excitement, especially when he is trying to regain an erection after orgasm. They can likewise be used to great effect during intercourse, especially in a woman-on-top position, where it is easy for the woman or her partner to apply the vibrator to her nipples or clitoris, or to the shaft of his penis.

Most vibrators are made of plastic or metal and range in length from about 5 to 12 inches (23 to 30 cm). The surface of the body, or "shaft," may be smooth, ribbed or grooved. Some models are covered with a thick layer of soft, fleshy latex molded into a lifelike representation of an erect penis. Some vibrators have a projection at the base that presses against the clitoris when the vibrator is inserted into the vagina.

Dildos

A dildo is similar to a vibrator, but it does not have a vibrating action and is usually used as an artificial penis during masturbation and lovemaking. Some dildos have a rubber or soft plastic bulb at the base that can be filled with warm water, which is then squirted out to simulate ejaculation.

Vibrators and dildos should always be carefully washed and dried before and after use or they will soon become a source of bacterial or fungal infection. For extra safety, they can be covered with a condom before use and the condom disposed of afterward. Sex toys, including vibrators and dildos, should never be shared by partners if one of them has, or may have, a sexually transmitted disease, especially HIV.

Clitoral stimulators

A woman's clitoris is usually the most sensitive part of her genitals, and her enjoyment of lovemaking and her chances of orgasm are greatly increased if it is stimulated directly during intercourse. It is possible for her or her partner to stroke her clitoris with a finger or a vibrator while making love, or a clitoral stimulator may be attached to the man's penis. This typically takes the form of a ring that fits around the base of the penis and has a small projection that rubs against the clitoris during intercourse. Certain condoms also incorporate projections with similar purposes; these usually have a ribbed or knobby surface texture designed to increase vaginal stimulation as well.

SEXUAL FANTASIES

Most people have sexual fantasies, in which they imagine what it would be like to make love—or indulge in other sexual or romantic activities—in a variety of situations and with various partners. These fantasies may be sexual daydreams, mental aids to masturbation, or scenarios that are played out in the mind before or during lovemaking. Like nonsexual daydreams, they provide a brief escape from reality into a realm of endless possibilities.

Common fantasies

Common fantasies of both men and women include having sex with someone—real or imagined—other than one's partner; making love with more than one person at a time; watching one's partner make love to another person; making love while someone else is watching; being coerced into having intercourse; and homosexual or bisexual lovemaking.

Daydreaming about different ways of making love, and mentally rehearsing them, helps a person to be a more imaginative, confident and fulfilling lover. Fantasies can trigger and help to maintain sexual desire, and so are often useful to people who have difficulty becoming fully aroused.

Some people fantasize only during foreplay. Others begin fantasizing during intercourse. Still others may have sexual daydreams, especially when with a new partner, but do not fantasize at all when making love. Men and women tend to use fantasy differently. Men may fantasize to help them get more aroused before intercourse, but they tend not to fantasize during it because the extra arousal can make it difficult to control ejaculation. Women, who may not be as readily aroused as men, often fantasize throughout lovemaking to help them achieve orgasm.

Sharing fantasies

While many people prefer to keep their sexual fantasies to themselves, others like to tell them to their partners, and some couples construct joint fantasies that they can enjoy together. This allows them to act out simple fantasy scenarios before and during lovemaking. Acting out sexual fantasies can be an exciting way to liven up a sexual relationship, as long as both partners consent fully.

The power of the imagination is a vital ingredient of an acted-out fantasy, but simple props such as soft cords, blindfolds and clothes can add to the sense of excitement.

◀ Sex in other settings Some people enjoy fantasizing about making love with their partner in an unusual or exotic setting. Popular locations include tropical beaches, waterfalls and airplanes.

Dominance and submission Partners who are accustomed to playing equal roles during sex can find experimenting with power games an erotic experience.

Sexual Intercourse

*Different couples make love in different ways. Some people use a
wide range of sexual positions and change position
several times during intercourse. Others have just one or two
favorite positions in which they habitually make love.*

**Missionaries and ▶
natives** *The mission-
ary position is so
called because it was
allegedly the sexual
position recommended
by Christian missionar-
ies to their Polynesian
converts in the era of
European colonialism.*

Each lovemaking
position has its
own particu-
lar advantages. In
several face-to-face
positions, such as
the missionary posi-
tion, the woman's cli-
toris gets direct stimu-
lation from the contact
with her partner's pubic
area, which helps to heighten her
arousal. This does not happen in rear-entry
positions, but when making love using a
rear entry position, the man or the woman
can more easily stimulate the clitoris manually. Rear-entry sex positions stimulate the
woman's G-spot (see page 98), according to
some, as do the woman-on-top positions.

MAN-ON-TOP POSITIONS

The missionary position, the basic man-on-
top position, is probably the best known
and most widely used of all lovemaking
postures. The missionary position allows
sexual partners to kiss,
embrace and main-
tain eye contact to
see the pleasure that
they are giving each
other. Penetration
can be shallow or
deep, and the pace of
lovemaking can vary
from slow and sensual to
wildly passionate. The main
drawback of the missionary posi-
tion is that it restricts the woman's freedom
of movement during sex. This means that
her ability to control the rhythm and speed
of intercourse and the depth of penetration
are fairly limited.

To adopt the missionary position, the
woman lies on her back with her legs parted, and the man lies on top of her with his
legs between hers and then gently inserts
his penis into her vagina. By supporting his
weight on his elbows or his hands, he can
allow her more freedom to vary the sensations for both of them as he thrusts. The
woman can move her pelvis up and down,
from side to side or in a circular fashion.

The woman can vary the depth and angle
of penetration in this position by lying with
a pillow supporting her buttocks, by opening her legs wider or by wrapping one or
both around her partner's torso. She can
also lie with her buttocks on the edge of
the bed and her feet on the floor, so
that her partner can make love

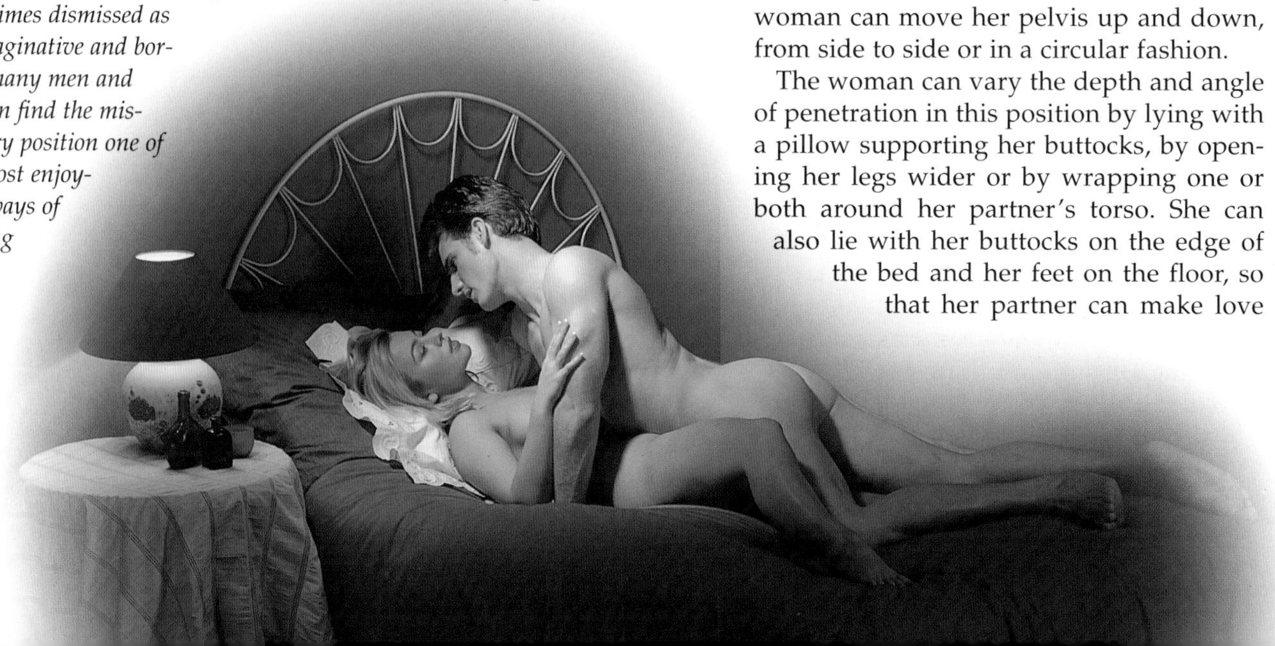

**The missionary
position** *Although it is
sometimes dismissed as
unimaginative and bor-
ing, many men and
women find the mis-
sionary position one of
the most enjoy-
able ways of
making
love.*

to her from a kneeling position. If the woman is sufficiently supple, she can draw her knees up to her chest so that when her partner enters her, his pelvis is against her buttocks. She can also place one or both of her feet flat against her partner's chest (in the *Kama Sutra*, this is known as the pressed or half-pressed position). This position allows the penis to penetrate the vagina very deeply, so the man should be careful not to thrust too hard.

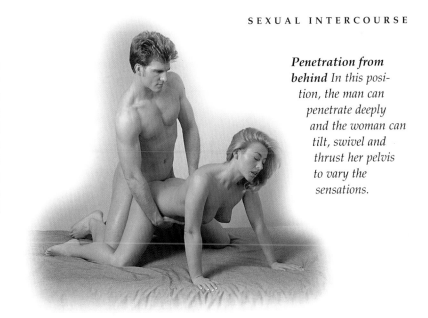

Penetration from behind In this position, the man can penetrate deeply and the woman can tilt, swivel and thrust her pelvis to vary the sensations.

The Language of Sex

In English-speaking countries, most sexual positions do not have names that are widely or consistently used, the exceptions being the missionary, doggie and spoons positions. This reflects an aversion to the open discussion of sex and means that when people want to mention a sexual position, they usually have to describe rather than name it. Attempts to borrow names from less reticent cultures have so far not met with much success.

Woman-on-top Kneeling astride her partner allows a woman to move freely and exert control over the angle and depth of penetration.

WOMAN-ON-TOP POSITIONS

In the various woman-on-top positions, the woman has greater control because she can decide the speed of the movements and the depth of penetration. The man assumes a relatively passive role. Some women find that a woman-on-top position is the easiest one in which to reach coital orgasm.

In the simplest type of woman-on-top position, a straightforward reversal of the missionary position, the man lies on his back and his partner lies on top of him, her legs straddling his, and she inserts his penis into her vagina. Then she moves her pelvis while her partner lies still or responds by thrusting. He has both hands free to stroke and caress her. To vary the sensations, she can bring her legs inside his to tighten the grip of her vagina on his penis.

Alternatively, the woman may sit or kneel astride her partner. She can alter the angle of penetration by leaning forward or back,

and if she is kneeling she can raise or lower her pelvis and so control the depth of penetration. In this position, both partners have their hands free to caress each other, and it is easy for the woman to increase her pleasure by stimulating her clitoris manually or with a vibrator.

The woman can further vary this position by sitting or kneeling with her back to her partner instead of facing him. This posture, which is actually a rear-entry position, makes eye contact difficult and kissing impossible, but many couples find it an erotic variation.

REAR-ENTRY POSITIONS

The best known of the rear-entry positions is the so-called doggie position, which gets its name from its similarity to the way in which dogs mate. The woman kneels on all fours on the bed or on the floor, and her partner kneels behind her, then he or she

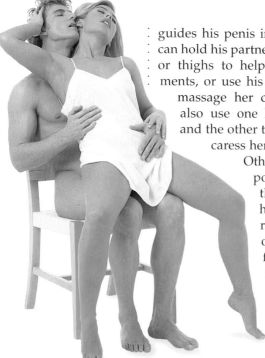

guides his penis into her vagina. The man can hold his partner's shoulders, waist, hips or thighs to help him control his movements, or use his hands to caress her and massage her clitoris. The woman can also use one hand to support herself and the other to stimulate her clitoris or caress her partner's testicles.

Other versions of the doggie position are achieved by the woman supporting herself on her forearms rather than on her hands or by her kneeling on the floor in a virtually upright position, perhaps supported by the edge of the bed. Rear-entry sex is also possible with the woman lying face down.

Sitting positions
Sensations can be enhanced by rhythmically contracting the vaginal muscles.

STANDING POSITIONS

Using a standing position can be an exciting change from making love on a bed, but it can also be awkward, especially if one partner is much taller than the other or if either partner is infirm. The simplest standing position in which to make love is that in which the partners stand facing each other, in effect creating an upright version of the missionary position.

If the woman is light enough, or if her partner is strong enough, he can lift her up after he has entered her and support her by locking his hands beneath her buttocks or holding her thighs. She can help him by putting her arms around his neck, crossing her ankles behind his back and gripping his body with her thighs. This is easier to achieve when the woman's back is supported by a wall.

In the rear-entry standing position, the woman stands with her legs slightly apart and bends forward from the waist, then her partner enters her from behind. This position is virtually the same as the doggie position but with the partners standing rather than kneeling; it allows the man similar deep penetration and freedom to thrust, and both partners the opportunity to use their hands to provide extra stimulation. As with the face-to-face standing position, however, height differences can be a problem, and if the difference in height is too great, the couple might not be able to use this position at all.

The woman can make penetration much easier and deeper if she bends fully at the waist so that her body is at right angles to her legs. For support, she can reach back and hold onto her partner, put her hands against a wall, or hold onto the bed, a table or any other stable object.

SITTING POSITIONS

Making love in a sitting position does not permit either partner a great deal of movement, but it allows a gentle, unhurried and very intimate form of intercourse, and the face-to-face sitting positions allow the partners to kiss, cuddle and caress each other.

To make love sitting on a bed, the man sits with his legs extended, and his partner sits in his lap, facing him and with her legs behind his back. She carefully slides her vagina onto his penis. When on a chair, the woman sits on the man's lap with her legs straddling his, either facing him or with her back to him.

Can We Talk About It?

ASKING FOR WHAT YOU WANT DURING SEX

When you start a relationship, you may be cautious about expressing some of your sexual wishes. Perhaps you feel embarrassed or anxious that you will shock your partner or make him or her feel like an inadequate lover. Or you may feel you should wait for the "right time." For some couples, though, the time never seems right, and before you know it, sex has become a routine performance, and it feels inappropriate to ask for changes.

First of all, define exactly what it is you want to add or change about your sex life. This will allow you to make positive suggestions to your partner instead of negative statements, such as "our sex life is boring" or "we never do anything different." Talking to your partner should never involve criticism of his or her past performance. Simply say that you are curious or that you think it would be fun to experiment.

Asking for what you want sexually can also be nonverbal. For example, during foreplay gently guide your partner's hand or mouth to the parts of your body where you want to be touched and caressed.

SIDE-BY-SIDE POSITIONS

The simplest version of a side-by-side position is the face-to-face style. A couple can reach this position by carefully rolling over onto their sides from a basic man-on-top or woman-on-top position, sustaining penetration as they do so, or they can lie beside each other and then insert his penis into her vagina. To vary this position, one of them can hook his or her uppermost leg over the other's, or the woman can raise her uppermost leg, allowing her partner to slide his legs between hers.

The rear-entry version of this position is known as the spoons position, because its shape can be likened to a pair of spoons nested together, one bowl inside the other. The woman lies on her side and her partner lies behind her, snuggled up against her back. Then she draws her knees up a bit and opens her thighs slightly to allow him to enter her from behind, and he tucks his knees into the back of hers. In this position, the man can kiss and nuzzle his partner's neck and shoulders and use his free hand to caress her breasts and gently massage her clitoris. Because of its restful nature the spoons position is a good way to have sexual intercourse during the later months of pregnancy or for older or infirm couples.

Spoons position
The man lies behind his partner and enters her from the rear.

Side-by-side sex This *type of sex position best serves tender, unhurried lovemaking.*

FACILITATING FEMALE ORGASM

Some sexual positions are more likely to facilitate female orgasm than others. Women who find it difficult to reach orgasm from intercourse alone—for instance without manual or oral stimulation—often find that a woman-on-top position is helpful.

The woman can use her hands to push herself backward and forward to create friction on the clitoris.

Maximum contact
Women-on-top positions can maximize the amount of friction between the clitoris and the man's pubic bone.

The woman can move horizontally by pushing against the man's feet.

The male and female pelvises are aligned so that his pubic bone puts pressure on her clitoris.

The man can use his hands to pull his partner close to him and increase the pressure on her clitoris.

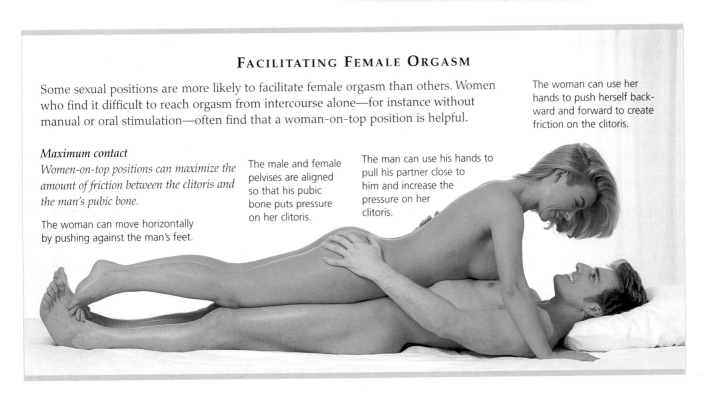

Prolonging Sexual Intercourse

The duration of a couple's lovemaking often depends on the man's ability to control his ejaculation. There are various techniques for sustaining intercourse that can help a couple prolong their sexual pleasure.

After a man ejaculates, he quickly loses his erection, which means that intercourse is over. He can continue to stimulate his partner in a variety of ways—"afterplay" can include all the same activities as foreplay—but some couples enjoy prolonging the act of penetrative sex itself.

There are some simple and enjoyable techniques that prolong sexual pleasure. They include delaying ejaculation and resuming intercourse immediately after ejaculation—many techniques derive from tantric sex.

TANTRIC AND TAOIST SEX

Tantra is an ancient doctrine that evolved in India at least 1,500 years ago. It is based on the idea that the power of sexual energy can be harnessed to unite the male principle or force (Shiva) within each person with its female counterpart (Shakti) to achieve spiritual liberation.

Taoism is an even older doctrine that developed in China and first appeared in written form more than 2,500 years ago. Based on the concept that health, longevity

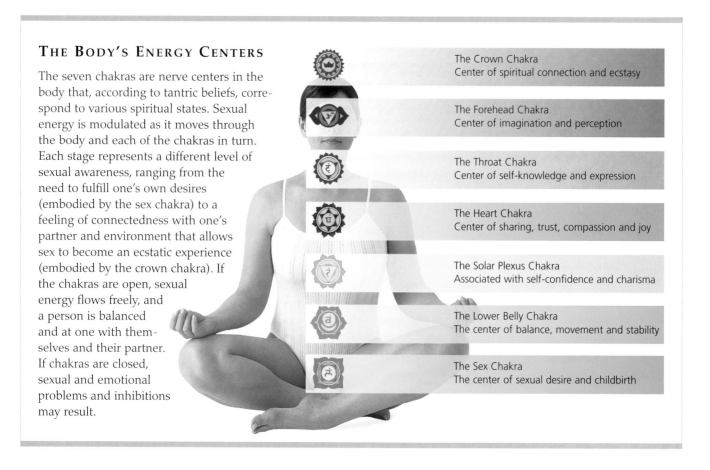

THE BODY'S ENERGY CENTERS

The seven chakras are nerve centers in the body that, according to tantric beliefs, correspond to various spiritual states. Sexual energy is modulated as it moves through the body and each of the chakras in turn. Each stage represents a different level of sexual awareness, ranging from the need to fulfill one's own desires (embodied by the sex chakra) to a feeling of connectedness with one's partner and environment that allows sex to become an ecstatic experience (embodied by the crown chakra). If the chakras are open, sexual energy flows freely, and a person is balanced and at one with themselves and their partner. If chakras are closed, sexual and emotional problems and inhibitions may result.

The Crown Chakra
Center of spiritual connection and ecstasy

The Forehead Chakra
Center of imagination and perception

The Throat Chakra
Center of self-knowledge and expression

The Heart Chakra
Center of sharing, trust, compassion and joy

The Solar Plexus Chakra
Associated with self-confidence and charisma

The Lower Belly Chakra
The center of balance, movement and stability

The Sex Chakra
The center of sexual desire and childbirth

and tranquillity can be achieved by harmonizing the male (yang) and female (yin) within each individual, it teaches that one way to attain this harmony is to use male self-control to ensure female sexual satisfaction. As a means to these ends, both Tantric and Taoist teachings include techniques such as shallow thrusting, muscle control and soft-entry sex, to make intercourse last for as long as the participants wish.

Shallow thrusting

One of the simplest methods a man can use to help him delay ejaculation is the shallow-thrusting technique. As he nears ejaculation during intercourse, he instinctively begins to thrust deeper and faster, but with practice he can prevent himself from ejaculating by resisting this instinct and making his thrusts slow and shallow. This technique becomes even more effective if combined with breath control. Very rapid breathing usually accompanies impending ejaculation. By taking slow, deep breaths, a man can curb the urge to ejaculate.

Other techniques

If shallow thrusting and breath control are unsuccessful, simultaneously contracting the anal sphincter and the *PUBOCOCCYGEAL (PC) MUSCLES* can often help to delay ejaculation. The ring of muscle called the anal sphincter keeps the anus closed; the PC muscles are the same ones that a man can use to stop the flow when he is urinating. Alternatively, he can partly withdraw his penis and grip its base, with his thumb on the underside just above the scrotum and two fingers on the upper side of the penis where it joins the body. By squeezing firmly for about four seconds, he can quell his urge to ejaculate.

A man can also try pulling down on his testicles to delay ejaculation. As ejaculation approaches, a man's scrotum tightens and his testicles are drawn up against his body.

Soft-entry sex

Sometimes a man will partly or completely lose his erection when trying to control his ejaculation and then have difficulty regaining it. He can continue to have intercourse without a full erection by using the technique known as soft-entry sex. The soft-entry technique can also be used when a couple want to make love again after the man has ejaculated, but masturbation or oral sex fails to bring about erection. It can also be of help if a man cannot achieve a full erection before lovemaking begins. Soft-entry sex does not, however, cure long-lasting impotence.

To perform soft-entry sex, the man uses his fingers to gently guide the end of his penis into his partner's vagina. When it is in, he firmly grips the base of his penis with his forefinger and thumb. This will trap blood in his penis, hopefully making it swell and stiffen enough for the man to be able to thrust gently inside his partner's vagina. This thrusting may be sufficient to produce a full erection. When the man feels that this is happening, he should release his grip on his penis so that lovemaking can continue.

Synchronizing heart rates The couple place their hands on each other's hearts and adjust their breathing rates so that they are synchronized.

◀ *Shiva Nataraja* The Hindu Lord of the Dance represents divine harmony between opposing forces and energies. The figure unites the male and female principles of Shiva and Shakti, in a gesture that embodies perfect balance.

Popular Variations

Kneeling Entry

In this simple rear-entry posture, the man has both hands free to give his partner extra stimulation by caressing her and stroking her clitoris. The woman can support herself on her hands, or vary the position by taking her weight on her elbows. This posture allows deep penetration, so the man should be careful not to hurt his partner by thrusting too hard.

Resting Position

During an active and very passionate session of lovemaking, it is wonderful to move into this position and just lie still for awhile. The man lies on one side, resting his head on one arm, with his legs straight and crossed at the ankles. His partner lies on her back at a right angle to him with her legs bent over his hips. After penetration, both partners remain still.

Low-level Entry

This rear-entry position allows deep penetration, especially when the woman puts one or more pillows under her pelvis to support herself and make it easier for her partner to enter her. As in any other lovemaking position, the woman should always let her partner know, with gentle words or gestures, if he is thrusting too hard or if she finds the position uncomfortable.

Yab Yum
A classic Tantric posture, this is a comfortable and loving face-to-face lovemaking position. The man sits in a lotus posture and his partner sits astride him. The name is Tibetan in origin, "Yab" meaning father, "Yum" meaning mother. The position thus represents the union of the male and female principles or cosmic oneness.

Yawning Position
This is a useful posture for the woman who finds it difficult to move her hips when she is making love lying on her back. By lying with her thighs raised and parted, she can vary the genital sensations for herself and her partner by, for instance, bending her knees, raising one or both legs, or crossing her legs behind her partner's back.

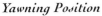

Front Kneeling
To get into this posture, the woman lies on her back and bends both knees into her chest before her partner enters her. By bending her knees against her chest, the woman is tensing her vaginal muscles, and many women find that this tension can lead to considerable sexual arousal.

Advanced Positions

Suspended Congress

The man stands on both feet and supports his partner by holding her buttocks, while she wraps her arms around his neck and her legs around his waist. The man may find it easier to support the weight of his partner if he bends his knees slightly, and this will also allow him to thrust more easily.

Three Feet on the Ground

The man stands with both feet on the ground while his partner stands, facing him, on one leg with her other leg wrapped around his waist or hooked around the back of his thigh. The man should help his partner to maintain the position, and her balance, by supporting her raised thigh with his hand. Most couples find that this an easier position than the Suspended Congress, mainly because the woman's stance is more stable but also because she can respond better to her partner's thrusting movements.

Forward Bend

This requires the woman to bend forward from a standing position so that she is supported on her hands and feet. Pillows, cushions, or some other form of support for her hands will reduce the amount she has to bend, and make it easier for her to maintain the posture without too much discomfort. When his partner is in position, the man approaches her from the rear.

Legs Raised

The woman first lies on her back with her les raised while her partner kneels in front of her and enters her. Then she places one foot on her partner's shoulder and stretches the other leg out, alternating the position of her legs throughout the posture. This posture is almost a dance, and requires the woman to cncentrate and feel her way to a satisfying rhythm as she alternates leg positions.

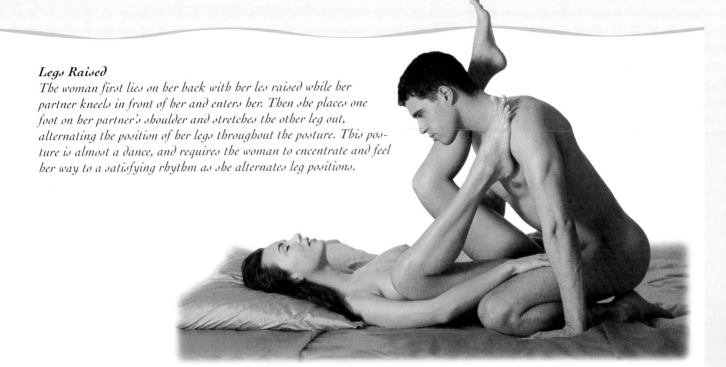

Tantric Tortoise

The woman lies on her back and the man kneels between her legs. Then she places the soles of her feet on his chest, and after penetration, he presses her knees together with his arms as he thrusts, helping her to grip his penis tightly inside her vagina.

Swing-Rocking

Both partners sit, facing each other, and put their arms around each other. After penetration, they use the weight of their bodies to create a back-and-forth rocking motion like that of a swing. This is a good posture for prolonged lovemaking.

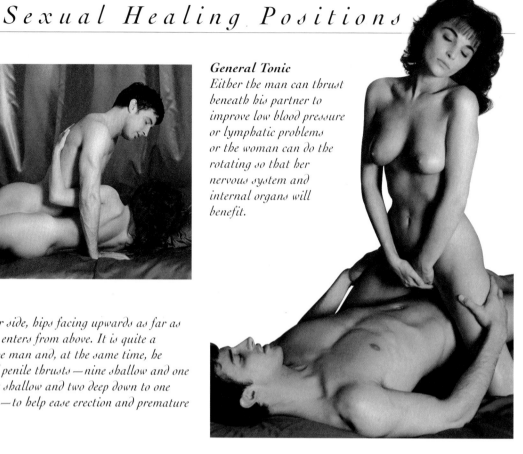

General Tonic

Either the man can thrust beneath his partner to improve low blood pressure or lymphatic problems or the woman can do the rotating so that her nervous system and internal organs will benefit.

Erection Problems

The woman lies on her side, hips facing upwards as far as possible, and the man enters from above. It is quite a difficult posture for the man and, at the same time, he needs to do two sets of penile thrusts — nine shallow and one deep, followed by eight shallow and two deep down to one shallow and nine deep — to help ease erection and premature ejaculation problems.

Energizing Position

The woman lies on her back, thighs raised and parted, with her head and shoulders supported by pillows, then her partner lies between her legs and penetrates her. The man should perform penile thrusts — nine shallow followed by one deep, eight shallow followed by two deep and seven shallow followed by three deep, etc. twice.

Weak Knees

Where there are joint weaknesses, the woman should lie on her back and wrap her legs around her partner's thighs. He should kneel and penetrate only shallowly. She should rotate her pelvis clockwise and counterclockwise alternately for as long as she can.

Positions for Pregnancy

Many men find their pregnant partners' changing bodies, particularly their enlarging breasts, extremely attractive and sexually arousing and sex during pregnancy, whether or not it is penetrative, can increase the feelings of intimacy and love between partners.

A number of women find that they have increased sexual desires during pregnancy, particularly in the second trimester, when many of the minor complaints have disappeared and they aren't too large. These increased feelings of desire are largely the result of the huge amounts of sex hormones that start to circulate around a woman's body early in conception. Pregnancy, too, results in an increased bloodflow, particularly in the pelvic region, and this can make a woman's genitals more sensitive which will, in turn, result in heightened sexual arousal.

Although a woman's sex drive can vary in pregnancy, many women discover that sex at this time can sometimes be far more exciting than in a non-pregnant state, and some women experience orgasm for the first time. Sex even can be seen as something that prepares a woman's body for childbirth because it exercises the pelvic muscles and keeps them strong and supple.

A few men worry that sexual activity will harm their unborn babies. But the amniotic fluid that surrounds the baby protects him or her from any bumps or bruising. There is also a protective plug at the entrance to the uterus which stops bacteria entering. So you need not abstain from intercourse unless otherwise advised by your physician.

Remember, though, that a woman's breasts may be particularly tender at this time and that the man should always be gentle. Vigorous sexual activity could result in abrasions or infection, so don't be too athletic at this time. If bleeding occurs, stop having relations and consult your doctor.

Intimate massage

If, for any reason, your doctor has advised you against having penetrative sex, you and your partner still can maintain physical and emotional intimacy with loving caresses and gentle abdominal massage.

Side-by-side positions

These are ideal during pregnancy because they prevent painful pressure being placed on a woman's abdomen and breasts. Make sure you are both comfortable during sex. Use plenty of pillows and cusions to support your bodies. If the man can support his own body weight with his hands, this will allow you to have face-to-face contact.

Oral Sex

In 1948, when sex researcher Kinsey produced his report on sexual habits, almost half of all married adults reported having had oral sex. More recent statistics show that roughly three-quarters of men and women have had oral sex.

The pattern of giving and receiving oral sex seems to have changed over the years. It used to be seen as an advanced or an experimental sexual technique that couples moved on to after intercourse as something more daring. Studies, such as *Sexual Behaviour in Britain* (1994), suggest that today oral sex typically happens before intercourse, sometimes instead of it—young women in particular will offer partners oral sex if they are not yet ready to allow penetration.

CUNNILINGUS

Cunnilingus
The clitoris and vagina are stimulated with the lips and tongue, as part of foreplay or afterplay.

Oral sex performed on a woman's genital area is known as cunnilingus. Cunnilingus includes any type of genital kissing, licking, sucking or nibbling. A partner may begin by licking a woman's labia to lubricate her and then move on to her clitoris, licking and sucking with perhaps downward strokes from root to tip or flicks from side to side. The tongue can also be inserted into the vagina, simulating intercourse, but this often is not as arousing as clitoral stimulation. Many women gain pleasure from oral sex because it directly stimulates the clitoris and often arouses women in ways that intercourse does not. In fact, some women may find it difficult to reach orgasm any other way The clitoris is packed with nerve endings and is the erotic center of the female body.

Emotionally, cunnilingus is an intimate act that can make many women feel desired and loved. It also allows them to receive pleasure without feeling any obligation to give. This is important for women who find reaching orgasm difficult because they focus on their partner's pleasure.

The Hite Report (1976) on female attitudes toward sexuality revealed that although many women surveyed gained enormous sexual pleasure from cunnilingus, some women disliked it because they felt it to be dirty or immoral, or that their partners would be repulsed by the smell of the genitals. A minority of men questioned were unwilling to perform cunnilingus, feeling it to be subservient and unmanly. However, many men reported that they enjoyed the experience and felt proud of their ability to give their partner pleasure. In *The Hite Report on Male Sexuality* (1981) one man was quoted as saying, "I feel that the genital kiss given by a man to a woman is one of the most intimate expressions of love there is. I often have dreams involving sex, most of which do not end with my orgasm or ejaculation but do include a protracted period of my kissing the woman's genitals."

FELLATIO

Oral sex performed on a man's penis is called fellatio; the word comes from Latin and means "sucking," although this action by itself may not be particularly arousing. More often, a woman uses one of two techniques: either she licks the man's penis and testicles with her tongue, or she thrusts the penis directly into her mouth and out again, simulating the movements of intercourse. Fellatio can be combined with manual stimulation of the penis.

According to *The Hite Report on Male Sexuality*, the majority of men enjoy fellatio. Some do find it distasteful, degrading for partners or morally wrong, due in part to their social upbringing or religious beliefs. But most men find fellatio emotionally rewarding. It is an act of intimacy, and the movement of jaw and lips, combined with the warm, moist skin of a partner's mouth, is intensely stimulating. Some men find that intercourse produces more intense sensations than fellatio, simply because it is a more mutual experience, but oral sex allows other men to relax, without the pressure to perform.

Many women say that they enjoy giving fellatio because they like the actual sensation, the intimacy or the pleasure that it gives their partner. But some women are wary of tasting body parts that are so close to those used for urination. Others become nauseous or gag, particularly if their partner's penis thrusts deeply into their mouth. Some women who feel happy to give oral sex to their partner feel unwilling to go as far as ejaculation. No health reason exists for why a man should not ejaculate into his partner's mouth—unless, of course, he has an infection—but many women dislike the texture and the taste of semen, and prefer to pull away just before ejaculation or spit the fluid out. Conversely, other women

feel it is the ultimate intimacy to swallow a lover's body secretions. Because of reservations about ejaculation, fellatio quite often happens as part of foreplay, a preliminary to sexual intercourse in which the woman arouses the man, but he then penetrates her before he actually ejaculates.

MUTUAL ORAL SEX

A position that is known as "sixty-nine" ("soixante-neuf" in French) enables a man and woman to give oral sex to each other simultaneously. The two partners—one kneeling on top of the other or the two lying side by side—can be likened to the numerals 6 and 9 in close proximity. Couples who practice this technique say that it is an exciting variation on normal lovemaking. Sixty-nine does have disadvantages. The positions can be uncomfortable, particularly if there is a big height difference between partners. Also, because neither partner can focus fully on giving or receiving pleasure, it can be problematic to continue sixty-nine through to orgasm; the spasms of climax in one partner can cause discomfort if he or she is still orally stimulating the other.

fact or fiction?

A woman can become pregnant by swallowing her partner's semen.

Fiction. Pregnancy from oral sex is impossible unless a woman somehow transfers semen, perhaps on her fingers, to her vagina and cervix. Even semen transferred in this way would be unlikely to cause pregnancy.

ORAL SEX AND LABOR

Some African tribes recommend that women who are due to go into labor drink their husbands' semen. This is based on the fact that prostaglandins (substances found naturally in semen) cause uterine contractions. Whether or not semen taken orally can induce labor is a subject for medical debate. Many doctors argue that the prostaglandins in semen would be destroyed by stomach acid and therefore have no effect on the uterus. Pregnant women are certainly not advised to avoid oral sex at any stage during pregnancy.

HEALTH RISKS OF ORAL SEX

Oral-genital contact should be avoided if either partner has a sexually transmitted disease. Herpes (see page 138) on the mouth, face or genitals can be transmitted through oral sex. Any kind of oral contact with a partner's feces may transfer bacteria that can lead to infection. It is important to wash thoroughly before oral sex if it is going to include the perineum and anal area.

The herpes virus
Genital herpes is caused by the herpes virus hominis, type 2 (magnified at right). It is a chronic condition, characterized by painful sores. There is no absolute cure for herpes.

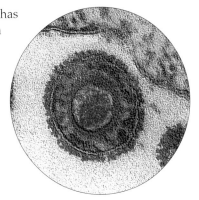

Anal Sex

Anal intercourse, in which a man puts his penis into his partner's anus and rectum, is common among homosexual men. Although some heterosexual couples experiment with anal sex, it is rarely practiced as frequently as vaginal intercourse.

In the past, before reliable contraception became available, anal sex was more common among heterosexual couples because it provided a sure way to avoid pregnancy. Today couples may experiment with anal intercourse because it is a novel technique, providing unique sensations. Many couples never try it, finding the idea unappealing or distasteful.

Some men report that being anally penetrated is intensely exciting because it stimulates the prostate gland, which is situated next to the rectum behind its upper wall (the side nearest the penis). In terms of sexual arousal, the prostate gland can be thought of as the male equivalent of the woman's G-spot (see page 98).

Many women find anal sex painful. One reason for this is that the anus, unlike the vagina, does not produce its own lubrication. Unless the anal sphincter muscle is very relaxed, tearing of the delicate tissues can occur. Deep penetration in particular can cause great pain or discomfort.

Some people experiment with anal stimulation rather than full penetration. This involves stroking the area around the *PERINEUM* and anus. To avoid any risk of infection, the hands must always be thoroughly washed immediately after giving anal stimulation, and a man should never touch his partner's genitals after he has touched her anal area.

HEALTH RISKS

For either sex, anal intercourse carries a high risk of injury and infection because the lining of the anus is not designed to withstand friction, and the blood vessels within it are delicate and easily broken. This causes bleeding, which is why sexually transmitted diseases, such as HIV and hepatitis, are transmitted more readily through anal than vaginal intercourse.

Doctors advise men who have anal intercourse to wear a condom and to make sure that the anus of the receiving partner is lubricated with a water-based lubricant (oil-based lubricants destroy condom rubber). The risk of infection makes using a condom an essential precaution, and it should be one of the extra-strong types designed specifically to withstand the rigors of anal intercourse. However, even extra-strong condoms cannot guarantee complete safety.

Vaginal intercourse must never follow anal intercourse unless the man has safely disposed of the condom and thoroughly washed his genitals and hands with soap and water. Otherwise a high risk exists of transferring bacteria from the woman's anus to her urethra and vagina.

The Kinsey Institute New Report on Sex (1990) recommends that "Anyone—male or female, heterosexual, bisexual or homosexual—who receives anal sex should have regular checkups that include examination of the anus and rectum."

Health considerations
Because of the high levels of bacteria found in and around the rectum, unhygienic anal sex can lead to infections in other parts of the urogenital tract. People practicing anal sex should always use a condom.

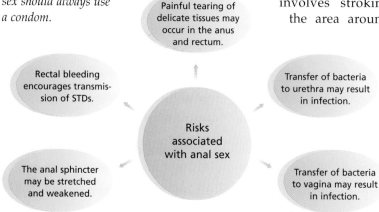

Painful tearing of delicate tissues may occur in the anus and rectum.

Rectal bleeding encourages transmission of STDs.

Transfer of bacteria to urethra may result in infection.

Risks associated with anal sex

The anal sphincter may be stretched and weakened.

Transfer of bacteria to vagina may result in infection.

LOVE & SEX THROUGHOUT LIFE

Sexual Statistics 68

Adulthood 70

Middle Age 76

Advanced Age 80

Sexual Statistics

How often do most people have sex? How often do they masturbate? Who has oral and anal sex? This kind of information interests people because it helps them understand where their own practices fit into their society's norms.

The last sexual event *Laumann and colleagues asked people what sort of activities they performed in their "last sexual event." This sort of question provides a snapshot of people's sexual behavior. This graph shows the percentage of people of different ages who engaged in oral sex in the "last sexual event."*

According to *The Social Organization of Sexuality* (1994), by Edward Laumann and others—one of the latest and most comprehensive research studies into adult sexual behavior in a long line of sex surveys—frequency of sex increases once a couple enters a monogamous cohabiting relationship. Perhaps surprisingly, the media-perpetuated idea that young single people have active and exciting sex lives is an exaggeration. Even married people who have extramarital affairs make love less often than those who remain faithful to one partner, whether married or cohabiting.

Aside from running counter to the impression given by the media, this finding was deeply ironic. The researchers had their initial funding withdrawn after North Carolina's Senator Jesse Helms and others forced through a change in the law to prohibit state financing of sex surveys, partly on the grounds that the information such studies uncovered would damage the moral fabric of society. Instead, the survey suggests that traditional moral values are as strong (and satisfying) as ever.

Most people, according to the Laumann study, want to settle down in a long-term relationship—usually marriage—once they reach adulthood and to remain faithful to that partner for life. While a significant number of marriages do end in divorce, with infidelity cited as the main reason in many cases, the evidence suggests that the underlying cause of marital breakdown is irreconcilable differences between the couple rather than any lack of commitment to the principle of monogamy.

In the Laumann survey, 80 percent of those questioned—the participants ranged in age from 18 to 59—had had a maximum of one partner in the previous 12 months (some had had no partner in that time). Half of all the adults questioned in the study had had no more than three partners over their entire lifetime.

Just 3 percent of adults reported having had five or more partners over the previous 12-month period. Clearly, most people are not promiscuous. The study found that the average length of a marriage among this age group is 25 years, with 4 years being the average interval between marriages.

Surveys such as the Laumann study, which attempt to chart the demographics of human behavior, can give only a "snapshot" of current social behavior during the period in which the research was carried out. Another survey, conducted 10 years before or 10 years after, may produce a different picture. This simply confirms that human behavior, especially sexual behavior, changes over time.

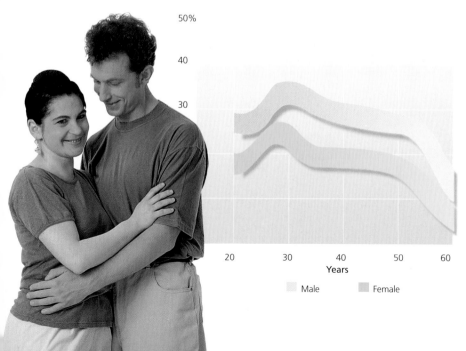

50%

40

30

20   30   40   50   60
Years

■ Male   ■ Female

CHANGING ATTITUDES

Cohabitation, once called "living in sin," is now common practice as a prelude or alternative to marriage, and, to many people, it is morally acceptable. Yet 30 years ago living together out of wedlock was almost unheard of, and even 20 years ago it was still generally frowned upon. Those couples who chose to cohabit rather than marry would often assume the outward appearance of respectability, even to the extent of wearing wedding rings. Today many couples choose to live together for a year or more as a form of trial marriage. Some couples reject the institution of marriage altogether, considering it outmoded and unnecessary.

Sex surveys may also influence society's attitudes toward sex and generally encourage more openness about sexual issues. Research by Kinsey, and that of Masters and Johnson shocked society by suggesting that sexual practices such as oral sex and mutual masturbation were more widespread, and therefore by implication more acceptable, than had previously been thought. For these researchers, just getting people to talk about these kinds of subjects was a major battle.

In the Laumann study, however, most of those surveyed were willing to discuss their sexual preferences, and few people found such activities morally wrong when practiced by consenting adults, even if they did not engage in them themselves.

Laumann discovered that in the previous year, 90 percent of male participants in the study and 86 percent of female participants had had vaginal intercourse, but only 27 percent of men and 19 percent of women had had oral sex. For most people questioned, oral sex was placed well below "watching partner undress" as a popular sexual activity. Even fewer had bought erotic videos to spice up their love lives (23 percent of men and 11 percent of women), and only 10 percent of men and 9 percent of women had had anal sex.

OTHER SEXUAL OUTLETS

When Laumann's team questioned the study's participants about masturbation, they made a surprising discovery. Conventional wisdom has been that masturbation is a substitute for sex with a partner; a way to relieve sexual tension among those—particularly teenagers and young adults—who are not currently in a sexual relationship. In fact, the evidence suggests that masturbation is practiced most often by men and women in their late twenties and thirties who are also enjoying regular sex with a partner.

In the Laumann study, 85 percent of men and 45 percent of women who were living with a sexual partner said that they masturbate. This social group also thought about sex more than did other groups. The findings also showed that women are more likely to begin masturbating after they have begun a steady relationship than before.

The results suggest that having a relationship with one person, whether through marriage or cohabitation, creates such a highly charged erotic environment that couples become more preoccupied with sex and therefore desire additional sexual outlets, such as masturbation.

FEMALE ORGASM

Laumann found that despite the many magazine articles explaining in detail how women can obtain sexual satisfaction, the majority of women do not regularly reach orgasm during sex. While 75 percent of men questioned always had an orgasm during sex, only 29 percent of women did. Yet over 40 percent of married or cohabiting women and 50 percent of married or cohabiting men said they were satisfied by sex. This suggests that, despite the media hype, there is much more to sex than achieving orgasm.

◀ The drive to marry Although cohabitation is increasingly popular as a test of compatibility, most couples eventually marry. Even older people who are beyond childbearing age and have been married before return to marriage as a way of expressing their love for one another.

How long does sex last? The length of time people devote to each sexual episode is a sensitive subject. The Social Organization of Sexuality study found that most people spent from 15 minutes to one hour making love, but as Laumann and his colleagues point out, many people overestimate the time that activities take.

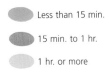

Less than 15 min.

15 min. to 1 hr.

1 hr. or more

Adulthood

*Adulthood is the time when sexuality becomes established.
Men and women become aware of their sexual needs, responses
and preferences, and usually sex becomes an important part of a
marital or other monogamous relationship.*

While sexual intercourse in adolescence takes place in the context of increasing financial, social and domestic freedom, sex in adulthood is commonly defined by growing responsibilities in these areas. Sexual behavior in adulthood typically changes from decade to decade. A couple who are in their twenties generally have sex more often than a couple in their thirties or forties. Couples in their twenties are also likely to be highly fertile.

Adulthood is the time when most people have their children, and the emotional highs and lows that accompany the presence of new family members transform relationships in ways both good and bad.

A WOMAN'S SEXUAL RESPONSES

The patterns of arousal and orgasm that women experience in their twenties will form the basis of their future sexuality. These years are a time for learning about sex and exploring the body's responses. Many women may be unfamiliar with their bodies and have great anxieties about their sexual performance. They may concentrate on their worries (about not reaching orgasm, for instance) rather than their pleasure. The study *The Social Organization of Sexuality* (1994) by Edward Laumann and others found that women in their twenties are less likely to reach orgasm from sex or to masturbate than older women.

By their thirties, most women have developed a good degree of sexual self-knowledge, and this is reflected in their enjoyment of sex and their ability to achieve orgasm. Laumann's study found that 88.5 percent of women in this age group reached orgasm regularly, compared with 79 percent of women in their twenties. Women in their thirties are often less inhibited about communicating their sexual needs to their partners. One problem that some women in this age group begin to experience is a lack of libido, brought about by stressful working conditions and/or fatigue related to pregnancy and childrearing.

The forties signal a time when hormonal changes may begin to affect a woman's sexuality (see page 77). Nevertheless, according to sex therapist Helen Singer Kaplan, women are more likely to experience multiple orgasm at this stage of life because they have resolved past sexual problems and attained sexual and emotional ease.

A MAN'S SEXUAL RESPONSES

Men in their twenties usually find that sexual arousal happens very easily. They often have short refractory periods, meaning that they can achieve an erection within minutes of their last ejaculation, and can have sex

Family life The decision to settle down and have children is a turning point in adult life. Many couples say that creating a family is one of life's most enriching experiences, bringing a sense of permanence, fulfillment and joy.

several times in succession. The main sexual problem that young men encounter is premature ejaculation (see page 213), since they may not have learned to exert control over their ejaculatory responses. They may also have little interest in foreplay.

Men in their thirties may notice that their sexual responses have slowed down slightly, and that they have more difficulty sustaining repeated erections. On the positive side, however, men are less likely to suffer from hyperarousal and premature ejaculation at this age, which means that sexual intercourse can last longer. Lack of libido as a result of work- or family-related stress is not uncommon at this time; nevertheless, it need not be a problem if neither partner sees it as such.

Men in their forties may notice that a full erection can take longer to achieve than previously, but only a tiny percentage of men of this age group suffer from impotence.

ROMANTIC LOVE

According to popular culture, adolescents have crushes and infatuations, while adults fall in love. Modern societies consider this feeling of romantic love to be sufficient justification for most, if not all, adult relationships.

The initial feeling of being in love with someone may lead to placing the loved person on a pedestal and thinking obsessively about him or her. This state of intensity may be accompanied by physical sensations such as weakness, sleeplessness and loss of appetite. Relationship counselors agree that adult relationships follow a natural evolution in which this state of being in love gradually transforms itself into a state of caring love. If this transformation does not occur, once the state of being in love has run its course, a couple generally splits up.

In a good relationship, being in love will evolve into a state of deep, reciprocal caring in which partners allow each other to express themselves and grow as individuals—this is known in psychological terms as the facilitating role of love. Often, however, couples panic when they realize that their initial feelings of passion and intensity are fading, taking this as a sign that they must be falling out of love and the relationship is losing its meaning. Relationship counselors say that this is the stage at which couples have to start contributing to

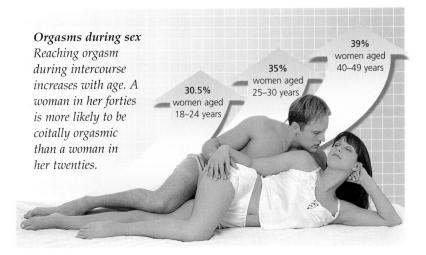

Orgasms during sex
Reaching orgasm during intercourse increases with age. A woman in her forties is more likely to be coitally orgasmic than a woman in her twenties.

30.5% women aged 18–24 years
35% women aged 25–30 years
39% women aged 40–49 years

the relationship in practical ways, rather than relying completely on the sheer force of their emotions.

The ways in which people respond to adult relationships depend strongly on the lessons they learned during childhood. Counselors usually try to help couples articulate their unspoken rules and expectations about love and sex in order to help them

THE COURSE OF LOVE

Adults measure the intensity of a relationship by how romantically attached or "in love" they feel.

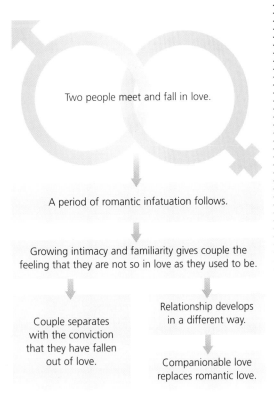

Two people meet and fall in love.

A period of romantic infatuation follows.

Growing intimacy and familiarity gives couple the feeling that they are not so in love as they used to be.

Couple separates with the conviction that they have fallen out of love.

Relationship develops in a different way.

Companionable love replaces romantic love.

The wedding day
Weddings are emotionally charged, romanticized occasions. But if a marriage is to last, companionship rather than romance must be the driving force.

Common pressures on a married couple
Psychologists say that the most common sources of stress in marriage are money, work and children.

work out problems within a relationship. Above all, they encourage people to cultivate good listening skills, whereby one partner is able to listen uncritically to what the other is saying, not what one wants or expects the other to say.

MARRIAGE

Although many societies no longer consider marriage the only way to sanctify sexual relationships, many couples still make this form of commitment to each other. About 75 to 80 percent of people who have been through divorce remarry, and in some cases more than once. In its ideal form, marriage represents a loving, nurturing relationship in which two people offer each other ongoing emotional support, security and commitment. Marriages are rarely perfect, but relationship counselors argue that a good or healthy marriage is one in which couples communicate well, acknowledge their differences and disagreements and are prepared to work at the relationship.

Despite the romantic associations that many people attach to marriage, long-term relationships can be stressful. Once a couple marry, money and children commonly become sources of pressure. Uncertainty

about their future level of income places a well-documented pressure on married couples. Current societal factors, such as unemployment and a move toward contracted, part-time, service-based work, mean that permanent employment can no longer be assumed. Another common source of stress comes from disagreements about when or even whether to have children.

Perceptions of the ideal marriage vary from culture to culture. A report in the *Journal of Social and Personal Relationships* (1993) suggests that, in Japan, socioeconomic factors such as the husband's income are very important in marital satisfaction. In Western cultures, the quality of spouses' interactions is thought to be a good indication of satisfaction.

Until the 1960s, pressures on marriage tended to result in affairs and marital collapse but not divorce. In the past 40 years divorce has become relatively easier, and the pressures on marriage are more clearly indicated by divorce rates. Statistics show that almost one in two marriages in North America end in divorce.

In the West, where love is emphasized as a reason for marriage, marital satisfaction declines with age. In other cultures, where love is seen as a consequence of marriage, this appears not to be the case. Yet even though satisfaction declines over the years, most long-term married couples in the West decide that, on balance, being married is preferable to not being married.

Adultery

Estimates of the incidence of adultery vary enormously. In the American study *The Social Organization of Sexuality* (1994), a dramatic downward revision occurred from earlier estimates of the number of couples engaging in extramarital sexual activity. The figures were revised from 65 percent of men and 50 percent of women to 26 percent and 21 percent, respectively.

The reasons offered by people who have had extramarital sex are diverse. Some cite revenge on an unfaithful partner or seduction by another person. Others claim they are naturally polygamous. The reasons offered respectively by men and women for indulging in extramarital sex point to clear gender-specific differences between them. Adulterous husbands give the desire for increased sexual excitement as the main rea-

What if my partner doesn't want me to work?

Should we have children? When is the right time?

If I lose my job will my partner respect me?

How many children should we have?

Child- and work-related marital stress

Suppose we can't have children?

What will happen to my partner if I lose my job or die?

Will I be a good enough parent?

Do we earn enough money? Should I work harder?

son for infidelity, while adulterous wives state that emotional dissatisfaction with their husband is the main reason.

A study in the *Journal of Social and Personal Relationships* (1995) found that when wives discover that their partner has been unfaithful, they are most likely to respond with self-doubt and disappointment, even though they feel just as angry and betrayed as husbands of adulterous wives. This is especially true of women who suffer from low self-esteem. The wife's sense of jealousy is reduced when she herself has already been unfaithful.

Although many people believe that adultery is sufficient basis to end a relationship, most marriages do manage to survive infidelity. Relationship counselors say that honest communication is one of the keys to recovery. The reasons for infidelity need to be established so that both partners can avoid a repeat of the circumstances that led to an affair in the first place.

PREGNANCY

Women may experience profound emotional and sexual changes during pregnancy. Some women report feeling fertile, energized and sensual, while others suffer from nausea and simply feel drained. Women's sexual desire may fluctuate during pregnancy, and frequency of intercourse tends to decline as pregnancy progresses, although some women report heightened desire in the middle stages of their pregnancy.

There is no physiological reason for couples to abstain from sex during pregnancy unless intercourse is painful or there is a risk of miscarriage. The fetus, suspended in amniotic fluid, is protected from any bumps or bruising. However, a protruding stomach and sore breasts can make face-to-face intercourse uncomfortable. Alternative positions such as side-by-side, rear entry and sitting may be more suitable during pregnancy.

Having children

The presence of a newborn baby may have dramatic effects on a couple's relationship and sex life, particularly in the first three to six months after birth. Couples often report feelings of intense love and joy alternating with fatigue and, sometimes, mild depression. Although women are able to have regular intercourse as soon as feels comfortable after giving birth, many couples take much

longer than this to resume an active sex life. The reasons for this delay include exhaustion, pain during intercourse (from stitches, for example), breast pain (from enlargement or cracked nipples during nursing), poor body image in women and lack of privacy. Some new fathers find it hard to reconcile the sexuality of their wife with the pain they may have witnessed her experiencing

THE PREGNANT BODY

The two most obvious changes to a woman's body during pregnancy are weight gain and a protruding belly, but many other changes occur as well. For example, the volume of blood in the body increases dramatically to provide an adequate supply to the growing fetus and the woman's vital organs. The pumping power of the heart likewise increases. The blood flow to the skin is greater than before, and many women notice that they feel hotter than normal. They may also find that their skin looks healthier, giving rise to the radiant glow often associated with pregnancy.

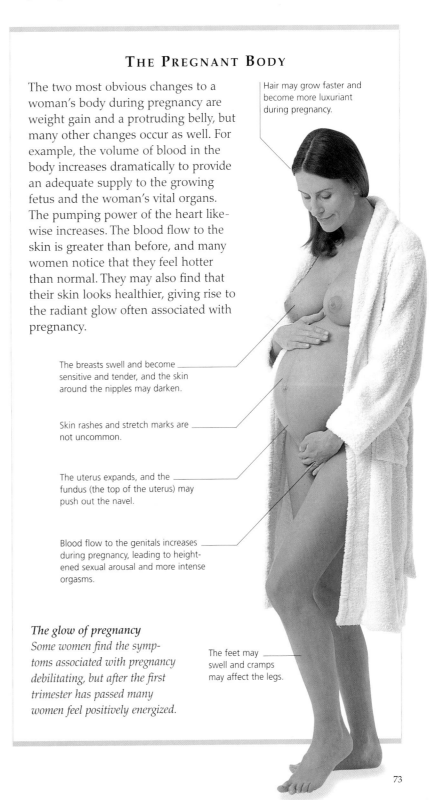

Hair may grow faster and become more luxuriant during pregnancy.

The breasts swell and become sensitive and tender, and the skin around the nipples may darken.

Skin rashes and stretch marks are not uncommon.

The uterus expands, and the fundus (the top of the uterus) may push out the navel.

Blood flow to the genitals increases during pregnancy, leading to heightened sexual arousal and more intense orgasms.

The feet may swell and cramps may affect the legs.

The glow of pregnancy
Some women find the symptoms associated with pregnancy debilitating, but after the first trimester has passed many women feel positively energized.

during childbirth. Nonpenetrative sex is ideal for regaining intimacy and can be just as satisfying as penetrative sex.

Children can cement and affirm a relationship between two people; an intense three-way bonding process can take place between mother, father and child. Although early parenthood can be hard work, many parents compare their feelings for a child to the sensations experienced when falling in love. To some extent, these loving feelings can be caused by hormones, because levels of a hormone called oxytocin are higher than normal in mothers with very young children. Nicknamed the "cuddle chemical," oxytocin encourages nurturing behavior. Levels of the hormone also rise, although to a lesser extent, in fathers.

In the first five years of marriage, children can sometimes undermine overall marital satisfaction. This may be due to the stress and demands inherent in childcare or to the shift in focus of a relationship from the emotional needs of the couple to the needs of a child. Men and women also experience stress over the new roles they adopt when they become parents. Are they "good" parents bringing up the child in the right way? How should they divide up the tasks involved in childcare? Who takes primary responsibility for the baby? What happens if the division of work leaves the man feeling excluded or the woman feeling overburdened? What happens if the woman wants to return to work? Some or all of these questions are likely to arise between partners who have become parents. Although some couples are lucky

New parenthood
Getting to know a new baby can be an exhilarating experience, but it can also be a tiring one. Combining work and parenthood is an acquired skill.

Sensual touch
Intercourse may be uncomfortable during pregnancy or after childbirth. Sensual massage is a good way to stay intimate with a partner.

enough to fall into a pattern that immediately suits both of them, others may need to work hard to negotiate solutions.

NONMARITAL RELATIONSHIPS

Although many adults choose to make the lifelong commitment of marriage, others retain their single status throughout adulthood. Some people decide that marriage will not provide the right context for their relationship—they may be unwilling to make a serious commitment or they may feel that a relationship does not need to be sealed with a public announcement and a ceremony. Alternatively, relationships may not evolve to the point where marriage becomes a possibility. Some people have experienced failed marriages and become disillusioned with intimate, long-term relationships. Other people find that their sexuality makes marriage impossible.

Cohabitation
An increasing number of adults are turning to cohabitation as an alternative to getting married. Often, however, this arrangement is a deferral rather than an actual rejection of marriage; most couples who cohabit do eventually marry

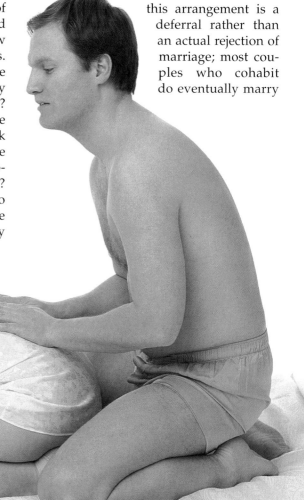

one another. Some couples perceive living together before marriage as advantageous. It lets them assess how they relate to each other before they actually commit themselves. When such couples marry, they have already developed common routines, habits and expectations.

A study in the *Journal of Social and Personal Relationships* (1994) reported a number of unexpected differences between cohabiting and married couples. Cohabiting couples reported having more sex than married couples, fewer affairs, a greater frequency of women initiating sex and a higher level of sexual satisfaction than in married women. Cohabitants typically either get married or break up within two years.

If cohabitants do get married, they are more likely to divorce than couples who did not cohabit before marriage. This may be because people with strong religious views tend neither to cohabit nor divorce.

Couples who cohabited before marriage seem to have a different set of values to those who did not. The former have wider sexual experience, employ more equal division of domestic chores and spend a greater amount of their leisure time together.

Celibacy

Since adulthood is the time when many people engage in long-term relationships, those who opt out of sexual relationships are often considered to be unusual.

People may give a number of reasons for being celibate. These include spiritual growth, waiting for the right partner, work pressure and mental adjustment after the breakup of an important relationship, fear of contracting a sexually transmitted disease or of becoming pregnant, a lack of interest in sex, sexual-identity questions, long-term physical separation from a partner, or being widowed or divorced in later life.

Celibacy has different significance for different individuals: some find it liberating and empowering; some accept it as the best available option; others find that celibacy is forced upon them when they do not want it.

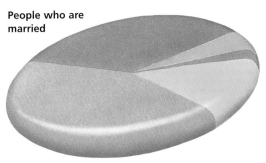

People who cohabit

People who are married

The Language of Sex

Many people use the word "celibacy" to refer to a lack of sexual activity through choice. In fact, the original meaning of the word "celibacy" was "unmarried."

By definition, people who are celibate do not have sexual intercourse but they can relieve sexual tension through masturbation and they can give and receive physical affection by touching and embracing.

Long-term homosexual relationships

Although some societies allow homosexual couples to marry (Norway and Denmark are two countries that have introduced legislation for this), this is not the most common way to express love and commitment in the homosexual community. Monogamy varies with gender in gay relationships: it is estimated that 18 percent of gay men and 72 percent of lesbians are monogamous in their relationships.

Sexually nonexclusive or "open" relationships are more common in long-term relationships between homosexual men, especially if a significant age difference exists between the partners. Research suggests that unlike partners in heterosexual open relationships (which are comparatively rare), gay men in open relationships are more likely to negotiate their own rules on safe sex with their partners.

How often do most people make love? Differences exist between the lovemaking habits of people who are married and people who cohabit. For example, people who cohabit are more likely to have sex four or more times a week.

Not at all

A few times a year

A few times a month

Two/three times a week

Four + times a week

SERIAL MONOGAMY

It has been suggested that people in Western societies, where monogamy is respected as the ideal, are effectively polygamous, because a significant number of people have long-term partners in succession. This behavior is referred to as serial monogamy.

In the U.S. the majority of young adults between the ages of 18 and 24 engage in serial monogamy. They have relationships that may be relatively short, but they remain sexually faithful to their partner for the duration of the relationship. This pattern can also apply to married relationships. People can marry and divorce several times during a lifetime.

Middle Age

Middle age can be a time when couples become closer, since lifestyle changes enable them to spend more time together. A marriage or relationship that has endured over years can confer a sense of great emotional security and sexual intimacy.

Entering midlife
Middle age may allow a more careful selection of priorities and activities than previously. It can mean focusing on relationships and spending more time on leisure.

Middle age can be a turning point for many people. Children grow up and leave home, and careers can become stabler and demand less primary attention than previously. People may choose this time to reassess the various elements in their lives, such as their relationships, their work and their long-term goals. Middle age is also a time when physical changes take place. For women, one of the biggest challenges of middle age is the natural decline in female sex hormones that occurs around the time of menopause.

MENOPAUSE

A wide range of physical and emotional symptoms accompanies falling estrogen levels during menopause, and these can have an effect on relationships. Some women see menopause as defeminizing, as an end not just to fertility but also to sexual attractiveness. They can experience anxiety and low self-esteem. Other women see menopause as freedom from reproductive concerns; a liberating experience.

Although hormonal decline in men (see page 109) does not follow such a clear pattern as female menopause, men may experience a "midlife crisis," in which they start to doubt their looks, virility and achievements.

The last menstrual period in a woman's reproductive life cycle is referred to as the menopause, and it marks the end of her fertility. All women will have experienced the menopause by the time they reach 60.

The years and months leading up to and following a woman's last menstrual period are referred to as perimenopause ("peri" means "around"). For most women, perimenopause is between ages 45 and 58. During this time, the ovaries produce fluctuating amounts of estrogen (the main female sex hormone) before stopping production altogether.

As menopause approaches, ovulation becomes less and less likely in each menstrual cycle. Menstruation becomes increasingly unpredictable: a woman may menstruate some months and not others, and the flow of blood may be heavy one month and light the next.

At the end of the perimenopause, when estrogen is no longer produced by the ovaries, postmenopausal symptoms may start to appear (see page 81).

A WOMAN'S SEXUAL RESPONSES

Women's sexuality in midlife may be characterized by increased sexual confidence and experience. Women in their forties and fifties have generally learned what sort of stimulation they require in order to become aroused and to reach orgasm. They also may feel more relaxed about expressing their needs and desires. While many women are able to use this self-knowledge to maximize their sexual pleasure, others find that the changes of menopause eclipse the positive aspects of growing older.

Physical and emotional changes during perimenopause sometimes combine to cause a loss of or decrease in sex drive. For example, night sweats may lead to insomnia, chronic fatigue and depression, all of which result in loss of libido. A woman may experience symptoms that directly affect the UROGENITAL TRACT, such as vaginal dryness, stress incontinence (see page 146) or genital itch, any of which can make intercourse uncomfortable. Lack of vaginal lubrication during sexual arousal is common during and after perimenopause.

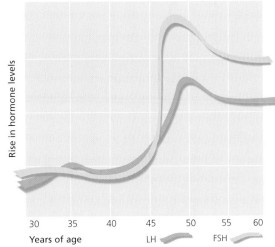

Rising hormone levels When menopause is about to happen, there is a dramatic increase in the amounts of luteinizing and follicle-stimulating hormones circulating in a woman's bloodstream. The average age at which menopause occurs is 51 years.

By contrast, some women notice that their sex drive increases at menopause. One reason for this is that during their fertile years women produce both male and female hormones. When estrogen levels fall at menopause, there is a comparative excess of the male hormone testosterone, which is largely responsible for sex drive in both sexes. This phenomenon does not occur in women who are on hormone replacement therapy (HRT), because their estrogen levels remain high. Occasionally, gynecologists use testosterone pills or implants to treat a decrease in a woman's sex drive.

SYMPTOMS OF THE FEMALE MENOPAUSE

PSYCHOLOGICAL	PHYSICAL
Depressed mood	Hot flashes and night sweats
Feeling nervous or anxious	Muscles that are easily fatigued and sore
Memory changes, particularly a tendency to be forgetful or distracted	Less vaginal lubrication, resulting in soreness and dryness around the vagina and vulva
Inability to concentrate	Bloated abdomen
Feelings of pessimism	Frequent urination
Irritability	An unusual taste in the mouth
Sudden changes in mood for no apparent reason	Increased tendency to stress incontinence and prolapse of pelvic organs
Inability to make decisions	Breasts prone to sagging
Tearfulness	Increase in breast pain

Tackling menopause Menopause should not be seen as a time of illness or sexual decline. A positive attitude will go a long way toward helping a woman cope with her symptoms.

HORMONE REPLACEMENT THERAPY

The main treatment for menopausal symptoms is hormone replacement therapy (HRT). This treats menopause as a hormone deficiency condition and serves to restore hormone levels to normal. HRT usually involves taking, in the form of pills, skin patches or creams, a combination of estrogen and progestogen (the synthetic version of progesterone—see page 129). The estrogen alleviates menopausal symptoms and offers long-term bone and heart health. The progestogen causes the uterine lining to be shed, as in a menstrual period, which is important in the prevention of endometrial cancer.

HRT protects the body from the long-term dangers of an estrogen deficit, which include osteoporosis and heart disease. Because estrogen contributes to the health of many organs, the body remains in its premenopausal state. The waist-to-hip ratio remains the same (whereas the waist would normally fill out after menopause), hair remains thick, muscles keep their strength and tone, and the skin retains its elasticity. HRT also maintains sex drive and the health of the sex organs.

HRT must be prescribed by a doctor. Not all women respond well to HRT—some experience a worsening of symptoms such as mood swings, while others are advised against taking HRT because it is thought to be linked with a very slight increased risk of breast cancer. Women with a previous history of breast, uterine or ovarian cancer are usually not offered HRT by doctors.

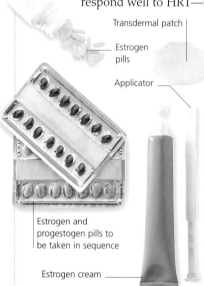

Transdermal patch

Estrogen pills

Applicator

Estrogen and progestogen pills to be taken in sequence

Estrogen cream

Types of HRT
The hormones found in HRT can be administered in a variety of ways: through the skin in the form of adhesive patches, via the vagina in the form of creams and suppositories or orally in the form of pills.

Low self-esteem during perimenopause can also create sexual problems. Some middle-aged women describe themselves as "out of the running" or "out of the mating game." They feel that menopause represents a loss of youth and beauty as well as fertility. As a result, they become self-conscious about sex. If a woman worries about how her body looks to her partner during lovemaking, she may find it difficult to become aroused or to reach orgasm. These

problems are compounded if the man is also experiencing low self-esteem associated with midlife changes.

Although fertility declines in midlife, a woman should continue to use contraception until she knows that she is no longer fertile. Most doctors say that this point is reached one year after the last menstrual period. Perimenopausal women need to pay attention to the type of contraceptive they use. The birth control pill (see page 164) carries a slightly higher risk of thrombosis in older women, especially if they smoke. Also, by maintaining an artificially high level of hormones, the pill may disguise the onset of menopause. Doctors may prescribe the progestogen-only pill or the intrauterine device (IUD; see page 123) for older women. Natural or rhythm methods of family planning are not effective in the perimenopausal period. The erratic nature of the menstrual cycle at this time makes predicting ovulation impossible.

A MAN'S SEXUAL RESPONSES

Men in their forties and fifties may notice a few minor changes in their sexual responses, but none of these have a serious impact on their ability to make love. For example, men may notice that the angle and hardness of their erections diminish, or they may feel that their orgasms are less intense. Having intercourse more than once a day may present more of a challenge at 50 than at 20, especially if a man is feeling tired or stressed. Also, middle-aged men often find that the quickest route to erection is direct stimulation of the penis, rather than fantasy. Middle-aged men also tend to ejaculate with much less force, which may in part explain why orgasms feel less intense.

Many of the men interviewed in Shere Hite's *The Hite Report on Male Sexuality* (1981) said that sexual enjoyment reached a peak in middle age, because they had gained an intimate knowledge of both their own and their partner's sexual responses. This gave them sexual confidence, enabling them to shed their inhibitions, to talk more openly about sex and to experiment more than they had in the past. Some men also said that the connection between love and sex had become more important to them. They appreciated and enjoyed the emotional intimacy of lovemaking. From a woman's perspective, the sexual changes that men

Performance anxiety
Feeling that they have to try especially hard to prove themselves in the work environment is an anxiety that many middle-aged men face.

experience in midlife may be advantageous: sex becomes more loving; there is more emphasis on foreplay; and men take longer to ejaculate, which means that intercourse can be slower and more sensual.

Male insecurity

For men who feel that their roles as worker, husband and father are slowly eroding, midlife can be a difficult time. During these years problems often converge, creating intense insecurity. Minor or major health difficulties—including those caused by poor diet and bad habits such as smoking—make men aware of their own mortality. They may compare themselves with younger, fitter men and feel that they are no longer sexually attractive. At work they may experience rivalry with younger colleagues. At home a wife or partner may be suffering from menopausal symptoms that affect not just the couple's sex life but their entire relationship. A man's role as father may also diminish as his children grow up and leave home.

Common questions arise for men in midlife: "Have I fulfilled my ambitions?" "Am I still attractive?" "Do I still command respect?" "What does the future hold?" "Can I still perform sexually?" Negative answers to such questions can lead to stress, depression and even sexual difficulties, including the inability to achieve and maintain an erection. A deterioration in midlife marital relationships sometimes causes men

to seek sex outside marriage. One frequently cited explanation for affairs—particularly those with younger women—is that they provide a way of recapturing feelings of youth. Affairs can reassure men of their virility and potency and provide the energy and sexual tension lacking in relationships with a wife or partner. Unfortunately, insecurity rarely provides a basis for a stable relationship; sooner or later most men are compelled to confront their real fears.

If emotional or psychosexual problems run deep, professional help from a relationship counselor or a sex therapist may be the best hope for resolution. Some couples find that honesty, frankness and mutual recognition that middle age is a time of transition helps to guide them through the changes.

Does male menopause exist?

Male menopause is a much more controversial subject than female menopause, which doctors acknowledge can have a profound effect on women's sense of well-being.

Men experience a gradual decline in testosterone levels from about age 45 to 70, followed by a marked decline after 70. Whether this causes menopause-like symptoms is debatable. Many doctors attribute male midlife symptoms (see below) to stress and declining health rather than hormones.

HRT FOR MEN

Men who are given replacement testosterone generally experience a sense of greater well-being and higher energy levels and sex drive.

In the U.S., testosterone can be administered as pills, injections, implants or skin patches; in Canada, it is available only in the form of pills and injections. Before HRT is prescribed, men need a thorough health check, including blood tests to give a hormone profile and screening for any liver abnormalities. An ultrasound study of the prostate gland should also be carried out to check for the presence of cancer.

SYMPTOMS OF THE MALE MENOPAUSE

PSYCHOLOGICAL	PHYSICAL
Depressed mood	Noise sensitivity
Inexplicable mood changes	Fatigue and decreased energy
Hyperanxiety (feelings of intense worry or panic)	Loss of strength and stamina
Reduction in alertness	Decreased facial hair growth
Failing memory	Dry skin
A sense of aging	Increased perspiration
Irritability and feelings of impatience and intolerance	Hot flushes
Reduced concentration span	Aches and pains in joints
A decline in libido: in sexual interest and sex drive	Erectile problems

Advanced Age

A misconception has long existed that older people cease to be interested in sex. Growing evidence suggests that many older people maintain the sexual desire of their youth, and although lovemaking may be less vigorous, it remains satisfying.

Jay and Fran Landesman *Married since 1950, this prominent couple from the beatnik generation said in 1996 that their marriage was better than ever. "It's as though the relationship has started over again."*

In *The Hite Report on Male Sexuality* (1981), 57 percent of men between ages 61 and 75 said that their desire for sex either increased with age or remained the same. When asked how age affected their enjoyment of sex, only 11 percent of men between 61 and 75 reported a decline. In Shere Hite's 1976 study of women's sexuality, the results were similar.

For many people, sexual desire and enjoyment seem to remain constant throughout life, though the frequency with which people have intercourse may decrease. In a survey conducted in 1994, titled *The Social Organization of Sexuality*, it was found that only 20 percent of American men and 12 percent of women in their fifties had sex at least once a week, compared with 35 percent of both men and women in their twenties and thirties.

A report in 1992 in the *Harvard Health Letter* suggests that although frequency of intercourse does decline with age, the best prediction of an active sex life after age 60 is high levels of desire and activity when young. Conversely, a couple who have never had an active sex life may be content with celibacy in their old age.

Some researchers have questioned the validity of statistics on the links between sexual activity and old age. They point out that elderly people were brought up in less permissive times and may be reluctant to provide accurate and honest information about their sex lives. In addition, they say, the meaning of celibacy in older people is easily misinterpreted. Not having sexual intercourse may indicate diminished desire, but it may also result from the death of a partner or failing health.

SOCIAL ATTITUDES

In the majority of cultures, sexual attractiveness is strongly identified with youth, health and beauty. Society does not consider aging to be beautiful or sexy, and many older people feel they are not expected to be sexual beings. In fact, they may feel pressured to deny their sexuality.

Leading feminist writer Germaine Greer argues that this is particularly true for women: "The older woman is simply not perceived as a sexual entity, unless she

makes an unsubtle display of herself, which amounts to a statement of availability, which is a turnoff to all but the least desirable partners."

Some cultures actively discourage older people from engaging in sexual activity. For example, the Meru of Kenya expect a woman's sex life to end on the marriage of her daughter, and the Hokkien in Taiwan insist that both men and women stop having sex when they become grandparents.

In Western society, an increasing number of older people are expecting and demanding a more active old age. They are rediscovering sex as a pastime, and workshops encourage them to relearn dating skills and brush up on sexual techniques.

PHYSICAL CHANGES

Three physical factors affect sexual activity in older people: the hormonal changes that affect desire and cause the aging of the UROGENITAL TRACT; muscle weakness and lower energy levels associated with advanced age; and the increased probability of chronic medical conditions such as DIABETES and heart disease. All of these pressures can take their toll on an individual's sex life. In addition, some of the medications used to treat conditions such as high blood pressure have an adverse effect on the libido or male erectile function.

A woman's sexual responses

Hormonal changes have the most direct impact on female sexual behavior. After menopause women stop producing estrogen in their ovaries, and this can give rise to a range of postmenopausal symptoms, including atrophy (the shrinking, thinning and drying) of the vagina, vulva and clitoris. Postmenopausal women produce a great deal less vaginal lubrication when they are sexually aroused—this can result in painful intercourse. The muscles that surround the sex organs can also weaken, leading to prolapse (see page 145) of organs such as the uterus and bladder into the vagina. The likelihood of vaginal and urinary infections also increases. If women continue to take hormone replacement therapy in the postmenopausal period, they should not suffer from these symptoms.

A man's sexual responses

In men, lower production of testosterone decreases sexual desire. Genital sensitivity declines, and as a result the penis needs more direct stimulation to become erect. Many men find that whereas they once had an erection within seconds of being physically or mentally stimulated, this now takes much longer. They may notice that their ability to ejaculate diminishes, and less semen is expelled with less force. Also, the refractory period (see page 110) usually becomes longer.

The physical changes associated with advanced age may be exacerbated by a couple's reaction to them. For example, the man who finds erection difficult becomes anxious, and this hinders arousal. Similarly, the woman who is slow to lubricate finds intercourse painful and may become reluctant to have sex as a result. In extreme cases, couples may even stop all sexual activity.

Desire increases.

Desire is unchanged.

Desire decreases.

Age and desire Shere Hite interviewed men between the ages of 61 and 75. Although some men said that libido declined with age, the majority thought that it stayed the same or increased.

fact or fiction?

Older men no longer become aroused by visual stimuli.

There is a small amount of truth in this. A young man can become sexually aroused very quickly when looking at something provocative, whether it is his partner undressing or a sexually explicit photograph. In contrast, an older man may find these things psychologically erotic, but he is less likely to respond by having an erection. Erections in older men are more often a response to direct physical stimulation.

Adapting sexual behavior

People in their later years are able to take advantage of their slower sexual responses by spending more time on both foreplay and lovemaking, so that sex becomes a more sensual experience. Sex does not always have to be penetrative—couples can try to be inventive and increase their repertoire of activities (see page 42).

Vaginal lubricants
Using a lubricant before sex can eliminate the problem of vaginal dryness. Lubricants are available as jellies or creams. Suppositories are available only in the U.S.

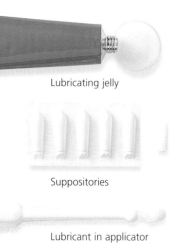

Lubricating jelly

Suppositories

Lubricant in applicator

The benefits of sex
There is a positive relationship between sexual activity in advanced age and a sense of well-being.

Older women may need different kinds of sexual stimulation than they previously required. For instance, the tissue covering the clitoris may shrink and thin, leaving the clitoris exposed and extremely sensitive. This can make direct stimulation painful, in which case cunnilingus (see page 64) and gentle touching using plenty of lubrication are alternatives. If a woman feels anxious because sex is sometimes uncomfortable, she may want to try sexual positions in which she is on top, which will allow her to control the depth and angle of penetration as well as the pace of lovemaking.

Although advanced age may cause physical impediments to sex, it also brings many sexual benefits. Birth control ceases to be an issue, and age and experience often give people the confidence to express their desires openly. Older couples have more time and privacy to devote to sex, with fewer distractions and worries. Sexual activity into old age also has positive implications for the health of the sex organs. For women in particular, regular intercourse or masturbation, combined with contracting the *PUBOCOCCYGEAL (PC) MUSCLES*, helps maintain vaginal muscle tone and the ability to produce lubrication.

Some long-term couples come to realize that they have made love the same way for years without experimenting or talking about sex; others have unresolved emotional problems within the relationship that have affected their sex life; still others find that sex has become routine and takes sec-

ond place in their relationship. Older couples can visit sex therapists for help with and advice about these issues.

Masturbation

Self-stimulation can be very important in old age. Masturbation enables women and men without partners or with infirm partners to release sexual tension (with the benefit of maintaining the health of the vulva and vagina). For men, masturbation can also help allay fears about impotence—if a man can achieve erection through masturbation, intercourse remains possible. In addition, since sexual activity aids the production of testosterone, masturbation can help to maintain sex drive.

Loving touch

If a long-term couple have always been physically and emotionally close, sexual touching and intimacy will probably carry on into old age. In her autobiography, *A Quest for Love* (1980), Jacquetta Hawkes described her early relationship with her husband, the English novelist J. B. Priestley, as "magnetic." They continued to make love until he was 85 years old.

Couples who have been able to express affection only in a sexual context find that as the frequency of lovemaking decreases, so too do all forms of affectionate expression. Most gerontologists believe that intimate, but not necessarily sexual, touching promotes a sense of happiness and well-being. Lack of touch can result in feelings of isolation and loneliness.

Loving physical gestures, such as holding hands, linking arms, hugging and kissing, become much more important during old age. A person who has lived a long time often craves something deeper than a sexually fulfilling relationship, and close friends or relatives can provide this. Loving gestures convey a sense of caring, acknowledgment and support, especially at an age when many elderly people may feel that their worth to society is limited.

Elderly people who have lost their spouse or who live a socially secluded life often focus their love and affection on their pets. Stroking, cuddling and caring for domestic animals may be as emotionally satisfying as the exchange of physical attention with a human being. Owning pets has also been shown to lower blood pressure and to

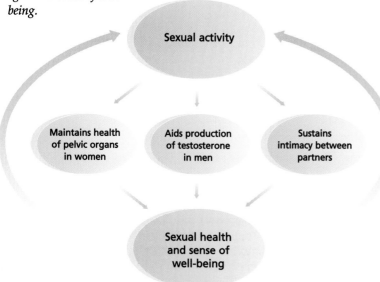

Sexual activity

Maintains health of pelvic organs in women

Aids production of testosterone in men

Sustains intimacy between partners

Sexual health and sense of well-being

release endorphins (these are chemical substances that are found in the brain; their release provides a sense of well-being).

NEW AND RENEWED RELATIONSHIPS

Older people can often look forward to the prospect of grandparenthood (it is estimated that three-quarters of North Americans over age 65 are grandparents). Relationships with grandchildren can be among the most fulfilling. Grandparents enjoy the luxury of giving their love freely without the burdens and stresses of domesticity, work and childcare. Because grandparents usually have more time than parents to talk and listen, they can act as valuable confidants. They can also provide a positive role model for aging and a link to the past. By relating stories of life several decades past, they can give their grandchildren an understanding of how society and attitudes change.

The birth of grandchildren often provides a sense of purpose to older people. A couple who have drifted apart over the years can be brought together by the mutual interest they have in their grandchildren. The presence of grandchildren may also help to heal any family discord between grandparents and their own sons or daughters, or sons- or daughters-in-law.

SEX IN SPECIAL CIRCUMSTANCES

Many people have continuing good health throughout their life. Some are not so fortunate, and their difficulties become more pronounced the older they get. It is estimated that three in five people over 85 suffer from a longstanding illness. Ailments that commonly afflict elderly people include heart disease, arthritis and diabetes. Fortunately, with a little imagination and some simple techniques, satisfying sex can be achieved no matter what degree of health impairment a person experiences.

Heart disease

Heart-disease patients may worry that an active sex life could be detrimental to their health, but the American Heart Association reports that a heart patient can resume usual sexual activity as soon as he or she feels ready to do so. Because many heart-disease patients suffer from fatigue and may be too tired in the evening, the best time for sex may be late morning or early afternoon. Sufferers should also wait at

LOVE IN ADVANCED AGE

Contrary to the myth that older people do not fall in love, new romantic relationships can and do happen. Advanced age can bring a sense of freedom to some people: they no longer feel accountable to their parents or their children, and, having spent a lifetime living up to society's expectations, they may feel that it is time to act self-indulgently, especially if they have been single for a number of years.

Romantic relationships can arise in the most unexpected ways: between people who have been friendly for years (perhaps all their lives); in retirement communities, when people are brought together for the first time; or through new activities such as bridge or exercise classes. Some older people may decide to vigorously pursue a new lifestyle in order to find a partner, others may join a specialized dating agency.

Some older couples entering new relationships want to marry or remarry, although this is a trend that is more likely for men than for women. Research has shown that a number of women reject marriage in later life because, having been on their own for a long time, their independence has become important and they do not want to resume the role of wife and caregiver.

Many gerontologists say that love promotes longevity because it gives

Reviving relationships
Romance can come in the form of a new relationship, or it can be revived in a current one. Taking up a hobby such as hiking can create a common interest and a new sense of intimacy.

meaning to life and prevents isolation and loneliness. Although any relationship involves a certain amount of stress, couples who meet in later life tend to express more tolerance toward each other than younger couples. There is also the benefit of being free from worries about pregnancy, settling down, childrearing, careers and social mobility—all factors that commonly threaten the relationships of younger couples.

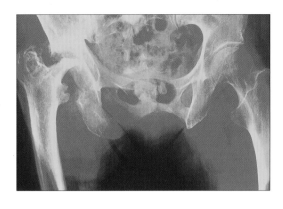

Arthritic joints A common affliction in older people, arthritis causes the slow destruction of the joints. The hip joints are commonly affected —in severe cases hip replacement surgery may be necessary.

Preparing for sex If joints are stiff, a shared hot bath can ease discomfort and improve flexibility.

least two hours after eating before making love to ensure that their bodies have properly digested the meal.

Arthritis

Stiff joints can make sexual intercourse painful. To ease the pain, the partner suffering from arthritis should sit or lie down to avoid bearing any weight on affected joints. If both partners suffer from arthritis, the side-by-side spoons sexual position (see page 55) is ideal. Heat makes the joints more mobile, so having sex in a well-heated room could be helpful. A gentle massage using warm oil can increase flexibility and relaxation. A warm bath can also help.

Diabetes

Noninsulin-dependent, or Type II, diabetes develops mainly in people over 40. In men the illness can cause damage to nerve fibers that affect erection, and in uncircumcised men and in women, it can cause genital yeast infections (see page 143).

Appropriate dietary and weight-control measures can decrease the fatigue of diabetes and help prevent nerve and heart damage. A doctor should be consulted to make sure that medications prescribed for diabetes do not affect libido. Individuals suffering from diabetes also have an increased risk of developing hypertension and cardiovascular disorders, in which case they should follow the recommendations for heart-disorder patients (see above).

Postoperative sex

Any abdominal or pelvic surgery involves the formation and healing of scar tissue. This can take up to eight weeks, during which time sexual intercourse should be avoided. Serious surgery, such as heart surgery or hip replacement, can require a recovery period of up to three months. Individuals vary greatly, so it is essential to follow the advice of a doctor. Unless otherwise advised, a patient who is recovering well and feeling relaxed should be able to partake in gentle sexual activity within a few weeks. A chair offers better support than a bed, and pillows can be used to cushion sensitive areas. Side-by-side positions, with the affected partner doing the least work, may be best.

Hysterectomy

After an *EPISIOTOMY*, a hysterectomy is the second most common surgery for women in the Western world. It has been estimated that approximately one woman in three undergoes hysterectomy by the age of 60. Hysterectomy consists of the removal of the uterus—and sometimes also the fallopian tubes and cervix—to remedy a number of female gynecological problems. These include cancers, endometriosis, fibroids, painful and heavy periods, prolapse, and pelvic inflammatory disease (see pages 190 to 198). If the ovaries are also removed, the surgery is known as a hysterectomy and oophorectomy.

After a hysterectomy, loss of libido is common. Sex should resume only after scar tissue and any internal bruising have healed and the woman feels relaxed and ready. When the cervix is removed, some women complain that they lose the ability to reach orgasm. This may be due to the loss of sensitive nerve endings in the cervix. Strengthening the *PUBOCOCCYGEAL (PC) MUSCLES* by repeatedly contracting them and massaging the G-spot (see page 98) can help revive orgasmic response.

Although some women experience long-term sexual problems after hysterectomy, most recover very quickly and feel more sexually confident after the operation. *The Maine Women's Health Study* (1989 to 1991) of 798 women found that hysterectomy left 71 percent of the women feeling better mentally, physically and sexually than they had before the operation.

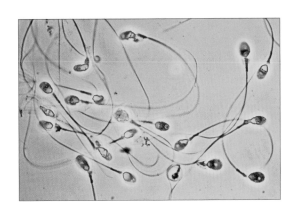

SEXUAL ANATOMY & PHYSIOLOGY

The Sexual Body 86

Puberty 88

Male Sex Organs 91

The Sperm Cell 94

Female Sex Organs 96

The Ovum 100

The Breasts 102

The Sexual Response Cycle 104

The Sexual Body

Some parts of the body function solely for sex and reproduction, but other body parts make vital contributions to successful sexual activity. Without hormones released by the brain, for example, sexual maturation would never even start.

The sensual body
The most intense site of erotic pleasure is the genitals, but many other parts of the body play important parts in arousal and sensual enjoyment.

The genitals are the focal point of sexual pleasure. During masturbation or intercourse, with the right stimulation, muscles around the genitals contract rhythmically, producing the pleasurable sensations of orgasm. Although the male genitals and the female genitals and breasts receive the most attention as sexual areas, all the parts of an individual's body, in one way or another, enhance sexual attraction and response.

Parts of the body far from the genitals, such as the lips, have their own responses to sexual arousal. The skin all over the body contains millions of nerve endings that make it highly responsive to touch, with skin-to-skin contact often triggering sexual arousal. Although orgasm is felt most strongly in the genitals, sexual pleasure radiates throughout the entire body. When a woman climaxes she may arch her feet and back and curl her toes. She may have involuntary muscular contractions all over her body, and her chest and neck may become covered in a fine rash (see page 104).

Other parts of the body act as sexual attractors. Pubic hair is a sign of sexual maturity, and the lips, buttocks and belly are full of erotic significance. Some anthropologists argue that they are examples of sexual self-mimicry: the lips mimic the labia; the breasts mimic the buttocks; and the navel mimics the vagina (self-mimicry is significant because human ancestors used to mate using rear-entry positions).

INSIDE THE BODY

A complex interplay of hormones is necessary to promote sexual desire and fertility. Hormones are responsible also for triggering sexual development and they also maintain masculinity and femininity. Testosterone is responsible for a man's characteristic muscle strength, facial hair and deep voice, while estrogen and progesterone stimulate breast growth and regulate a woman's cycle of fertility.

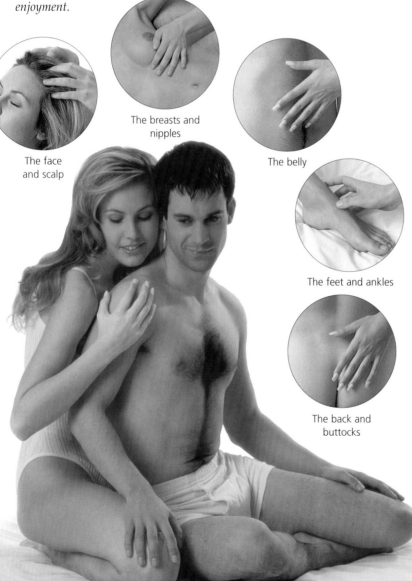

The face and scalp

The breasts and nipples

The belly

The feet and ankles

The back and buttocks

The cardiovascular system also plays a vital role in sexual arousal and function. During arousal, the heart pumps faster, sending an increased blood flow to the genitals and causing them to become engorged. This makes the penis erect and causes physical changes in the vagina and clitoris that enable orgasm and may even aid conception (see page 107).

THE BRAIN

The brain plays both a conscious and subconscious role in the process of sexual arousal. Some people claim it is the most important sexual organ.

Before arousal takes place, a person usually perceives something as sexy—a photograph, a smell or the proximity of another person. This perception initiates sexual desire and is followed by physical changes in the genitals or the rest of the body.

An area in the brain known as the limbic system processes information received from the senses of sight, smell, taste, hearing and touch, as well as emotional stimuli such as thoughts, desires and fantasies. If the signals sent to the brain are positive ones, then the person experiences feelings of pleasure. If the information relayed to the limbic system has a positive sexual component, messages will be sent from the brain to increase blood flow (vasocongestion) to the genitals. This sort of arousal is termed psychogenic, because it originates in the mind.

Sexual arousal also can occur without any perception of pleasure to start the process and without involving the limbic system. A direct touch or pressure on the genitals can cause the blood flow to increase to this area, a phenomenon known as reflex arousal. While it is a much simpler response than psychogenic response, it is just as important. During sexual intercourse, psychogenic and reflex responses work together. A man's reflex response tends to override his psychogenic response during sex, and continuous stimulation of his genitals will almost certainly lead to ejaculation and orgasm. A woman, however, can be distracted by the sound of a telephone ringing or a child crying, which can block her progression to orgasm despite continuous physical stimulation of the genitals.

At the moment of orgasm, both men and women suddenly release substances called beta enkephalins (a type of endorphin). These chemical messengers resemble opiates such as morphine. Beta-enkephalins latch on to receptors in the brain, known as opiate receptors, and cause the diffuse rush of pleasure and euphoria felt during orgasm.

◀ **Homunculus**
Some parts of the body are more responsive to touch than others. The proportions of this body reflect the amount of space devoted to them by the cerebral cortex in the brain. One of the functions of the cerebral cortex is to respond to touch.

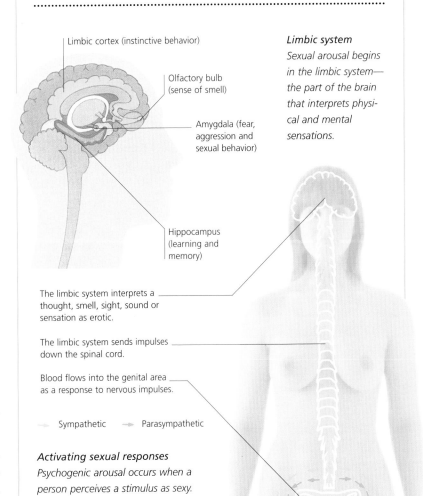

SEX AND THE BRAIN

Limbic cortex (instinctive behavior)

Olfactory bulb (sense of smell)

Amygdala (fear, aggression and sexual behavior)

Hippocampus (learning and memory)

Limbic system
Sexual arousal begins in the limbic system— the part of the brain that interprets physical and mental sensations.

The limbic system interprets a thought, smell, sight, sound or sensation as erotic.

The limbic system sends impulses down the spinal cord.

Blood flows into the genital area as a response to nervous impulses.

⟶ Sympathetic　　⟶ Parasympathetic

Activating sexual responses
Psychogenic arousal occurs when a person perceives a stimulus as sexy. The brain transforms this perception into nervous impulses that travel through the body's nervous system to "instruct" blood to flow to the genitals, causing sexual arousal.

Puberty

Sometime between childhood and adulthood, a surge in sex hormones triggers sexual development. The sex organs mature, and associated hormonal activity makes sexual intercourse and reproduction possible.

The physical changes that characterize puberty make male and female bodies both fertile and attractive to the opposite sex. Puberty usually starts between ages 8 and 14 in girls and between 10 and 15 in boys. For girls, the first sign is the beginning of breast development, while boys notice that their genitals start to enlarge. For both sexes, these changes are followed by the appearance of hair in the genital area and armpits.

Puberty is often a time of rapid physical growth. After body hair appears, the hormone somatotropin is released by the pituitary gland in the brain to trigger bone and muscle growth.

Girls normally experience this growth spurt earlier than boys. Around age 12, they are often taller than boys of the same age, but by age 15 boys tend to be taller. Most girls are close to their adult height when they start to menstruate. Body shape also changes: girls gain body fat and their hips become wider; boys gain more lean body tissue, so their overall percentage of body fat drops, and their shoulders and chests become broader than their hips.

MALE SEXUAL DEVELOPMENT

In boys, follicle-stimulating hormone (FSH; see box, right) triggers development and production of sperm, and luteinizing hormone (LH) triggers production of testosterone. Testosterone, which is the most important of all male sex hormones, is responsible, in one form or another, for the development of most of the male *SECONDARY SEXUAL CHARACTERISTICS*.

Ninety-five percent of testosterone is secreted by the testicles and 5 percent by the *ADRENAL GLANDS*. In addition to sexual changes, testosterone causes bone ends to fuse, or close over, terminating growth in both boys and girls. The testicles and scrotum respond to testosterone by increasing in size. The surface of the scrotum becomes

| STAGE 1 | STAGE 2 | STAGE 3 | STAGE 4 | STAGE 5 |

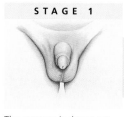
The scrotum is drawn up close to the body.

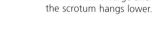
The testicles enlarge and the scrotum hangs lower.

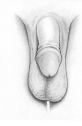
The testicles continue to enlarge and the penis grows longer.

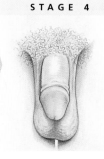
The penis increases in girth and pubic hair grows. The skin of the penis and scrotum deepens in color.

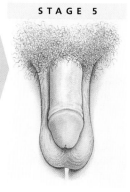
The penis grows in length and girth to reach its adult state. The testicles are fully functional.

Genital development in a circumcised male
There are roughly five stages in the development of the penis and testicles. Stage one is the immature genitals of babyhood. By stage five the sex organs are sexually mature, making reproduction possible.

ONSET OF PUBERTY

The way in which puberty begins is not fully understood. Scientists believe that an inhibitory mechanism exists in the brain, which at puberty is removed. The part of the brain known as the hypothalamus then releases a surge of hormone that triggers puberty. This is how puberty starts in both girls and boys.

The trigger hormone is known as gonadotropin-releasing hormone (GRH). It travels to the pituitary gland—located beneath the hypothalamus. The pituitary gland then secretes two important hormones known as follicle-stimulating hormone (FSH) and luteinizing hormone (LH). These hormones travel through the bloodstream and trigger the ovaries and testes to become active for the first time.

Before she can begin to menstruate, about a quarter of a girl's total body weight must be composed of fat. This is why the development of wider hips and fuller breasts during puberty is thought to be important in triggering menstruation. When girls have low body fat, the pituitary gland does not release the required amount of FSH and LH for normal menstruation to take place.

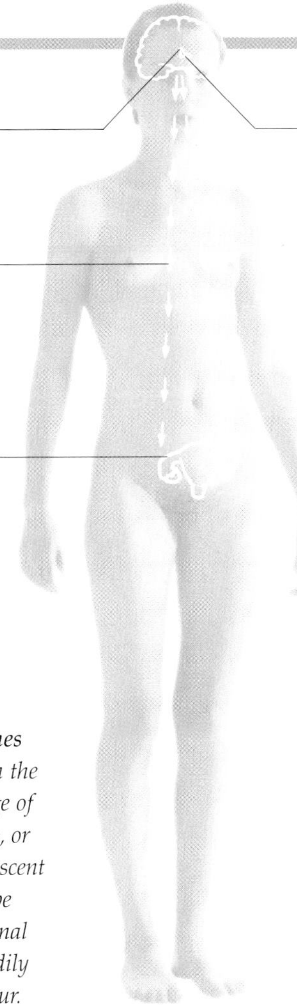

The hypothalamus releases GRH.

FSH and LH travel through the bloodstream to the ovaries.

FSH causes the egg follicles in the ovaries to start maturing for the first time.

The pituitary gland is stimulated to produce FSH and LH.

Ovulation
When the ovaries become active for the first time, an egg, or ovum (shown below), is released from the ovary. This is an event that will continue to happen periodically for the rest of a woman's reproductive life span.

The flow of hormones
Puberty begins when the brain releases a surge of chemical messengers, or hormones. The adolescent girl or boy will not be aware of this hormonal activity until the bodily changes begin to occur.

more wrinkled, redder and darker. The penis grows longer and then increases in width. After this, pubic and axillary (armpit) hair grows, followed by facial and chest hair. The testicles, scrotum and penis continue to enlarge.

Testosterone also causes the prostate gland (see page 93) and the voice box, or larynx, to enlarge. The vocal cords become longer and thicker, eventually causing a deepening of the voice. While this is taking place, some boys have an uncomfortable feeling in their throats for a few weeks, but for most, the change is gradual and free of any symptoms.

fact or fiction?

Erections occur even when you're not sexually aroused.

Fact. During puberty boys have high levels of testosterone causing spontaneous erections. This can be embarrassing, but it is not unusual or abnormal. It can also happen in prepubescent boys.

Between 30 and 50 percent of pubescent boys develop a slight increase in size in one or both breasts. Known as gynecomastia, this results from an excess of estrogen in the body and can cause a great deal of anxiety among boys and their families; doubts about masculinity are a common concern. Most cases disappear spontaneously within a year.

Ejaculation
The male equivalent of a girl's first menstrual bleed is a boy's first ejaculation. This is called spermarche and is usually experienced at about age 13. The first ejaculation

CHANGES AT PUBERTY

At puberty, both sexes undergo rapid physical development as their bodies change to become sexually mature.

Changes in girls include the following:

Breasts and nipples enlarge.

Menstruation begins.

Vaginal secretions increase.

The inner and outer lips of the vulva enlarge.

The vagina becomes longer and wider.

Changes in boys and girls include the following:

Height increases.

Sebaceous (oil) glands become active, and acne becomes common.

Body and pubic hair grows.

Sweat glands in the armpits and genitals become active, and adult body odor is produced.

Changes in boys include the following:

The voice becomes deeper.

Muscle mass starts increasing.

The penis and testicles enlarge.

Ejaculation becomes possible.

Facial hair develops.

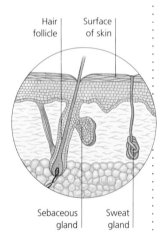

Hair follicle | Surface of skin

Sebaceous gland | Sweat gland

The cause of acne
Sebum is an oily substance secreted onto the skin by the sebaceous glands. Excess sebum production at puberty can result in oily skin and acne.

often occurs at night during sleep and is known as a nocturnal emission or, more commonly, a "wet dream." Wet dreams are experienced by about 75 percent of pubescent males (but rarely by adult males). They typically occur during the rapid eye movement phase of sleep.

Ejaculation during puberty does not guarantee fertility; it simply indicates that seminal-fluid production is beginning and that the testicles and prostate gland (see page 93) are adequately performing their secretory functions.

FEMALE SEXUAL DEVELOPMENT

In girls, the release of FSH and LH tells the ovaries to produce estrogen, which triggers the development of female sexual characteristics. The breasts begin to grow, although rarely evenly. It is common for one breast to be slightly larger than the other until sexual maturity is reached, when they may roughly even out. Pubic hair begins to appear on the pubic mound in a flat-topped triangular shape and on the outer lips (labia majora) surrounding the genitals. In about 45 percent of girls, pubic

hair growth occurs before breast growth. Hair also starts appearing in the armpits, and the fine, downy hair on the legs becomes thicker and longer.

The uterus enlarges and the external genitals become darker and more prominent. The vagina also enlarges and a slight discharge may be noticeable. The surge in estrogen levels that comes with puberty can make the skin oilier and prone to blocked pores, blackheads, spots and acne.

Menarche

The most dramatic development in puberty is the onset of menstruation, an event called the menarche. It normally occurs between ages 9 and 17. In Western societies it usually occurs after the age of 11. There are several causes of late menarche, or primary amenorrhea (see page 142). Low body weight caused by ANOREXIA NERVOSA or overexercising can inhibit menarche.

After menarche a girl's menstrual periods may be very irregular for a while, since she may ovulate some months but not others. It may take a couple of years for the menstrual cycle to become regular.

Male Sex Organs

Unlike the female sex organs, the male genitals are clearly visible. Because of this, most men have a good knowledge of their external sexual anatomy. What both sexes may be less aware of is the function of the structures inside the male body.

The most obvious male sexual organ is the penis. It has two functions: transporting urine out of the body and carrying sperm-containing semen for fertilization of the ovum. Most of the time the penis rests in its relaxed, or flaccid, state and hangs down in front of the testicles. While a flaccid penis is convenient for passing urine, it cannot penetrate the vagina to deposit sperm during sexual intercourse. For intercourse to be possible, the penis must become at least partially erect.

THE ANATOMY OF THE PENIS

Externally, the penis consists of a body, called the shaft, and a head, called the glans. The shaft is covered in loose skin that wrinkles up when the penis is flaccid. In uncircumcised men this skin forms a hood, or foreskin, over the glans.

The shaft

The tube that carries urine and semen along the length of the penis is called the urethra. It begins at the bladder and ends at the opening in the glans. Three columns of spongy tissue in the shaft of the penis are responsible for its great erectile ability. The smallest column is the corpus spongiosum, which surrounds and protects the urethra and expands at the tip of the penis to form the glans. It also thickens at the base of the penis, where it is encircled by a muscle that contracts rhythmically during ejaculation to force semen out of the penis.

On top of the corpus spongiosum lie two other columns, called the corpus cavernosa, that run parallel along the length of the penis. They are attached to muscles that are connected to a bone in the pelvis. When a man is sexually excited, these muscles pull

the penis into its erect position and blood rushes into the columns of spongy tissue, making them swell. The blood vessels leading away from the penis virtually close so that the blood is trapped and the penis becomes engorged and firm. As the penis becomes erect it not only changes in size, it also darkens; large blue veins stand out on its surface, and the shaft may become slightly curved. This curved shape helps the penis fit into the vagina. Although rare, an unusually curved penis may be due to a condition known as Peyronie's disease. Advanced age can affect the angle and firmness of a man's erection.

Average penis length when flaccid is between 2½ and 4 inches (6.5 to 10.5 cm) from the tip of the glans to the base. This length varies from one man to another, and is affected by conditions such as temperature. The average length of the erect penis is 6 to 7 inches (15 to 18 cm). The size of an erect penis can be affected by alcohol consumption, fatigue and degree of arousal. Penis girth and shape vary greatly: some have a wide base and taper to a point, whereas others are the same width throughout their length.

Contrary to popular myth, penis size has no effect on sexual ability or virility, nor does it correlate with body size or the size of the hands, feet or nose. In fact, sex therapists Masters and Johnson reported that penis size had less relation to the skeletal and muscular size of a man than any other organ in the body. Also, it is rare for an

X-ray of the penis During arousal the tissues inside the penis fill up with blood, making it hard and erect.

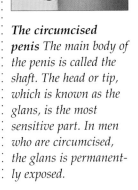

The circumcised penis The main body of the penis is called the shaft. The head or tip, which is known as the glans, is the most sensitive part. In men who are circumcised, the glans is permanently exposed.

91

adult male not to have an erect penis within the usual size range. Nevertheless, many men worry that it is less "manly" to have a small penis. One reason men may perceive their own penis to be smaller than other men's is because when they look down they see a foreshortened view. Doctors advise men who are anxious about penis size to look at themselves in profile in a mirror.

The glans

The smooth, conical tip of the penis is the glans, and the opening of the urethra in the center of the glans is where urine and semen exit the body. The ridge where the glans joins the shaft of the penis is the coronal sulcus, and during infancy the foreskin is attached to this. There may be tiny white bumps in this area; these are quite normal, but they can be mistaken for genital warts. The skin of the glans has many sensory nerve endings, making it one of the most erogenous areas of the male body.

The foreskin

Also called the prepuce, the foreskin is the loose fold of skin covering the glans. When the penis becomes erect, the foreskin retracts to expose the glans. At birth the foreskin is still partially fused to the penis. It gradually separates and, by the age of four, more than 90 percent of boys can move the foreskin over the glans, even if it cannot be fully retracted. The foreskin should never be forcibly retracted because it can lead to scarring and permanent damage. After puberty, the foreskin attaches to the glans only at the frenulum, a small, triangular fold of highly sensitive skin on the underside of the penis. On rare occasions poorly lubricated sex can cause the frenulum to tear or bleed.

The foreskin is thin and hairless and has small glands on the inner surface that produce an oily substance which, when mixed with dead skin cells, is called smegma. Freshly secreted smegma is colorless and odorless, but if it is not washed away it becomes white and foul-smelling and can even become infected. Boys should be taught to gently retract the foreskin and wash underneath it with warm water.

Circumcision is the surgical removal of the foreskin, a procedure widely performed for medical, cultural and religious reasons.

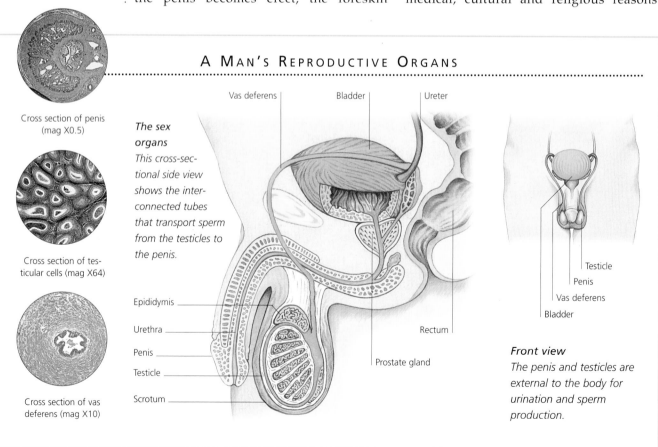

Cross section of penis (mag X0.5)

Cross section of testicular cells (mag X64)

Cross section of vas deferens (mag X10)

A MAN'S REPRODUCTIVE ORGANS

The sex organs
This cross-sectional side view shows the interconnected tubes that transport sperm from the testicles to the penis.

Vas deferens

Bladder

Ureter

Epididymis

Urethra

Penis

Testicle

Scrotum

Rectum

Prostate gland

Testicle

Penis

Vas deferens

Bladder

Front view
The penis and testicles are external to the body for urination and sperm production.

According to a U.S. organization called NOCIRC, up to 3,000 circumcisions are carried out daily. Although this indicates a decrease over past years, circumcision remains common in the U.S. and Canada, particularly with newborns. In the U.K., the National Health Service abandoned the routine practice of circumcision of newborn boys in 1949. Circumcision is a traditional practice among Jews, Muslims and many African tribes. Female circumcision, a much more brutal procedure, is still carried out in some African cultures.

THE TESTICLES

The male sex glands, or testicles, are two oval-shaped organs contained in a pouch of skin, the scrotum, and are the male equivalent of the female ovaries. The testicles hang loosely behind the penis, but in cold temperatures or during sexual arousal the skin of the scrotum contracts to draw them up close to the body. It is normal for the left testicle to hang lower than the right and for one testicle to be larger than the other. The skin of the scrotum is wrinkled and hairy.

The testicles produce sperm and the male sex hormone testosterone. To make sperm, the testicles must be slightly cooler than the rest of the body, which is why they hang just outside the body. Sperm formation begins in the seminiferous tubules—hundreds of tiny tubes that are tightly coiled inside each testicle. These tubules open out into the epididymis, which is another tightly coiled tube where sperm mature and are stored until ejaculation. Scattered between the seminiferous tubules are the cells of Leydig, where testosterone is made.

INSIDE THE BODY

Hidden inside the pelvic cavity is a complex system of ducts, tubes and glands that either carry sperm out of the body or bathe it in nutritious fluid to aid it in the journey through the female reproductive system (see page 97).

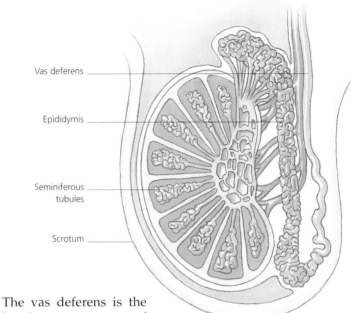

Vas deferens

Epididymis

Seminiferous tubules

Scrotum

Inside a testicle
Sperm are manufactured inside many tiny convoluted tubes known as the seminiferous tubules. They are then stored in the epididymis.

The vas deferens is the tube that carries sperm from the epididymis to the urethra. One such tube ascends from each testicle up and around the bladder and then descends to the urethra. A wider part of the vas deferens that sits just under the bladder—the ampulla—holds sperm just prior to ejaculation.

Both the prostate gland and the seminal vesicles secrete fluids that make up the whitish semen propelled from the penis during ejaculation. The seminal vesicles produce the bulk of the semen. The prostate gland contributes a small amount of fluid containing sugars, vitamins, minerals and enzymes, which all keep sperm healthy and help to stimulate movement.

Cowper's glands, also known as the bulbourethral glands, sit just below the prostate gland and secrete a clear, alkaline mucus that neutralizes any urine left in the urethra. This mucus lubricates the tip of the penis before ejaculation and may contain some sperm. When a man is about to ejaculate, the ampulla squeezes its sperm into the urethra, where sperm mix with the milky secretions. The semen is then pumped down the urethra, along the penis and out of the body.

fact or fiction?

Men should practice Kegel exercises.

Fact. Kegel exercises maintain the strength of the pelvic-floor muscles that surround the sex organs in both men and women. Men can exercise their muscles by repeatedly contracting and relaxing them (the pelvic-floor muscles are the same muscles used to stop the flow of urine).

The Sperm Cell

Sperm are the male sex cells that fertilize a female egg. Each sperm carries information that will determine a baby's sex and some of its physical characteristics. After puberty, millions of sperm are made daily in the testicles.

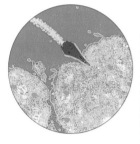

Penetrating the ovum *This microscopic picture shows the sperm entering the outer layer of cells of the ovum.*

Acrosome cap

Head containing chromosomes

Mature sperm *These healthy mature sperm cells are shown at 300 times their actual size.*

Midportion

Tail

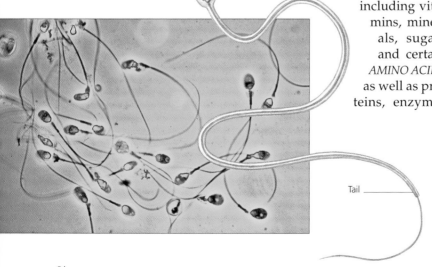

Every sperm cell has three parts: a head, a midportion and a tail. The oval or round head contains genetic information that, on fertilization, unites with the mother's chromosomes, ensuring that children inherit traits from both parents. The head of the sperm is capped by a structure called the acrosome, which contains enzymes to help penetrate the ovum.

The midportion of the sperm contains mitochondria, structures that convert nutrients in semen into energy the sperm can use to swim toward the ovum. The whiplike tail of a sperm is a protein structure that has a complex corkscrew motion, propelling the sperm forward at an average speed of 0.1 inch (3 mm) every minute.

SEMEN

A man ejaculates more than just sperm. In fact, sperm form only a fraction of the ejaculate. The milky fluid that sperm are bathed in is known as semen or seminal fluid. This liquid is very rich in nutrients, including vitamins, minerals, sugars and certain *AMINO ACIDS* as well as proteins, enzymes and alkaline substances. All of these components nourish and energize the sperm and help protect them from the acidic environment of the vagina.

The amount of semen released during ejaculation is roughly equivalent to one teaspoonful (5 ml) and usually contains 100 million to 500 million sperm.

Substances known as prostaglandins are found in semen. Experts believe that when semen comes into contact with a woman's cervix (see page 98), the prostaglandins soften the cervix, allowing the sperm an easier passage into the uterus. Prostaglandins may also increase contractions of the uterus, not only aiding sperm on their journey to the fallopian tubes but also possibly enhancing female orgasm. Other chemicals that play an important part in sexual reproduction are produced by the sperm. For example, the acrosome, covering the head of each sperm, produces chemicals called lysosomes that help the sperm to penetrate the ovum during fertilization.

THE DEVELOPMENT OF SPERM

Spermatogenesis, the creation of sperm cells, is a process that begins in the tight coils of the seminiferous tubules inside each testicle. The first stage is the production of germ cells—simple cells that are capable of evolving into highly specialized cells. These cells, which are also known as spermatogonia, develop into cells called spermatocytes. Spermatocytes divide in such a way that they contain only one-half of the normal pair of chromosomes. By spermatocyte stage the potential sperm cells are becoming increasingly specialized. After more divisions the spermatocytes become spermatids and finally sperm, at which point they move away from the supporting cells—known as Sertoli cells—and into the central cavity of the seminiferous tubules.

Next, sperm move to the epididymis, where they mature fully and grow their characteristic tails. Owing to the coiled length of the epididymis—20 to 23 feet (6 to 7 meters)—it takes sperm three weeks to complete their journey through it. Sperm then spend at least six days in the vas deferens, waiting to be ejaculated. If this does not happen, they die and are replaced by fresh ones. The development from germ cell to ejaculated sperm takes three months.

Sperm production first begins in puberty (see page 88) as a result of stimulation by hormones that are released from the pituitary gland in the brain. Thereafter, sperm production is continuous throughout a man's life, until he reaches old age, when his fertility gradually starts to decline. On average, each testicle manufactures approximately 1,500 sperm every second.

THE DIVERSITY OF SPERM

Research conducted on animals by Dr. Robin Baker, research biologist at the University of Manchester in the U.K., has led to the suggestion that men may produce several different types of sperm, each with a unique role to play in fertilization. "Killer" sperm are the most athletic—after ejaculation, they swim around the female's reproductive tract attempting to destroy alien sperm (those from another male) by producing a poisonous fluid. "Blocker" sperm also try to defeat alien sperm, but using a more passive technique: they become lodged around the cervix which prevents the entry of rivals. Both killer and blocker sperm exist to facilitate the relatively few sperm, known as the "egg getters," that are capable of fertilizing an ovum in the fallopian tube. Baker has also identified a fourth type of sperm known as "family-planning" sperm. These are thought to act as a natural contraceptive by destroying a male's own sperm. Males are believed to produce a particularly large amount of family-planning sperm when they are under stress. Baker's theory that sperm act as a kind of army—each type having a specific task—has challenged the notion that all sperm are capable of fertilization. His theories about the different roles of sperm remain controversial.

MALE SEX HORMONES

Hormones are chemical substances that are secreted into the blood by specialized glands or gland cells. They are transported in the blood to specific target sites in the body where they take effect. The male sex hormones, or androgens, are manufactured in the testicles and adrenal glands (located just above the kidneys). Several types of androgens exist, the main one being testosterone.

Testosterone is a steroid hormone that is made in the body from cholesterol. It is produced almost entirely (95 percent) in the testicles by the cells of Leydig (see page 93). If one testicle is lost or is badly damaged, the other testicle is still able to take over, producing twice as much testosterone when required.

Testosterone levels rise and fall during a man's lifetime. Although the hormone is very important in the development of the fetus, after birth its levels in the blood remain very low until puberty (see page 88). Hormone production then rises, peaking dramatically in the late teens and early twenties, as testosterone triggers the physiological changes of manhood. From the twenties on, testosterone levels gradually decline with age.

fact or fiction?

The male sex hormone testosterone is present only in men.

Fiction. Women manufacture testosterone in both their ovaries and adrenal glands. Testosterone is thought to be important in maintaining female sex drive.

Testosterone drives the development of sexual anatomy of the fetus.

Testosterone initiates male sexual development in puberty.

The sex drive (libido) in males and females is maintained by testosterone.

Testosterone stimulates the testicles to produce sperm.

Testosterone and other androgens stimulate muscle growth.

Testosterone may help influence sexual orientation early in fetal life.

Testosterone *The most important male hormone is testosterone. It gives men some of the features associated with masculinity, such as body hair and muscles.*

Female Sex Organs

In contrast to the breasts and buttocks, a woman's genitals and sex organs are mostly hidden from view. This may be why, in the past, knowledge of the vulva and vagina was shrouded in mystery. Even today, ignorance about the sex organs persists.

A woman's pubic and genital area is marked by a triangle of hair that first appears during puberty. Also at this time there is a thickening of the flesh over the pubic bone, causing the mound to protrude more. Pubic hair, which is coarser in texture and darker than head hair, may be sparse and neat, or cover a large area that stretches down to the upper and inner thighs.

The clitoris

At the front of the vulva is a soft fold or hood of skin that covers the clitoris. The clitoris is the erogenous center of the female body—it is packed with sensory nerve endings, and stimulation of it during sexual intercourse or masturbation can lead to orgasm.

The only visible part of the clitoris is the tip, or glans, which appears as a small pinkish bud under the clitoral hood. Internally, however, there is a large amount of erectile tissue. The clitoris and the penis both develop from the same structures in the embryo —an organ known as the genital tubercle.

The labia

The folds of skin that enclose the clitoral area and VESTIBULE are called the outer lips, or labia majora. Hairy on the outside and containing sweat glands on the inside, they protect the entrance to the urethra and vagina. The size of the labia majora varies considerably with age and from person to person. Although small in childhood and in old age, during the reproductive years the labia majora are full and fleshy.

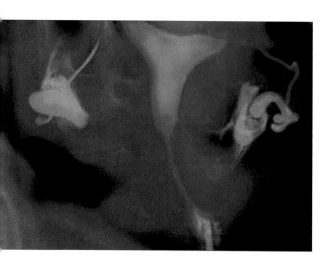

An X ray view of a woman's pelvic organs This colorized X ray shows the uterus in blue, the ovaries in red and the vagina as a pale blue tube. The fallopian tubes extend from either side of the top of the uterus.

THE EXTERNAL SEX ORGANS

The female genitals run from the pubic mound at the front of the body to the area behind the vagina known as the perineum. The vulva consists of two sets of lips, or labia (the labia majora and the labia minora), and includes the mons veneris (pubic mound), clitoris, and the vaginal and urethral openings.

The vulva The collective term for the female genitals is the vulva. The moist area enclosed by the labia minora is called the vestibule.

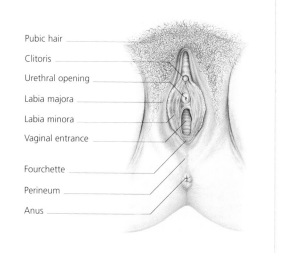

Pubic hair

Clitoris

Urethral opening

Labia majora

Labia minora

Vaginal entrance

Fourchette

Perineum

Anus

A WOMAN'S REPRODUCTIVE ORGANS

Cross section of cells lining fallopian tube (mag X1,100)

Cross section of vaginal wall cells (mag X50)

Cross section of uterine lining cells (mag X30)

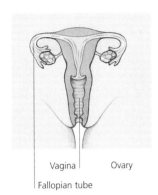

Vagina
Ovary
Fallopian tube

A front view of the female pelvic organs
The vagina extends upward and back into the pelvis. The top end of the vagina forms a curved vault around the cervix. The cervix leads into the uterine cavity.

The pelvic organs in profile
The vagina is situated between the urethra and bladder at the front and the rectum at the back.

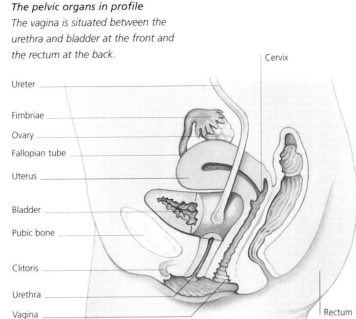

Cervix

Ureter

Fimbriae

Ovary

Fallopian tube

Uterus

Bladder

Pubic bone

Clitoris

Urethra

Vagina

Rectum

Flattened within the labia majora are the delicate, hairless inner lips, or labia minora. The labia minora extend from the clitoral hood to the back of the vulva, where they fuse to form the fourchette. They are full of sebaceous glands and apocrine (scent) glands that secrete lubricants that make the genitals smell sexually attractive.

In some women the labia minora extend outside the labia majora; this is a normal variation in size. The labia minora are very sensitive and when stimulated become engorged with blood and darker in color.

The hymen

This thin membrane, which surrounds part of the entrance to the vagina, is rich in sexual significance. Historically, an intact

The Language of Sex

The fleshy pad of fat at the front of a woman's genital area that cushions the pubic bone is known as the mons pubis, meaning "pubic mound," or the mons Veneris. In Latin, the word "mons" means "mound" and "Veneris" refers to Venus, the Roman goddess of love, so "mons Veneris" may also be translated as "mound of love."

hymen was a sign of virginity and chastity, whereas a broken hymen indicated lost virginity and promiscuity.

Some women, in countries such as Japan and India, have been known to have their hymens reconstructed with plastic surgery to indicate (or pretend) that they are virgins. A hymen may be ruptured through means other than intercourse—inserting tampons or engaging in strenuous physical activity, such as horseback riding. In some girls the hymen is absent at birth.

To allow vaginal secretions and menstrual blood to pass through, the hymen has a small opening. A very small number of girls have an imperforate hymen—one that completely obstructs the vaginal opening. Often not discovered until a girl fails to start menstruating at puberty, an imperforate hymen can be cut to allow the passage of menstrual blood. A thick hymen may prevent a girl from using tampons or having vaginal intercourse until surgically broken.

Occasionally the tearing or rupturing of the tissue may cause discomfort, slight pain or bleeding when a woman has sexual intercourse for the first time.

The vestibular glands

There are two small, rounded structures on either side of the vaginal opening known as vestibular, or Bartholin's, glands. During sexual arousal they secrete a few droplets of fluid to lubricate the vulva in preparation for sex. The vestibular glands occasionally become infected, making intercourse painful (see page 194).

The vagina

Its name derived from the Latin word meaning "sheath" or "scabbard" of a sword, the vagina is an elastic, muscular tube. It has three functions: to receive the penis during intercourse, to channel the flow of blood out of the body during menstruation, and as a birth canal during delivery of a baby. In an adult woman the vagina is normally about 3.5 inches (9 cm) in length, but its elasticity allows the length and width to vary greatly. The ridged inner walls of the vagina are surrounded by strong muscles that can be contracted around the penis during intercourse. They contain an extensive network of veins that fill with blood during arousal. The vaginal walls also have many sensory nerves that respond to deep pressure (but none that respond to light touch). The vaginal walls thin out in old age.

The G-spot

First described by Ernst Grafenburg, a German obstetrician and gynecologist, the Grafenburg spot, or G-spot, is reputed to be a highly erogenous area located on the front wall of the vagina. Since Grafenburg's apparent discovery, there has been intense debate among doctors and sex therapists as to whether the G-spot actually exists.

Anatomists have failed to find any gland or any area of tissue that they can identify as the G-spot, even though it has been claimed that the G-spot contains glands and nerve endings involved in female ejaculation. It is possible that the G-spot is a remnant of a gland equivalent to the prostate in men (see page 92) and is present or partially present in only some women.

Some women claim that pressure on the G-spot, about 2 inches (5 cm) up on the front wall of the vagina between the back of the pubic bone and the front of the cervix, produces the urge to urinate, followed by sexual arousal. Continued stimulation of this area may result in engorgement of the G-spot, followed by orgasm. When stimulated in this way, the G-spot may be felt as a lump or protrusion that is roughly the size of a small bean. Women who do not appear to have a G-spot should not be considered abnormal. Sexual pleasure and orgasm are dependent on stimulation of the clitoris rather than the G-spot.

The cervix

The neck of the uterus is known as the cervix and can be felt 4 to 6 inches (10 to 15 cm) into the vagina. It is round and quite firm, with a very small dimple the size of a pinhead (in women who have not been pregnant), known as the cervical os, in its center. The cervical os is the opening into the uterus that allows sperm to enter and menstrual blood and other secretions to leave. During childbirth the os opens widely to allow the baby's head to pass out of the uterus. After she has had one or more pregnancies, a woman's os becomes slit-shaped instead of round. Just before ovulation, the cervix becomes softer and moves farther down in the vagina.

The cervix produces a special type of mucus that varies throughout the menstrual cycle. At ovulation, the mucus becomes clear and stretchy—women can identify their fertile days in each cycle by watching for this change.

A Pap test (see page 148) involves taking a sample of cells from the cervix and examining them microscopically for abnormalities that may increase the risk of cervical cancer.

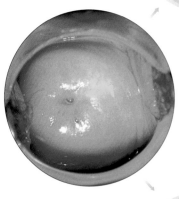

The cervix provides a passage for menstrual blood to leave the uterus.

The cervix softens and descends during a woman's most fertile days.

At ovulation the cervix produces mucus that is hospitable to sperm.

Contractions of the cervix during orgasm may draw sperm into cervical canal.

During pregnancy the cervix stays closed to protect the fetus.

During childbirth the cervix dilates to allow the baby into the vagina.

The cervix Situated at the top of the vagina, the cervix acts as the gateway to the rest of the female reproductive tract, and performs the numerous functions described above.

The uterus

Also known as the womb, the uterus is a hollow muscular organ the size and shape of an upside-down pear. It lies in the pelvic cavity between the bladder at the front and the rectum at the back. The primary functions of the uterus are to support and nourish a developing fetus during pregnancy. It can stretch by an incredible amount: enough to hold at least a 10-pound (4.5-kg) baby, plus the placenta and more than 2 quarts (2 liters) of AMNIOTIC FLUID.

The uterus has three layers: the lining, which builds up and breaks down each month in the menstrual cycle, is called the endometrium; the strong layer of muscle, which contracts to expel the baby during childbirth, is the myometrium; and the fibrous tissue, which forms the outer layer of the uterus, is known as the parametrium.

The ovaries

Located on either side of the uterus, the two small, almond-shaped organs called the ovaries produce female GAMETES, or ova. The ovaries are the female equivalent of the male testicles, and each measures about 1½ inches (3.8 cm) long and ¾ inch (2 cm) wide. In addition to producing an ovum during most menstrual cycles in a woman's reproductive life span (as a woman ages, some menstrual cycles are ANOVULATORY), the ovaries release the two sex hormones estrogen and progesterone.

The ovaries are as sensitive to pain as the male testicles. For example, deep penetration during sexual intercourse can bump them painfully into the pelvic wall. This problem can usually be overcome by a change in sexual position.

The fallopian tubes

Two fine tubes about 4 inches (10 cm) long, known as the fallopian tubes, run from close to each ovary and open into the upper part of the uterus. The ends of these tubes are bell-shaped and lined with fimbriae— fingerlike projections about 1 inch (2.5 cm) long. At ovulation, the ends of the tubes move toward the emerging ovum and the fimbriae wave in unison to sweep the released ovum into the tube. The ovum travels down the fallopian tubes to the uterus.

Externally, the fallopian tubes are the size of drinking straws; internally, the canals that carry the ova are the size of thin pieces of wire. The thick, muscular outer walls of the fallopian tubes protect the inner canals and their lining of cilia (hairlike projections) that beat rhythmically to move the ovum toward the uterus. An abundance of specialized cells in the inner lining of the fallopian tubes nourish the ovum or fertilized egg during the three-day journey to the uterus. Fertilization of the ovum most commonly occurs in the part of the tube nearest to the ovary.

The position of the uterus The uterus is usually tipped forward over the bladder, but about 20 percent of women have a retroverted uterus that lies backward against the rectum. Doctors once thought that this caused problems such as infertility. It is now recognized to be completely normal.

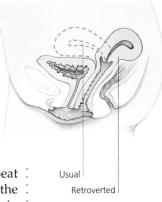

Usual

Retroverted

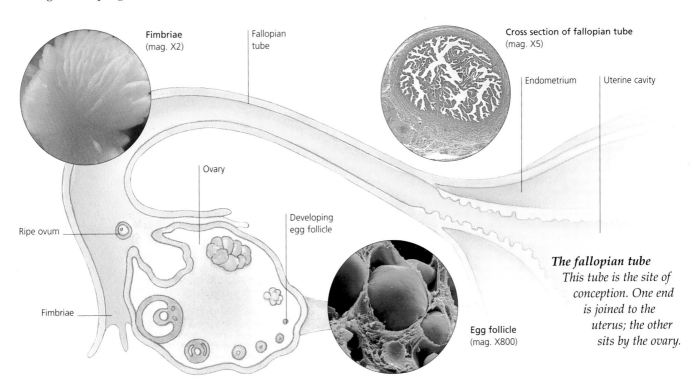

Fimbriae (mag. X2)

Fallopian tube

Cross section of fallopian tube (mag. X5)

Endometrium

Uterine cavity

Ovary

Developing egg follicle

Ripe ovum

Fimbriae

Egg follicle (mag. X800)

The fallopian tube This tube is the site of conception. One end is joined to the uterus; the other sits by the ovary.

The Ovum

When a girl reaches puberty her ovaries begin to release egg cells, or ova. "Ova" refers to more than one egg cell; "ovum" is singular. Each tiny cell contains all the genetic material necessary to combine with a sperm cell and create a life.

Unlike the male body, which produces sperm continuously, the female body contains all the ova it needs at birth. The ova mature and are released at the approximate rate of one every 28 days.

As a female fetus is growing in the uterus, several million structures called primordial follicles are developing in her ovaries. Each one of these follicles has the potential to become a mature ovum, yet almost as soon as they are formed, thousands of follicles begin to die. In fact, by the time a baby girl is born, only about one million of several million follicles have survived. Thousands more degenerate before puberty, and this process continues throughout adulthood. Since only about 400 to 500 ova can be released in a lifetime—more than enough for a woman to become pregnant many times—this does not constitute a problem.

Only when a girl reaches puberty do the primordial follicles, present in her ovaries since she was a fetus, start to develop into ova. During puberty, the chemical follicle-stimulating hormone (FSH) initiates the development of these follicles each month. Around the beginning of each menstrual cycle, approximately 20 to 30 primordial follicles start to mature, producing the hormone estrogen as they do so. Follicular maturation is a complex three-stage process in which usually only one follicle ultimately develops into a mature ovum while the others degenerate.

OVULATION

A mature ovum is contained in a fluid-filled structure called a Graafian follicle. This moves toward the surface of the ovary and then, stimulated by a surge of luteinizing hormone (see page 101), bursts to release the ovum into the pelvic cavity. This is ovulation. The ovum is swept into the fringed, funnel-shaped end of its companion fallopian tube. The journey to possible conception has begun.

The remnants of the burst Graafian follicle undergo several important changes. First, they collapse. Then the space inside the fol-

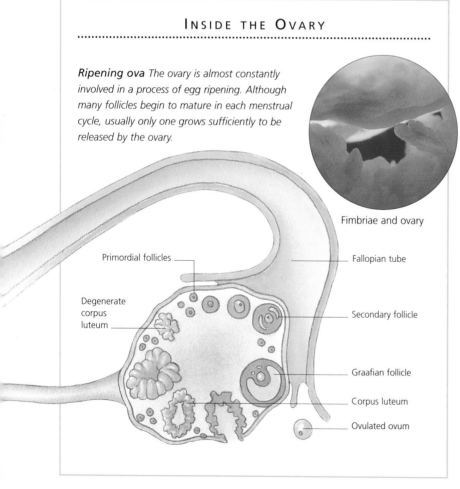

INSIDE THE OVARY

Ripening ova *The ovary is almost constantly involved in a process of egg ripening. Although many follicles begin to mature in each menstrual cycle, usually only one grows sufficiently to be released by the ovary.*

Fimbriae and ovary

Primordial follicles

Degenerate corpus luteum

Fallopian tube

Secondary follicle

Graafian follicle

Corpus luteum

Ovulated ovum

licle fills up with blood, and a glandular structure called a corpus luteum forms. This starts to secrete the hormone progesterone (it also secretes estrogen, but in lesser amounts), which helps the uterine lining thicken to receive a fertilized ovum. If conception does not take place, progesterone levels begin to fall in the last week of the menstrual cycle. The corpus luteum degenerates and the uterine lining starts to break down, to be shed during menstruation.

FEMALE SEX HORMONES

Hormones are chemical substances produced by parts of the brain, the ovaries, the endocrine glands and various other specialized cells in the body. Female sex hormones are secreted into the blood, where they circulate to target organs, affecting the development of SECONDARY SEXUAL CHARACTERISTICS, the menstrual cycle, pregnancy and breast-feeding.

Estrogens

Although people refer to estrogen as a single hormone, the estrogens are, in fact, a group of hormones. Types of estrogen include estradiol, estriol and estrone. Responsible for the development of female secondary sexual characteristics, they also help stimulate the development of the uterine lining each month for the possible implantation of a fertilized ovum. Estrogens are produced mainly by the ovaries but also by the placenta in pregnant women and in small amounts by the ADRENAL GLANDS.

Doctors prescribe synthetic estrogens in hormone replacement therapy (see page 78), the contraceptive pill and the so-called morning after pill. Doctors also use the synthetic estrogens in the treatment of certain prostate and breast cancers.

Progesterone

This hormone is released by the corpus luteum of the ovary after the ovum has been released. It is also produced by the adrenal glands and by the placenta during pregnancy. Like estrogen, progesterone prepares the uterus for implantation of a fertilized ovum, maintains pregnancy and causes development of the breasts during pregnancy. If fertilization does not occur, a fall in progesterone levels causes the shedding of the uterine lining during menstruation. Progesterone also affects the cervix and cervical

mucus during the menstrual cycle and the production of sebum and deposition of fat on the body during puberty.

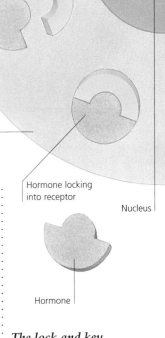

Progestogens are natural or synthetic forms of progesterone. In the U.S. and Canada they are used in the contraceptive pill; in the U.S., in some types of IUDs. Doctors also use progestogens in tests to find the cause of amenorrhea (see page 142). They may be combined with estrogens for use in hormone replacement therapy (HRT) and in the treatment of premenstrual tension and endometriosis (see page 145). Certain uterine cancers are treated with progestogens.

Prolactin

The secretion of prolactin, also known as lactogenic hormone, is regulated by the hypothalamus in the brain. Released by the PITUITARY GLAND, prolactin stimulates production of milk from the breasts after pregnancy. Sucking by the baby stimulates prolactin production during breast-feeding.

The gonadotropins

The term "gonadotropins" refers to any hormones that influence the functioning of the gonads (ovaries or testes). One of the main gonadotropins, follicle-stimulating hormone (FSH), is produced by the pituitary gland in the brain. In women, FSH stimulates the follicles in the ovary to become mature ova. It also promotes the secretion of estrogen.

The other main gonadotropin is luteinizing hormone (LH). This hormone triggers the release of the ovum from its ovarian follicle at ovulation and promotes the secretion of progesterone in women. In men, LH stimulates the production of male sex hormones (see page 95) in the testicles. Like FSH, LH is produced by the pituitary gland.

The hormone human chorionic gonadotropin (hCG) is produced in early pregnancy by the developing placenta. It prevents the corpus luteum from degenerating, so that progesterone continues to be produced and the uterine lining thickens to support a growing fetus. Most home pregnancy tests work by detecting the hCG that is excreted in urine.

The lock and key mechanism Hormones are able to affect only those cells that have receptors that exactly match the shape of the hormone molecule. This is known as the lock and key mechanism. Receptors may be inside or outside a cell.

The Breasts

The breasts are one of the most erotically charged areas of a woman's body and play a key role in defining her femininity. Breasts also have an important biological function—to sustain a child during infancy by producing milk.

A woman's breasts will change during her lifetime and even, as part of her menstrual cycle, from month to month. The breasts are made up of fat cells, connective tissue and special secretory cells. During childhood the breast area is usually flat except for the nipple, which protrudes slightly from the surrounding skin. At puberty high estrogen levels lead to an accumulation of fat in the connective tissue beneath the nipple, causing the breasts to enlarge. During adulthood the skin and fine ligaments within the breasts gradually lose their elasticity, and after menopause the breasts may shrink and droop. Many women notice that their breasts swell each month immediately before menstruation.

THE FUNCTION OF THE BREAST

Secretory cells in the breast are responsible for milk production. In anatomical terms, the breasts are similar to sweat glands, except that they secrete colostrum and milk rather than sweat. Colostrum is a thin white liquid that is produced for the first few days after a baby is born. It is high in protein and antibodies and makes an ideal first food for a new baby's digestive system. Milk pro-

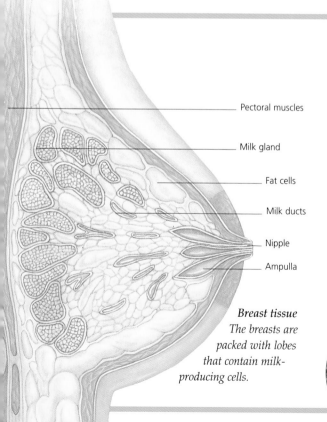

Pectoral muscles

Milk gland

Fat cells

Milk ducts

Nipple

Ampulla

Breast tissue
The breasts are packed with lobes that contain milk-producing cells.

THE STRUCTURE OF THE BREAST

Within the breast there are 15 to 20 grapelike clusters of secretory cells, where milk is produced, divided by the supporting connective tissue into lobes. Each lobe contains a system of minute ducts that collect milk secretions. These join up to form about 15 larger ducts, all leading to the nipple. Just behind the nipple, each duct widens to form a collecting pouch called the lactiferous ampulla.

The breasts are made largely of fat cells and apart from the nipples, they do not contain any muscle. They sit outside the rib cage on top of the pectoral muscles, and the breast tissue merges into the surrounding body fat on the front of the body. The size and shape of a woman's breasts are determined by their fat content. Developing the pectoral muscles makes only a slight difference to breast appearance.

Cross section of normal breast cells (mag. X64)

Cross section of breast cells during pregnancy (mag. X64)

Cross section of lactating breast cells (mag. X64)

BREAST DENSITIES IN WOMEN OF DIFFERENT AGES

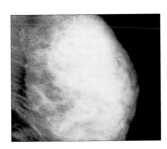

Under 30 years old
The younger a woman is, the denser her breast tissue (shown here on a mammogram as a white mass).

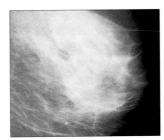

30 to 40 years old
Around this time, fatty tissue becomes more apparent. On a mammogram it appears as dark areas around the white mass.

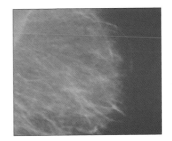

Mature (40-plus years old)
Approaching the menopause, breast tissue steadily decreases and any abnormalities can be more easily detected.

duction starts around the third day after birth. Milk provides all the nutrients needed for a baby's development. Milk also contains antibodies to protect the baby against disease. The lobes in a lactating breast become swollen with milk, giving breast-feeding women larger breasts than normal. When breast-feeding ceases, the breasts may return to their normal size, although from 30 to 50 percent of women have permanently larger breasts after breast-feeding.

THE NIPPLE

At the tip of the breast is the nipple, where a baby suckles breast milk. There are 15 to 20 milk-duct openings in the nipple, each bringing milk from the lobes. The shape of the nipple varies from woman to woman: it can be flat, protruding, cylindrical or conical. Some women have inverted nipples, a normal variant that can be corrected—if the woman chooses—with suction devices or cosmetic surgery. Inverted nipples do not impair breast-feeding (although cosmetic surgery does). If a nipple suddenly becomes inverted, however, it may be a sign of disease, such as breast cancer, and should be investigated immediately by a doctor.

The nipples contain many muscle fibers that contract during sexual arousal and breast-feeding and in response to cold temperatures. The contraction of these fibers makes the nipple elongated and hard to the touch. The nipple is an erogenous zone.

The areola

The area of skin around the nipple is the areola. Its color can vary from light to dark pink to almost black. It darkens during pregnancy and stays dark afterward. The tiny bumps on the areola are sweat and sebaceous glands that help to keep the nipple area lubricated during breast-feeding. When the muscles of the nipple contract, the areola also contracts, becoming small and puckered in appearance.

Can We Talk About It?

SEX AFTER A MASTECTOMY

A woman undergoing a mastectomy (surgical removal of a breast as treatment for cancer) experiences not only physical pain and a loss of sensitivity in a highly erogenous zone, but also frequently a loss of self-esteem and perceived sexual attractiveness. If you have undergone this procedure and are in a relationship, your partner may be feeling hesitant about initiating or expressing sexual intimacy and will need guidance and reassurance from you. It is important to discuss your feelings openly and honestly with him. Including your partner in your surgery and its aftercare—especially the moment when you see your scar for the first time—can also help to bring you closer together.

If you are single and have had a mastectomy, you may not want to date for fear of rejection. However, you need not discuss your surgery until the relationship is becoming serious or physical. Be prepared for some men to react with initial shock, and try to remember that breasts, or lack of them, should not determine the quality of a relationship.

The Sexual Response Cycle

The human sexual response cycle is a bodily process that begins with arousal. Before this physical arousal occurs, however, there must be a mental anticipation of sexual activity or the perception that something is attractive or stimulating.

Each person experiences sexual desire in a way unique to him- or herself, and many different stimuli can trigger the feeling. For some people simply sitting next to someone they find attractive will be enough to initiate sexual interest. It has been well documented that reading about sex or looking at photos or erotic movies can stimulate sexual feelings; but even the sound of someone's voice or the smell of their clothes may be enough to initiate feelings of sexual desire.

THE STAGES OF SEXUAL RESPONSE

Once the mind has recognized a conscious or subconscious sexual attraction, the sexual responses of the body follow. One explanation of sexual response, proposed by psychologist David Reed, concentrates on how the mind perceives and responds to arousal. He named this the Erotic Stimulus Pathway Model. In Reed's model, the psychological

changes that take place during arousal are more or less the same for men and women. The seduction stage consists of a person's experience of a conscious or subconscious sexual attraction to someone (whether a new or existing partner) and his or her attempt to interest or attract them. Sensation is the stage when the five senses—sight, hearing, taste, touch and smell—send signals of sexual pleasure and arousal to the brain. These sensations are then processed and can be acted upon consciously. The surrender stage describes the mental "letting go" that is necessary for orgasm to take place. Finally, the reflection stage involves thinking about the physical events that have taken place. If the feelings are positive, there will be a subconscious and conscious desire to repeat the cycle.

FEMALE SEXUAL RESPONSE

Sexologists Masters and Johnson were the first to explain in detail how human beings respond sexually. Their four-stage sexual cycle describes the physical changes that the body experiences at different levels of arousal. In their theory, after an initial period of desire, men and women go through four phases: excitement, plateau, orgasm and resolution. In females, the following changes take place.

Excitement

During the excitement phase, the clitoris and vagina become engorged with blood, and there are changes in the size and position of the vagina and uterus (see page 97). Changes also occur to the breasts—they enlarge slightly, while the nipples become erect and the *AREOLAE* swell and darken. Some women develop a skin flush or fine

Sexual responses in the mind and body
For every stage of physical sexual arousal, there is an associated cognitive or mental stage during which the brain responds to sexual stimuli.

Physical stages

Psychological stages

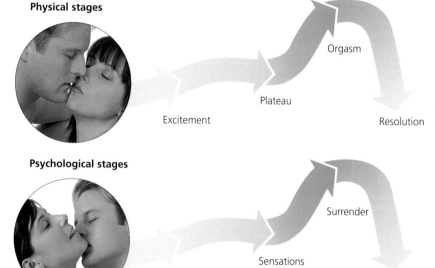

Orgasm

Plateau

Excitement

Resolution

Surrender

Sensations

Seduction

Reflection

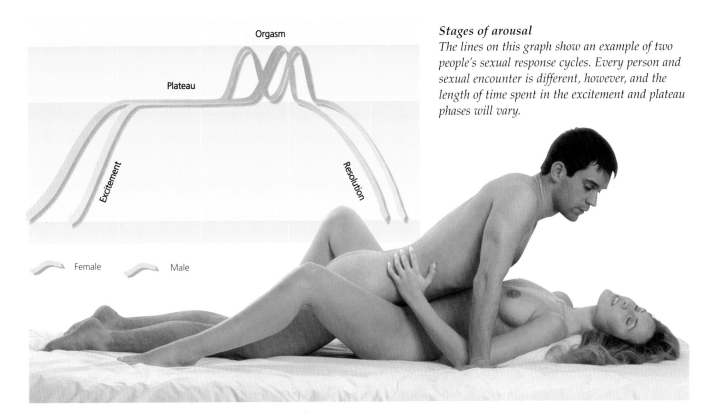

rash on the chest, known as a sex flush, that can appear at any time during sexual arousal. In addition, sexual excitement causes an increase in blood pressure, heart rate, breathing rate and muscle tension. Excitement lasts a variable length of time and may lead either to the plateau phase or to a return to rest.

Plateau

If sexual excitement and stimulation continue, a woman will enter the plateau phase. This is characterized by further blood flow to the entire genital area. The outer (or lower) third of the vagina decreases in diameter, which helps the vagina to grip the penis during intercourse, and the inner two-thirds of the vagina becomes more distended, providing a good receptacle for semen.

The uterus rises from the pelvic cavity and pushes into the abdominal cavity in a process called "tenting." Tenting results in the expansion of the vaginal cavity and creates an area where semen can pool after the man has ejaculated into the vagina. It also straightens the path from vagina to uterus to fallopian tubes, which facilitates the movement of sperm through the woman's reproductive tract. There is some evidence that stimulating the clitoris causes tenting.

Also during the plateau phase, the labia minora deepen in color, and the clitoris shortens and withdraws under the labial hood. A few drops of fluid may be secreted by the vestibular glands.

The duration of the plateau phase varies depending on the degree and type of sexual stimulation involved. The culmination of the plateau phase may be orgasm—the third and shortest of the four phases—or it may just slowly resolve. While some couples find this frustrating, others are comfortable with nonorgasmic resolution.

Orgasm

Although the intense, reflexive release of sexual tension that has built up during sexual stimulation and arousal may be centered in the genitals, it also affects the rest of the body. Female orgasms can feel intense, but they rarely last longer than 10 to 15 seconds. An orgasm begins with rhythmic contractions in the lower third of the vagina. The first contractions occur every 0.8 second—the same frequency with which the penis expels semen. After the initial contractions, the interval becomes progressively longer.

Penetrative sex
The penis fits snugly into the vagina, which becomes lubricated with slippery mucus during the excitement stage of female arousal.

Sexual Arousal and the Female Body

During sexual arousal, a woman experiences physical changes in and around the genitals. In a process called vasocongestion, blood rushes into the clitoris, which becomes erect; the labia minora flatten and move apart; the labia majora deepen in color and enlarge; the inner (or upper) two-thirds of the vagina lengthens; and the vaginal walls become moist and slippery.

EXCITEMENT

One of the first signs of sexual arousal in women is the wetness around the opening to the vagina. This allows penetration in a later stage of sexual response.

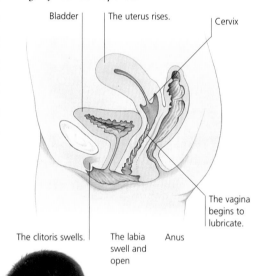

Bladder | The uterus rises.

Cervix

The vagina begins to lubricate.

The clitoris swells. | The labia swell and open | Anus

PLATEAU

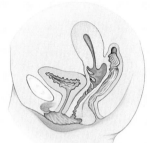

The upper part of the vagina is greatly expanded, while the lower part tightens up.

The genitals are fully engorged with blood.

The uterus reaches full elevation.

The lower vagina constricts.

The clitoris retracts behind its hood.

ORGASM

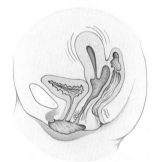

A series of contractions, or spasms, occur in the vagina and uterus.

The rectal sphincter contracts.

The uterus contracts.

The upper vagina balloons (a process called tenting).

The lower vagina contracts rhythmically.

RESOLUTION

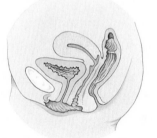

The uterus, vagina, clitoris and labia gradually return to their relaxed state.

The lower vagina relaxes.

The uterus lowers.

The upper vagina returns to normal size.

Postcoital glow
Following arousal, women experience the changes of the resolution stage. They may feel relaxed and tired or they may want to become aroused again. Unlike men, women do not have a refractory period.

Orgasmic contractions spread from the outer third of the vagina to the inner two-thirds and then up to the uterus. The uterine contractions start at the cervix and move toward the top of the uterus. These contractions may help to move sperm into the uterus and fallopian tubes and aid fertilization. The muscles of the pelvis and perineum and around the opening of the bladder and rectum also contract.

Some women may thrust their hips and pelvis as the muscles in the pelvis contract. Women usually experience 5 to 15 orgasmic contractions, depending on the intensity of the orgasm. The clitoris withdraws under its hood during orgasm, and although it may feel as though it is pulsating, it does not appear to contract rhythmically in the way the penis does.

Muscles in the back and feet may also undergo involuntary spasms during orgasm, causing the back to arch and toes to curl. The heart rate can rise to as much as 180 beats per minute and the breathing rate to as much as 40 breaths per minute. The blood pressure also rises. The pupils and nostrils dilate, and a woman may breathe rapidly or hold her breath for the duration of the orgasm. The more intense the orgasm, the greater the total body reaction. Masters and Johnson reported that immediately after orgasm, the area around the nipple starts to contract and wrinkle.

Outward behavior during orgasm varies from woman to woman. Some women have a contorted facial expression, as though they were in pain, and may moan or cry out. Other women clutch at the nearest object, be it their partner or a pillow, and some women make no sound and remain perfectly still, but report just as intense an orgasm.

Different types of female orgasm were first ranked by the Austrian psychoanalyst Sigmund Freud, who postulated that women experienced either a clitoral (or immature) orgasm or a vaginal (or mature) orgasm. He maintained that women who only had clitoral orgasms were sexually and psychologically immature.

This misconception survived for a long time, until Masters and Johnson used scientific equipment and many human volunteers to show that there is no physiological difference between an orgasm achieved by clitoral stimulation or vaginal penetration.

Subsequent research on the area known as the G-spot (see page 98) has shown that some women do seem to have two different types of orgasm. It is thought that one type of orgasm results from direct or indirect clitoral stimulation, whereas the other is achieved by G-spot stimulation.

Orgasms that originate from clitoral stimulation are sometimes referred to as tenting orgasms and lead to the contraction of the *PUBOCOCCYGEAL (PC) MUSCLES*. G-spot orgasms are sometimes referred to as uterine, or A-frame, orgasms and center around the uterus. They originate from stimuli carried by the pelvic nerve to the spinal reflex center. The deeper muscles of the pelvis and the uterus contract. Most women probably experience a combination of the tenting orgasm and the A-frame orgasm. Some women experience multiple orgasms (see below).

Resolution

After the last contractions of orgasm fade, the resolution phase begins. The breasts decrease in size, muscles all over the body relax, the heart rate and breathing pattern return to their resting state, and skin flushing begins to fade. The clitoris resumes its pre-excitement state within 10 to 20 seconds of orgasm, but the rest of the genital area takes longer—about 15 to 30 minutes.

If stimulation continues after orgasm, women can return to the plateau phase instead of entering resolution. This means they may be able to have more orgasms.

The stages of sexual response can vary between women and also from one sexual encounter to the next. On one occasion a woman may experience quick excitement and plateau phases, followed by orgasm and then resolution. On a second occasion the same woman may experience the excitement and plateau phases but not orgasm. This would be followed by a slow resolution. On a third occasion the woman may have repeated orgasms and keep returning to the plateau level before resolution.

MALE SEXUAL RESPONSE

The four stages of the male sexual cycle affect not only the penis and scrotum but also the internal sex organs and the blood flow and muscle tension in the entire body.

The G-spot There has been much debate about whether the G-spot exists. Some women report that they derive intense sexual pleasure from this area on the front wall of the vagina.

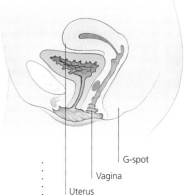

G-spot

Vagina

Uterus

MALE VERSUS FEMALE ORGASM

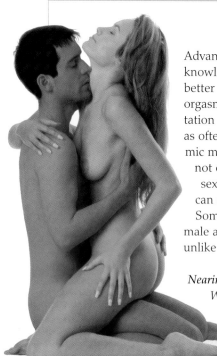

Advances in research and increased general knowledge about sex have made people much better informed about female sexuality and orgasm. One consequence of this is the expectation that women should experience orgasm as often as men. Women who are highly orgasmic may find this easy, but many women do not experience orgasm with each episode of sexual intercourse. Nonorgasmic intercourse can still be enjoyable.

Some fundamental differences exist between male and female orgasm. Female orgasm, unlike male orgasm, does not have a recog-

Nearing orgasm
Whereas men experience "ejaculatory inevita-
bility," women can be distracted from
orgasm right up until the last moment.

nized biological function. In fact, a woman can enjoy sex and conceive without ever experiencing orgasm. Psychological factors play a much greater role in determining whether a woman reaches orgasm. For example, if she is not completely relaxed, orgasm becomes difficult. Common psychological barriers to orgasm include feeling pressured to reach orgasm (or to reach orgasm quickly), worrying about something unrelated to sex, or concentrating on a partner's pleasure to the detriment of one's own. Whereas the thrusting movements of sexual intercourse cause many men to ejaculate easily, women may need additional or alternative types of stimulation. Intercourse does not always stimulate the clitoris enough to bring about orgasm.

FEMALE EJACULATION

Research suggests that a few women may ejaculate fluid at the time of orgasm in response to stimulation of the G-spot (see page 98). Those who analyzed the ejaculated fluid claim it resembles male prostatic fluid (see page 93) and is secreted by Skene's glands, near the urethral opening—the female equivalent of the male prostate gland. Female ejaculation is still controversial. It should not be confused with urine, which can leak when the sphincters of the bladder and urethra contract during orgasm, nor with vaginal lubrication.

Excitement

When a man becomes sexually aroused, there is a sudden increase in the blood flow to the penis and scrotum, and the penis becomes erect. The ADRENAL GLANDS also release adrenalin during the excitement phase, and this causes the heart rate, blood pressure and breathing rate to rise.

Plateau

If excitement or stimulation continues, the penis becomes more engorged, and the man has a full erection. The glans of the penis deepens in color, becoming deep red or purple, and there may be secretions of fluid from the BULBOURETHRAL GLANDS. The testicles increase in size by up to 50 percent and are pulled tightly against the body wall.

The series of events leading to ejaculation starts with the movement of sperm from the testicles to the ampulla, which is the flared end of the vas deferens. When the other constituents of semen have been squirted into the urethra by the seminal vesicles and the prostate gland, ejaculation is imminent. It is at this stage that a man experiences a sensation known as "ejaculatory inevitability." This means the man knows that even if all stimulation of the penis ceased, ejaculation would still occur. Ejaculatory inevitability lasts for about three seconds.

Orgasm

Ejaculation is the expulsion of semen through the penis, and it is usually, but not always, accompanied by orgasm. When a man experiences ejaculatory inevitability, the muscle sphincters at both ends of the urethra are closed and a pleasant sensation of pressure occurs. Then the outer muscle sphincter opens, and semen moves to the urethral bulb at the base of the penis. A man may experience orgasm without ejaculation, particularly if he experiences orgasm more than once in a short space of time.

Ejaculation occurs when several intense contractions of the muscles in the urethra and around the base of the penis pump semen out of the body. The contractions may be strong enough to expel the semen farther than 11 inches (28 centimeters). There are usually three to five main contractions at intervals of 0.8 second (this is the same interval as the vaginal contractions during female orgasm). These contractions may continue but become progressively weaker and irregular. Waves of contractions occur in the pelvic-floor muscles, and the inner thigh muscles may contract involuntarily. Male orgasm rarely lasts longer than 15 seconds and is generally between 4 and 10 seconds—this is shorter than most female orgasms.

Sexual Arousal and the Male Body

The first sign of arousal in men is penile erection, due to vasocongestion (engorgement with blood). The skin and muscles of the scrotum thicken as the testicles are drawn up toward the body, and secretions may leak from the tip of the penis.

PLATEAU

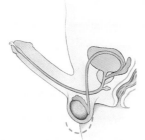

At the plateau stage the man's body is preparing itself for ejaculation.

The glans deepens in color.

The testicles increase in size and the scrotum thickens.

Droplets secreted by the bulbourethral glands appear at the tip of the penis.

The testicles are drawn up tightly against the body.

EXCITEMENT

An erect penis is usually a clear sign of male sexual excitement. Erections occur very quickly after a man feels aroused or stimulated.

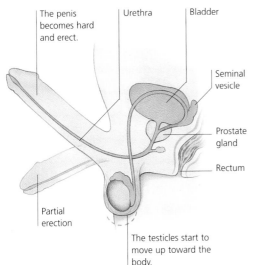

The penis becomes hard and erect.

Urethra

Bladder

Seminal vesicle

Prostate gland

Rectum

Partial erection

The testicles start to move up toward the body.

ORGASM

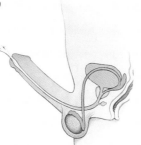

Male ejaculation and orgasm are usually simultaneous. As semen is expelled, the penis rhythmically contracts.

The penis and urethra contract.

Semen is expelled from the tip of the penis.

The bladder sphincter closes.

The prostate gland contracts.

The seminal vesicles contract.

RESOLUTION

Blood flows away from the genitals, and the penis gradually becomes flaccid — this is called detumescence.

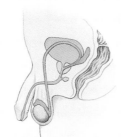

Blood flows out of the penile tissues and the erection slowly disappears.

The scrotum thins and the testicles descend.

Postcoital fatigue
It is common for men — and women — to feel relaxed and drowsy after making love.

The average volume of semen expelled during ejaculation is usually about one teaspoonful containing 100 million to 500 million sperm. The volume of semen and the sperm count are markedly reduced by repeated ejaculation within the space of a few days. If a man has not ejaculated for some time, a relatively large volume of semen will be produced. It is thought that the more semen a man ejaculates, the more enjoyable his orgasm is. (This contrasts with the female orgasm. Many women claim to have smaller, less powerful orgasms if they have not experienced one for a while.) Changes in the body include a rise in the breathing rate, heart rate and blood pressure, all of which reach a peak at the moment of orgasm. The breath-

fact or fiction?

Men cannot urinate and ejaculate at the same time.

Fact. As soon as a man feels that he is about to ejaculate, the sphincter muscle at the neck of his bladder contracts tightly so that urine cannot pass through into the urethra, and he will not be able to urinate until after he has ejaculated. The closing of the sphincter muscle prevents the backward flow of semen into the bladder.

ing rate may go up to 50 per minute and also the heart rate may increase to around 180 beats per minute.

The sensation of orgasm can be overwhelming, starting in the pelvic region and then spreading through the whole body. Men characteristically begin to thrust their hips during intercourse when they feel they are about to ejaculate. At the moment of ejaculation a man may thrust his pelvis forward very hard, pushing the penis as deep into the vagina as possible. Some men make involuntary noises during orgasm and grimace and clutch at their partner. Men may clench their toes and arch their feet in the way that some women do during orgasm; this is less likely if the man is on top of his partner during intercourse. A few men experience dilation of small blood vessels in the skin, giving rise to a sexual flush or rash, but this is seen more often in women.

SHOULD SEX BE SYNCHRONIZED?

The stages of arousal can take variable amounts of time, but generally, the younger a man is, the quicker he becomes aroused. Because of the slower arousal times of women, couples may find that their sexual responses are out of sync. For instance, this can create a situation when a man has reached an advanced stage of the plateau phase and his partner may only just be feeling aroused. Similarly, during penetration, when both partners are in the plateau stage, a man may progress rapidly to orgasm and ejaculation but his partner may need much more time and stimulation. Sex therapists Masters and Johnson suggest that: "In couples who have come to recognize that one usually reaches orgasm much more quickly than the other, deliberate alterations in their sexual routines may be called for to compensate for a discrepancy in timing."

Sexual timing
Sex can be prolonged by delaying penetration and concentrating on foreplay. The discrepancy between arousal times may diminish with age.

Resolution

After orgasm, the penis and testicles quickly decrease in size and return to their pre-aroused state within 10 minutes. This process is called detumescence. During this phase, a man's penis is relatively insensitive to sexual stimulation.

Most men are not thought to experience multiple orgasms with a single erection. The period between ejaculating and being able to have another erection is called the refractory period. Young men may have very short refractory periods (sometimes a matter of minutes) and potentially can achieve one erection after another in quick succession. In contrast, older men may find that the refractory period lasts much longer, so that it takes several hours or even days to achieve another erection after having sexual intercourse.

A man's breathing rate and heart rate slow down during the resolution period, and his blood pressure drops. It is common for men and women to feel relaxed and sleepy after orgasm.

MAINTAINING SEXUAL HEALTH

Sexual Health 112

Contraception 116

Safer Sex 128

HIV and AIDS 130

Other STDs 134

Female Disorders 140

Male Disorders 149

Abnormal Sex Organs 154

Sexual Health

Today people are more informed about sexual health than ever before. Safer sex practices, good sexual hygiene and awareness of how infections are spread have enabled individuals to take control of their sexual and reproductive health.

For those who think they may be at risk of contracting a sexually transmitted disease, sexual health means having regular checkups—the sooner a disease is diagnosed, the sooner it can be treated and the fewer the people who will become infected. For others, sexual health means practicing good day-to-day personal hygiene. The importance of this cannot be overstated. For example, poor genital hygiene can be a risk factor for some male genital cancers (see page 152), especially if a man works with substances such as oil and soot or is not circumcised.

GENITAL HYGIENE

People are taught that cleanliness and hygiene are an important part of staying healthy. To a large extent this is true, but over the past few decades, cosmetic and deodorant companies have exploited this fact, making many individuals believe that their natural body smells are unhygienic and should be washed away or disguised with other smells.

Women in particular have been targeted by the companies that manufacture fragranced feminine hygiene products, such as vaginal deodorants and scented genital wipes and sanitary napkins. The message conveyed by these products is that the normal smell of the vulva and vagina is unpleasant and undesirable. In fact, as long as a woman does not have a gynecological infection, the natural odors and secretions produced by her genitals are not only healthy and natural but also important for sexual desire and arousal.

The tissue lining the labia and the vagina is very sensitive; it provides a home to the healthy bacteria that help keep the vagina—and to some extent the inner labia—clean. Using deodorants or highly perfumed soaps upsets the pH and delicate bacterial balance around the vulva and the vagina, making yeast infections more likely. Even adding bubble bath or bath salts to bath water can upset the bacterial balance in the vagina, killing the "good" bacteria and encouraging the growth of "bad" bacteria. In fact, doctors have reported an increase in the number of women complaining of yeast infections just after the holiday season, when such products are widely received as gifts.

All that a woman needs to do for daily genital hygiene is to wash the vulval area with plain water and the anal area with unscented soap and water. Using soap on the vulva is unnecessary, although many women say that plain water does not make them feel clean. If women do wash with soap, they should choose an unscented

Disrupting the pH balance in the vagina *Certain bacteria live in the vagina and keep the area clean. These bacteria produce lactic acid, which kills unwanted bacteria and yeasts. If the balance of healthy bacteria is changed—by highly fragranced bath products, for example —a woman becomes more prone to vaginal infections.*

These factors alter pH and upset bacterial balance

- Bubble bath
- Spermicide
- Douching
- Infection
- Synthetic underwear
- Antibiotics
- Chlorinated pools
- Unusual increase in dairy consumption

- Healthy diet
- Cotton or silk underwear
- Specific medications for vaginal infections
- Avoiding scented hygiene products

These factors maintain healthy pH and bacterial balance

Sanitary Protection

The two most common methods women use to absorb the menstrual flow are sanitary napkins and vaginal tampons. Many girls begin by using napkins and later move on to a combination of napkins and tampons. Some women use napkins at night and tampons during the day, especially when playing sports or swimming. Modern napkins are very slim and absorbent, attach to underwear with a peel-back adhesive strip, and are invisible through clothing.

Women of any age can use tampons, as long as insertion causes no discomfort. Girls and women who have never had intercourse may find it easier to use small tampons.

Different absorbencies of tampon should be worn to suit the degree of blood flow. Super-absorbency tampons may be needed for the start of a period, followed by regular or light absorbency for subsequent days. Tampons should be changed every four to six hours and removed before sexual intercourse.

Fragranced tampons may cause irritation and lead to vaginal infection. A tampon that is left in the vagina too long eventually produces a strong-smelling, colorless discharge. This form of bacterial vaginosis (see page 143) should go when the tampon is removed, but a doctor should be consulted nonetheless.

Some women use contraceptive caps and diaphragms to catch menstrual blood flow during their period. Although convenient, this practice can cause abrasions in the membrane that lines the vagina and increase the risk of toxic shock syndrome (see page 114). For sex during menstruation, however, caps and diaphragms with spermicide will conveniently reduce the blood flow.

Some women use natural sea sponges to absorb menstrual blood flow as an alternative to tampons. Doctors discourage this method of protection because it is difficult to ensure that sponges are adequately free of pollutants, both natural and man-made.

Sanitary napkins
Napkins come in many different shapes and thicknesses.

Padded for heavy flow

Shaped for comfort

Wings for extra security

Slim for light flow

Applicator tampons
Cardboard or plastic applicators help guide the tampon into the vagina.

Tampon for heavy flow

Tampon for medium flow

Plastic-applicator tampon

Fragranced tampon
(may cause irritation to the vaginal lining)

Finding the best position
Often it helps to relax the vagina by placing one foot on a higher surface or squatting down.

INSERTING A TAMPON

Tampons are inserted high into the vagina, where they absorb the menstrual blood that flows through the cervical opening. Once it is inserted, a woman should be unaware that she is wearing a tampon. If it is uncomfortable, then it has probably been incorrectly inserted.

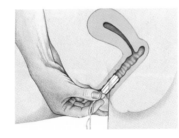

1 Push the applicator-free tampon into the vagina with the fingers. Aim toward the small of the back.

WITH AN APPLICATOR

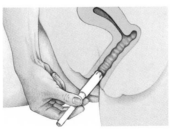

1 Holding the outer tube where it meets the inner one, insert the tampon into the vagina.

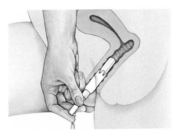

2 Push in the plunger with the index finger and then remove both tubes.

TOXIC SHOCK SYNDROME

This rare but life-threatening illness occurs primarily in women using tampons. If a tampon is too absorbent for the degree of menstrual flow or is left in too long, it can dry out the vagina and cause abrasions. These tiny cuts allow the *Staphylococcus aureus* bacterium to enter the body, where it starts producing poisonous toxins. Symptoms of toxic shock syndrome include high fever, sore throat, aching muscles, vomiting, diarrhea and a reddening of the skin. The illness can also lead to kidney failure. Doctors treat toxic shock syndrome with antibiotics. To prevent occurrence of toxic shock syndrome, women should use tampons of the correct absorbency for the degree of menstrual flow and change them at least every four to six hours. Tampons made of cotton or non-enhanced rayon are least likely to cause the illness.

Menstruation in other cultures In northern Nepal, a menstruating woman is believed to pollute those around her and is segregated from everyone except her younger children.

brand and make sure the soap lather is completely rinsed away. Postmenopausal women in particular should try to avoid soap, since the skin of their *UROGENITAL TRACT* becomes thin and sensitive and more susceptible to infection (see page 81).

It is important that girls and women are aware that some amount of vaginal discharge is normal and not a sign of poor hygiene or infection. There is cause for concern only if a vaginal discharge becomes profuse, discolored or smelly.

Male genital hygiene is very straightforward. Uncircumcised men—and boys old enough to retract the foreskin—should gently wash under the foreskin with water every day. They may or may not need to use soap depending on how much *SMEGMA* they produce. Some men find that soap dries the sensitive skin of the glans and causes rashes and irritation. Circumcised men usually need only to use water on the glans. All men should wash the anal area with soap and water daily.

The type of underwear worn also plays a role in the general health and cleanliness of male and female genitals. Both men and women should avoid underwear made from synthetic fabrics because these encourage sweating in the genital area, which in turn encourages the growth of bacteria and yeasts. Natural fibers such as cotton and silk absorb sweat and allow air to circulate. Some women who suffer from recurrent yeast infections (see page 143) can avoid the problem by wearing pure cotton underwear and stockings instead of pantyhose. Men's tight-fitting polyester or nylon briefs have also been found to lower sperm count.

MENSTRUAL HYGIENE

Menstruation has been perennially shrouded in myth: some women still believe that menstrual blood is dirty; some are superstitious about what they can and cannot do while they are bleeding. In some Arab cultures, women are forbidden to prepare or cook food while they are menstruating, and some orthodox Jewish and Muslim women undergo elaborate cleansing rituals after each menstrual period. Although myths and taboos persist, no medical or scientific reason exists why menstruation should be thought of as dirty.

The volume of fluid loss varies from woman to woman and month to month, averaging between two and six fluid ounces (60 and 175 ml). The fluid that is lost is a mixture of unclotted blood, mucus and cells. Enzymes inside the uterus unclot the blood, which allows it to drip through the cervical canal. Sometimes the blood reclots in the vagina and passes out of the body in that state—a menstrual flow with some blood clots is normal. An unusually heavy blood flow with many large clots, however, should be investigated by a doctor.

No specific hygiene needs to be practiced during menstruation beyond washing with unperfumed soap and water and using plenty of water around the entrance to the vagina. Women who use douches around the time of their period may actually encourage yeast infections.

PREVENTING SEXUALLY TRANSMITTED DISEASES

Sexually transmitted diseases (STDs) are diseases that are passed on by sexual contact (see page 134). The most threatening STD—HIV—is passed on by unprotected sexual intercourse (sex without a condom). While a definitive cure for HIV continues to elude researchers, experts have known how to treat other types of STD, such as *SYPHILIS* and *GONORRHEA*, for some time. But whether or not STDs are treatable, they should be avoided—they are frequently uncomfortable and can cause dangerous health complications, including infertility.

STDs can be communicated in a number of ways: genital-to-genital contact (such as vaginal sex); genital-to-oral contact (oral sex); genital-to-anal contact (anal sex); and oral-to-oral contact (kissing). Some types of sexual intimacy pose more of a risk than others (see page 129). There are also non-sexual ways of passing on diseases; for example, HIV can be transferred by sharing infected needles, and *CHLAMYDIA* and *TRICHOMONIASIS* can be passed on by a mother to her child during childbirth.

While antibiotics can cure many STDs, no existing vaccines prevent infection. The only way to avoid catching an STD is to be confident about the sexual history and health of sexual partners, though most doctors working in the field of sexual medicine would argue that even this is impossible. Some barrier contraceptives such as male and female condoms (see page 121) can help to protect against infection, but people whose behavior is considered to be particularly high-risk (see page 129) should have regular checkups at a clinic.

STD testing

People may attend a clinic specializing in sexual medicine for any of a variety of reasons. They may have had casual sex (on one occasion or frequently) and want to eliminate the possibility that they have been infected with an STD. They may have symptoms that they suspect are due to an STD, or they may have been warned by a sexual partner that they could be infected. Some people have checkups just to be reassured about their sexual health.

It is important to investigate a suspected STD as soon as possible—the longer an infection goes untreated, the greater the chances of permanent damage to the infected individual (for example, untreated gonorrhea can go on to cause infertility) and transmission to other people.

Most clinics will ask for a full sexual and medical history, including details of any travel abroad, before checking for STDs. It is important to provide information on all sexual contacts to be sure they can be informed if need be. People should not urinate for at least two hours before attending a checkup so that no bacteria are washed away. In some U.S. states and Canadian provinces, teenagers can request diagnosis and treatment of STDs without parental permission.

A number of STD clinics now have resident counselors who can help patients come to terms with the fact that they have an STD. Counselors can give advice on safer sex and the repercussions of an STD and will discuss with the patient any lifestyle changes that are considered to be necessary.

Culturing a swab
Many STDs are caused by bacteria. A swab allows a small sample of bacteria to be grown, or cultured, on an appropriate medium in a test tube or dish and identified under a microscope. The doctor takes a swab, using a metal loop or a cotton-tipped stick, from the urethra, the vagina, the cervix, the anus, the rectum or the throat.

DIAGNOSING STDS
Depending on the patient's symptoms and sexual history, various tests will be carried out to determine sexual health.

Checkups for women may include some or all of the following:

Examining the breasts

Taking a swab from the cervix and vaginal walls

Palpating the uterus from inside the vagina

Checkups for both men and women may include some or all of the following:

Taking a swab from the throat (when oral-to-genital contact has taken place)

Taking a swab from the urethra

Feeling the lymph glands in the neck, armpits and groin

Examining the pubic region for parasites, ulcers, abnormal lumps, bumps and rashes

Taking a urine sample

Examining the anal area and inside of the rectum

Taking a swab from the anal area and/or rectum

Taking a blood sample

Examining the external pubic and genital area

Checkups for men may include some or all of the following:

Examining the testicles for abnormal lumps or signs of tenderness

Examining the penis for visible discharge, ulcers or growths

Taking a swab from the tip of the penis

Contraception

Although women are highly fertile for only a short time every month, much research is devoted to trying to prevent conception from occurring. Effective methods of contraception have been sought not only in modern times but throughout history.

The ability to control fertility has been a great liberating force, particularly for women in the 20th century. Before effective contraceptives were available, efforts concentrated on identifying ovulation and avoiding sexual intercourse during this time. Nowadays, sophisticated hormonal contraception can totally suppress a woman's ovulation.

HISTORY OF CONTRACEPTION

Despite limited physiological knowledge, people throughout history have connected the ejaculation of sperm into the vagina with pregnancy. In the ancient world, coitus interruptus (the withdrawal of the penis from the vagina before ejaculation) was the most widely practiced form of contraception, although its effectiveness was limited.

By the 19th century coitus interruptus, although widely used, was beginning to lose popularity as a birth control method,

The 19th-century family Compared with the small nuclear families of today's society, 19th-century families tended to be extensive. Although having many children was the social norm, unreliable methods of contraception undoubtedly played a part in determining family size.

perhaps because alternatives were becoming available. Men felt that it destroyed their pleasure in sex and so found it difficult; women felt that it allowed them no control over their fertility; and physicians argued that it led to physical and psychological illness.

Abstinence from sexual intercourse was also widely used to control the number of pregnancies a woman had. People who practiced abstinence sometimes used herbal anaphrodisiacs to suppress their libido or searched for alternative sexual outlets, such as oral or anal sex, homosexual sex and, occasionally, bestiality.

Some couples tried to abstain from sex when they believed that a woman was in her fertile phase—the practice now known as the rhythm method. However, women's fertile periods were often miscalculated. For example, the ancient Greeks believed that conception was most likely to take place immediately before or after menstruation; the Romans thought that the days just after menstruation were the riskiest; and in 1847 a French physician claimed that women were safe from conception from the 12th day after menstruation to the beginning of their next period. A woman's fertile period was not accurately plotted until the 1920s.

Over the centuries, numerous suggestions for contraceptive practices, potions or mechanical devices have been recorded. In ancient Rome, the Greek physician Soranus of Ephesus suggested that a woman should squat down and induce sneezing after having sexual intercourse. Centuries later Casanova was reported to have placed half a squeezed lemon over a woman's cervix—presumably it acted as a crude forerunner of the diaphragm.

The condom

The design of the first condom is attributed to the Italian anatomist Gabriello Fallopio (after whom the fallopian tubes were named). In 1564 Fallopio designed a small linen covering to put over the glans of the penis during sexual intercourse. Fallopio intended his condom to protect the wearer against venereal disease, however, and not against pregnancy.

By the 19th century condoms were made from sheep's intestines. They did not fit well, had to be put on very carefully and were secured at the open end with a ribbon. Because condoms were stocked only in brothels or by specialist wholesalers, they were hard to obtain. At least one advice book provided instructions on how to make condoms from intestines.

It was not until the discovery of the process to vulcanize rubber in 1844 that condoms became available. By the 1850s they were easy to buy, but had a negative image, condemned as inconvenient, unesthetic and unsafe. Some birth control advocates warned of condoms bursting and advised people to inflate them with air or water before use. There was also a lingering assumption that condoms were to prevent promiscuous men from contracting syphilis.

During the 1920s and 1930s condoms became increasingly popular and sales began to surge and did not fall off until the advent of the birth control pill. Today, with the increase in sexually transmitted diseases such as HIV, condom sales have risen again. Refinements in design have resulted in condoms varying in thickness, shape, size, color and even flavor. The female condom, which is now widely available, was first introduced in 1992.

The diaphragm

Stopping the passage of sperm by blocking the cervical opening is an age-old method of contraception, but a scientifically designed diaphragm was not proposed until 1838. Its German pioneer, Friedrich Adolphe Wilde, suggested making a wax mold of the cervix and using this to make a rubber shield. Unlike today's diaphragm, which is inserted only before intercourse, the rubber shield was worn by a woman all the time when she was not menstruating. Perhaps because diaphragms had to be individually fitted, the idea failed to take off.

OLD CONTRACEPTIVE DEVICES

Before hormonal contraceptives were invented, most birth control devices aimed at preventing pregnancy either by covering the penis with a condom or by shielding the cervix with a sponge or a crude cap or diaphragm. Douches were devices that propelled water into the vagina after intercourse in an attempt to wash away the semen. They have since been proved ineffective, but barrier methods of contraception (see page 121) are still used today.

Sheep-gut condom
Before the vulcanization of rubber, people had to use other materials, such as animal intestines, to make condoms.

The sponge
A small piece of sponge attached to a ribbon was widely used as a contraceptive at the beginning of the 20th century.

Tortoiseshell condoms
Condoms made from tortoiseshell were used in 19th-century Japan. The smaller ones were designed to cover the glans.

Vaginal douche
Made from rubber and vulcanite, this vaginal douche was used in the early 20th century.

U.S. Patent Office records from the 1850s show many patents for rubber pessaries. These were mainly doughnut-shaped devices that were prescribed by doctors to correct a malpositioned or a prolapsed uterus (conditions now believed to have been very common at the time). Before long, however, these pessaries were modified to act as contraceptives.

In 1864 a rubber device known as a womb veil was introduced. The literature that accompanied the womb veil described its benefits: "Conception cannot possibly take place when it is used. The full enjoyment of the conjugal embrace can be indulged in during coition. The husband would hardly be likely to know that it was being used, unless told by the wife."

Natural methods
Plants, oils and substances such as honey and lemon were once used as spermicides.

The two main selling points—invisibility and infallibility—may have been appealing to women in the 19th century, but limited knowledge of anatomy may have made them uncomfortable with the idea of inserting a diaphragm and fearful that, once inserted, it would be irretrievable. The devices did not achieve major popularity until the 20th century.

The sponge

Mention of the contraceptive sponge appears in birth control literature dating back to the 14th century, and it became a popular method of contraception in the 18th and 19th centuries. Women would take a small piece of sponge, dampen it with water, tie a ribbon around it and insert it high in the vagina before sexual intercourse. They hoped that the dampened sponge would absorb the man's semen during intercourse. After intercourse the sponge was withdrawn, washed and stored for next time. With the sponge, women believed that they gained unobtrusive control over fertility.

Advice about the way sponges should be used varied immensely. Some 19th-century birth control experts advised moistening the sponge with chloride of soda or other chemicals. Others recommended that it be repeatedly reinserted and rinsed after intercourse in order to soak up all the semen. Another suggestion was that the sponge be left in for several hours after intercourse.

Many doctors told women to use a douche after withdrawal of the sponge. Women in the 19th and early 20th centuries often douched routinely with water and a spermicidal agent, such as vinegar, baking soda or bichloride of mercury. Many relied on this as their sole contraceptive.

The intrauterine device (IUD)

The first known intrauterine device was a pebble placed in the uterus of a camel to prevent the animal from becoming pregnant during long trips across the desert.

Research on the IUD for humans was first carried out by German scientists early in the 20th century. The prototypes were made of silk, then later of gold and silver (birth control advocate Marie Stopes called her early IUD device the gold pin). However, they caused severe internal irritation, and research on the IUD soon stopped. Not until the early 1960s did development of the IUD recommence. The first of the new generation of IUD devices, the Lippes Loop, was made of plastic. More recent types contain copper or hormones, which are slowly released over a period of 1 to 10 years.

Hormonal contraceptives

When the oral contraceptive pill first became available in the early 1960s it was embraced wholeheartedly by both women and the medical profession. It was

THE WORK OF MARGARET SANGER

The most influential figure in the history of U.S. family planning, Margaret Sanger was born in New York in 1879 to a middle-class family of 11 children. Sanger was thus aware of the many health problems associated with large families.

During her career as a nurse she saw the terrible problems women faced—including fatal self-performed abortions—in their attempts to control their fertility. The Comstock Act of 1873 made it a criminal offense to distribute material that even mentioned birth control.

Frustrated at this lack of information, Sanger traveled abroad to learn about family planning. In 1914 she founded the National Birth Control League, and, with gathering support from doctors, she founded the National Committee on Federal Legalization for Birth Control in 1923.

The campaign for contraception
When Sanger opened her first birth control clinic in New York in 1916, she was promptly arrested. It was not until the 1950s that U.S. laws were revised to allow contraception and the provision of contraceptive advice.

considered revolutionary because, for the first time, women were given total control over their fertility.

The first research into hormonal contraceptives was a U.S.-funded project in Austria in the early 20th century. The results showed that ovulation in animals could be prevented with estrogen injections.

In the late 1930s an American, Gregory Pincus, continued the research. By the early 1950s he had gained the support of Margaret Sanger, who organized more funding for him. As early as 1951 Pincus proved that progesterone inhibited ovulation, and he began a search for a synthetic hormone to emulate it.

In 1956, extensive clinical trials of a combined estrogen-progesterone contraceptive pill were undertaken in Boston and Puerto Rico by John Rock, a Harvard gynecologist. Finally, in 1960, the U.S. Food and Drug Administration approved the pill as an oral contraceptive, and it was released onto the American market.

Since the advent of the contraceptive pill, there have been intermittent scares about its possible side effects, such as an increased risk of blood clots, heart attacks, high blood pressure and breast cancer. Despite this, the pill remains one of the most popular forms of birth control for North American women under the age of 30.

Research into hormonal contraception has led to the introduction of injections and implants that deliver hormones to the body.

Abortion and infanticide

Throughout history, abortion and infanticide have been used as last resorts when contraceptive measures have not been used or have failed. In some early civilizations abortion was a punishable offense, while infanticide was acceptable—perhaps because it targeted female babies, whereas abortion put the more highly valued male fetus at risk. Other societies accepted abortion in the belief that fetuses were not human—in ancient Greece the philosopher Aristotle taught that human life did not begin until 40 days after conception.

In the 19th century there was an upsurge in the number of abortions, presumably because people saw advantages in limiting family size. In 1869 (until 1969) abortion was a criminal code offense in Canada. Canadian women continued to have abor-

tions during this period, however, these illegal abortions were clandestine and usually unsafe, posing a considerable threat to women's health.

CONTRACEPTION TODAY

The large variety of contraceptive products available from doctors and pharmacies today allows couples to choose the method that best suits their sexual needs, age and reproductive history.

Hormonal treatments

The two main hormones that rise and fall each month in a woman's menstrual cycle are estrogen and progesterone. When a woman becomes pregnant, the levels of

---

THE BODY'S RESPONSE TO THE PILL

Progesterone
Women who take the pill have artificially high levels of this hormone. Usually progesterone is released only after ovulation.

Estrogen
In non-pill users estrogen is released by developing egg follicles in the ovary.

How the pill works
Increased levels of the hormones estrogen and progestogen stop the pituitary gland in the brain from releasing FSH and LH (see page 129). This stops ova from maturing in the ovary, thus preventing ovulation. It also temporarily changes the fallopian tubes, uterine lining and cervical mucus to make conception and implantation of a fertilized ovum unlikely.

The pill is taken orally, usually in cycles of 21 or 28 days.

↓

The pill suppresses pituitary hormones.

↓

Ovulation is suppressed.

↓

Cervical mucus becomes hostile to sperm.

Contraceptive pills
Doctors will prescribe the pill with the individual needs of the woman in mind. Some pills have very low doses of hormone, some have variable amounts, and some contain the hormone progestogen, but not estrogen.

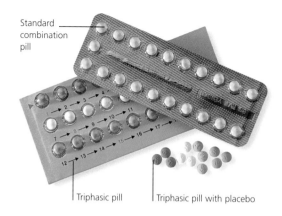

Standard combination pill

Triphasic pill

Triphasic pill with placebo

Implants Silicon rods are inserted under the skin of the upper arm. Once in place, they are invisible, although most women can feel them through the skin.

these hormones remain high instead of rising and falling. Hormonal contraception works by using synthetic versions of natural hormones to trick the body into thinking it is already pregnant. This prevents ovulation and makes fertilization impossible.

Hormonal contraception also makes the cervical mucus hostile to sperm and alters the uterine lining to prevent the implantation of a fertilized ovum. Hormonal methods of contraception are among the most effective and are available in several forms.

The combined pill contains both progestogen (a synthetic type of progesterone) and estrogen. If it is taken in the correct way, the combined pill is 99 percent effective in preventing pregnancy. Women who do become pregnant while taking the pill may have taken it irregularly or taken medication (antibiotics, for example) that interferes with the pill's efficacy. Stomach upsets that cause vomiting and diarrhea also make the pill unreliable.

There are three types of combined pill. These are the monophasic pill, in which each pill in the pack contains the same dose of progestogen and estrogen; the biphasic pill, in which the first 7 pills contain less progestogen than the remaining 14; and the triphasic pill, in which there are three different types of pills in each pack. Particular types of hormonal combinations suit some women and not others.

Contraceptive pills can be taken in 21- or 28-day regimes. In a 21-day regime, a pill is taken daily for 21 days, followed by a pill-

free break of 7 days. During the pill-free break a withdrawal bleed occurs. This is similar to menstruation, but it is not the same as a true menstrual period because it is the body's response to the withdrawal of the hormones found in the pill. A withdrawal bleed is usually lighter and shorter than a menstrual period.

Women who follow a 28-day regime take pills continuously, but the pills they take between day 21 and day 28 are placebos (they do not contain any hormones). The women experience a withdrawal bleed while they are taking the placebo pills in just the same way as women who follow a 21-day regime. Following a 28-day pill regime prevents the woman from becoming confused about when to stop and start taking pills in each cycle.

The combined pill allows convenience and spontaneity in lovemaking, lighter and more painfree and regular periods as well as some protection against various disorders, such as ovarian and endometrial cancer, ovarian cysts, endometriosis and pelvic inflammatory disease (see pages 144 to 148).

Although it rarely causes any undesirable side effects, some women do experience nausea, headaches, increased appetite, weight gain or a slightly increased risk of heart problems and high blood pressure. Unlike barrier methods of contraception, the pill does not protect against sexually transmitted diseases.

The progestogen-only pill (POP) is also known as the mini-pill. The POP does not contain estrogen, and only 10 percent of pill users take it. Unlike the combined pill, the POP does not prevent ovulation. Instead, it works by turning the cervical mucus into a barrier against sperm, making the uterine lining inhospitable to a fertilized ovum and interfering with the muscular action of the fallopian tubes so that the journey of the ovum is made difficult.

The POP has fewer side effects and health risks than the combined pill and is suitable for smokers, women over 40, diabetics and breast-feeding women. The main disadvantage of this contraceptive is that a pill must be taken within the same 3 hours every day, compared with the 8 to 12 hour range for the combined pill. Also, many women taking the POP can develop amenorrhea (see page 142) or spotting.

USING A MALE CONDOM

It is important to remember that a condom should be put on as soon as the penis becomes erect. It should then be worn during any penis-vagina contact, whether or not this includes penetrative sex.

1 Carefully remove a condom from its packet and pinch the air from the teat between thumb and forefinger.

2 Still pinching the teat with one hand, hold the condom in place on the glans of the penis and, using the other hand, slowly roll the rim of the condom down the length of the shaft.

3 Roll the rim as far down the shaft of the penis as possible. Remember to hold the rim in this position during withdrawal after intercourse, before the penis becomes flaccid.

Implants come in the form of six small silicon rods that are inserted under the skin of the upper arm. Once in position they release a low dose of progestogen into the bloodstream and provide contraception for up to five years. Fewer than 1 in 100 women become pregnant while using implants. The insertion, which is carried out in a doctor's office, involves making a small incision in the skin of the arm under local anesthetic. If a woman wants to conceive during the five-year life span of the implants, they can be removed by a doctor.

Although implants provide very effective contraceptive cover, a number of side effects, such as irregular bleeding, mood swings, weight gain, nausea and hair loss,

have been reported. Some women have also experienced discomfort and scarring when the silicon rods are removed.

Injectable hormones work on similar principles to the pill, but they are injected rather than taken orally. The injection contains one of two long-lasting progestogens, which prevent ovulation, thicken cervical mucus and thin the uterine lining. Depending on the type, women are given repeat injections at two- or three-month intervals.

While injected hormones provide freedom from menstrual pains and allow sexual spontaneity, they occasionally produce irregular periods, acne, mood swings and loss of interest in sex.

Barrier methods

Condoms, diaphragms and caps—all barrier methods of contraception—provide a physical barrier that prevents sperm from completing their journey to the fallopian tubes. Barrier methods afford very effective protection against disease and infection. The condom in particular has come to be associated with safe sex and helping to prevent transmission of the HIV virus.

The condom is made of thin latex rubber. It is unrolled onto a man's erect penis before intercourse and contains the semen when he ejaculates. After ejaculation, the man should immediately withdraw his penis, holding on to the rim of the condom, and dispose of the condom. If this is done after the erection subsides, the condom can slip off and semen can leak into the vagina. Condoms are the most popular method of contraception—45 million couples worldwide use them as their main contraceptive.

Condoms are readily available in most countries; they have no side effects and offer good protection from sexually transmitted diseases. Although many couples use condoms successfully, some find putting them on disruptive. Couples also complain that they have to plan ahead to use them; some men claim a loss of sensation during intercourse; and condoms can occasionally split or slip off on withdrawal.

Condoms should always be used with a water-based lubricating jelly rather than an oil-based one, since latex breaks down when in contact with oils (see page 128). Some people are allergic to the latex used in

The range of condoms Condoms come in many different colors and flavors. The latest type is made from plastic rather than latex, which means it will not degenerate in the presence of oil.

condoms. A relatively recent innovation is the plastic condom, which is made from strong, thin polyurethane. This is suitable for men and women with allergies to latex, and, it is claimed, because the polyurethane is so thin, it does not decrease sensitivity during sexual intercourse. The plastic condom is as effective at preventing pregnancy and protecting the user against sexually transmitted diseases as the conventional latex condom.

The female condom is a loose polyurethane tube designed to line the inside of the vagina. It has two flexible rings, one at each end of the tube. The top ring fits high inside the vagina against the cervix and the bottom ring lies flat against the labia. The condom is inserted before intercourse and gently removed after the man has ejaculated. As long as the penis remains inside the condom during intercourse, no semen will escape into the vagina. The female condom also protects against most sexually transmitted diseases (STDs).

Female condoms are less likely to interrupt lovemaking than male condoms, but a woman using one for the first time may have difficulty inserting it properly and is advised to practice alone a couple of times.

Caps and diaphragms, unlike male and female condoms, allow semen to enter the vagina but prevent it from passing through the cervix. The diaphragm is a soft latex dome with a flexible metal rim that fits around the cervix and holds the diaphragm in place against the pubic bone. The cap is a smaller rubber device that covers the opening in the cervix that leads to the uterus. There are three types of cap: the cervical cap is thimble-shaped; the vault cap, which is not available in Canada, is shallow and semicircular, more like the diaphragm, but without the metal rim; and the vimule cap is a combination of the other two. Although both cervical and vimule caps stay in place by suction, cervical caps are rarely used because they are harder to insert, and few doctors and nurses are trained to fit them.

Diaphragms and caps come in different sizes to suit individual women. They must be fitted by a nurse or doctor and refitted if a woman loses or gains weight or has a baby. During fitting, the doctor or nurse teaches a woman the correct procedure to insert her cap or diaphragm. The woman follows this procedure before every episode of sexual intercourse. The device must be used with spermicidal jelly or cream and left in place for at least six hours after inter-

INSERTING A FEMALE CONDOM

It takes practice to insert a female condom. New users may find it helpful to use the hand to guide the penis into the vagina. This avoids the penis missing the condom or causing the condom to bunch up.

Made from fine polyurethane, the female condom ensures maximum sensitivity.

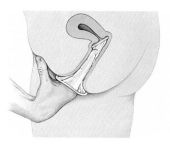
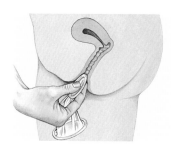

1 Hold the condom at the closed end, squeezing the inner ring between a thumb and middle finger.

2 Still squeezing the inner ring, gently push the condom into the vagina and then up past the pubic bone.

3 Let one inch of the condom sit outside the body. Check that the outer ring is lying flat against the labia.

course. Caps and diaphragms are reasonably durable and, if properly cared for, can last for up to two years.

Diaphragms and caps are often recommended for women who live with their partners. They have few long-term health risks and are suitable for women who cannot use hormonal contraception. They can be left in for renewed lovemaking, but extra spermicide is necessary after three hours.

Some women dislike the intrusiveness of inserting a device every time they have intercourse. Caps and diaphragms also carry a risk, although extremely low, of toxic shock syndrome if left in for too long, and some women using the diaphragm find they suffer frequently from *CYSTITIS*.

Intrauterine devices (IUDs)

The IUD is a small plastic device wrapped in thin copper wire that is inserted into the uterus by a doctor. Once fitted, it can provide contraceptive protection for up to 5 years. The IUD appears to work by making the uterine lining hostile to both sperm and fertilized ova. Even if conception does take place, the implantation of a fertilized ovum cannot.

Most women who use IUDs are older women who do not want to have any more children. While the IUD offers complete sexual freedom, it is associated with a slight risk of pelvic infection (see page 144), which can cause complications such as damaged fallopian tubes. Insertion of an IUD may be uncomfortable for a couple of hours afterward, and some IUD users complain of heavy and painful periods. IUDs may cause cramping and significant discomfort in women who have not had a baby.

Progestogen-containing IUDs are small T-shaped plastic devices that are inserted into the uterus, where they release the hormone progestogen. Progestogen thickens the cervical mucus, which prevents sperm from traveling to the fallopian tubes. It also thins the uterine lining, making pregnancy difficult to achieve, and causes some women to stop ovulating.

Unlike conventional IUDs, progestogen-containing IUDs cause periods to become light and often painless. They are effective immediately and give protection for one to three years. Progestogen-containing IUDs are available in the U.S. but not in Canada.

HOW TO INSERT A DIAPHRAGM

Find the easiest position for insertion. This may be lying down, squatting or with one foot raised on the edge of the bath or toilet.

1 Hold the rim between thumb and forefinger and squeeze spermicide into the diaphragm.

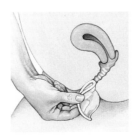

2 Squeeze the rim into an oval shape and insert it into the vagina. Push the diaphragm as high into the vagina as possible so that its front lies behind the pubic bone.

3 To check that the diaphragm is sitting in the correct position, insert the middle finger high up into the vagina. The cervix should be felt as a firm rounded shape through the latex.

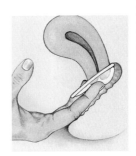

Can We Talk About It?

USING A CONDOM

Knowing when to raise the issue of using a condom with a new partner is difficult. You may worry that if you broach the subject very early, you are making the assumption that intercourse is definitely going to happen. If you broach the subject when you are already in bed together, however, it may be too late to take precautions. The best idea is to talk about the issue when you feel sure that you and your partner want to have sex but before you become too intimate.

Your partner may feel relieved that you have broached the subject. If not, point out that using a condom will make you feel safer and able to relax and enjoy yourself. If your partner resists, you may need to reconsider your relationship. Remind yourself and your partner that condoms are not optional but are a vital form of protection against pregnancy and STDs (see page 134). Don't be made to feel selfish.

Men produce vast numbers of sperm. In order for a male contraceptive to work, it must stop the production or the delivery of every single sperm. (Preventing ovulation in women is comparatively simple, since only one ovum is released every month.) Current research centers around injecting male hormones (androgens) into the bloodstream. This would halt the sequence of events that leads to sperm production, since high levels of androgens instruct the brain to secrete less gonadotropin-releasing hormone (GRH). The problem with this method is that it causes such side effects as irritability and acne, although adding a female hormone, progestogen, may eliminate these problems. Scientists are also looking at the possibility of blocking gonadotropin-releasing hormone with molecules other than androgens.

Disadvantages may include slight bleeding between periods and temporary side effects such as acne, headaches and tenderness of the breasts. Cysts can sometimes appear on the ovaries during the first few months after insertion of the progestogen-containing IUD. These are not considered dangerous and usually disappear without treatment.

Chemical methods

In North America, spermicides are available as creams, foams and gels, and in the U.S. as suppositories and film. Although they chemically destroy any sperm they come into contact with, they are not effective contraceptives on their own and should always be used in conjunction with a cap or a diaphragm. The contraceptive sponge—a round piece of polyurethane foam that is inserted high in the vagina—is also impregnated with spermicide. Some women use the sponge as their sole method of contraception, but this is not recommended unless they have low fertility.

The active ingredient in most spermicides is nonoxynol-9, which increases protection against some sexually transmitted diseases, including human immunodeficiency virus (HIV). Some types of condom are impregnated with nonoxynol-9. Men and women who have an allergic reaction to nonoxynol-

9, resulting in irritation to the vagina, vulva or penis, are advised to choose a different spermicide and check condoms before use.

Natural methods

Understanding the way that conception occurs allows people to use natural methods to prevent it. This can mean avoiding sex during fertile periods or not ejaculating during intercourse. The latter, however, is notoriously ineffective.

The rhythm method, also known as the safe period method, has a reputation for being highly unsafe. However, if couples are taught by an experienced family-planning expert, they can become quite skilled in recognizing the bodily changes associated with ovulation. It is essential that a couple either avoid intercourse during the entire period around ovulation, when a woman may be fertile, or use a barrier method of contraception. The main clues to ovulation are changes in cervical mucus, the position and firmness of the cervix, changes in body temperature, and predictions based on a menstrual calendar. As the technology available to detect ovulation improves (see page 170), the rhythm method may become more widely used. The rhythm method may be easiest for those women who have regular, established menstrual cycles.

HAVING AN IUD FITTED

An IUD should be fitted and removed by a doctor. The device is inserted into the uterus via the cervical canal through a special inserter tube. Threads attached to the IUD hang down into the vagina. IUDs can be fitted at any time, but some doctors prefer to fit them at the end of a period, when the cervix is softer and pregnancy is unlikely.

What are IUDs made from?
IUDs are small plastic devices wrapped with pure copper. Some contain progesterone.

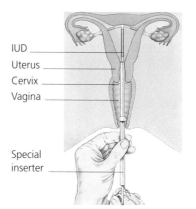

IUD
Uterus
Cervix
Vagina
Special inserter

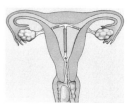

Checking an IUD
Insert a finger high into the vagina to feel the threads of an IUD at the entrance to the cervix.

Inserting an IUD
The IUD is gently pushed through the hollow tube into the uterine cavity. It springs into its normal shape and sits high up in the uterus. The inserter tube is then removed and disposed of.

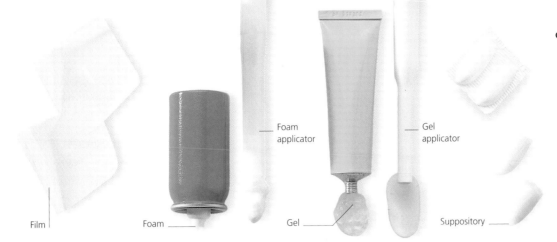

Foam
applicator

Gel
applicator

Film

Foam

Gel

Suppository

Types of spermicide
Spermicides are chemi-
cals that destroy sperm.
Spermicides should be
used in conjunction
with barrier methods of
contraception.

The withdrawal method, also known as coitus interruptus, is an ancient practice involving withdrawal of the penis from the vagina immediately before ejaculation. Because the semen is deposited outside the body, people have routinely assumed that conception could not occur. During arousal, however, men release drops of pre-ejaculatory fluid that contain sperm, making coitus interruptus highly unreliable as a method of contraception. A recent Oxford University study showed that 6.7 percent of married women between the ages of 25 and 39 using the withdrawal method for a year became pregnant. Other studies have put this figure at as high as 25 percent.

Breast-feeding fully—that is, giving two- to four-hourly feedings to a baby day and night—is thought to protect a woman from becoming pregnant. This is because breast-feeding helps to raise levels of the hormone prolactin, which prevents ovulation. This form of protection is not always reliable, however, and most doctors would recommend using an additional contraceptive during breast-feeding.

Emergency contraception

A woman who has had sex without using contraception or who thinks her method of contraception might have failed has two emergency options.

The postcoital pill is a type of hormonal medication given after unprotected sex. It is popularly referred to as the morning-after pill. "Morning-after" is slightly misleading, however, because the first dose can actually be taken at any time within 72 hours of having unprotected sex. If unprotected sex has resulted in conception, the postcoital pill will prevent the fertilized ovum from becoming implanted in the uterus.

The postcoital pill must be prescribed by a doctor. Four pills are taken—two right away and two 12 hours later. The hormones are of the same type contained in the normal contraceptive pill, but the doses are much higher, which can make some women vomit or feel nauseous. The treatment is not designed for regular use, and patients must have a follow-up checkup. The postcoital pill is 95 to 99 percent effective.

The IUD can be fitted within five days of unprotected sex (the sooner the better) to prevent pregnancy. It can also be used as an ongoing method of contraception if desired. Insertion of an emergency IUD requires a follow-up checkup.

Contraceptive reliability

The efficiency of any contraceptive method depends on the diligence and care that is taken when using it. All forms of contraception are more effective for couples who are highly conscientious (remembering to take the pill every day, for example). Methods that need practice, such as the diaphragm, may have an above average failure rate during the first year of use.

THE FUTURE OF BIRTH CONTROL

The ideal contraceptive is safe, inexpensive and 100 percent effective. It should have no side effects, be unobtrusive to love-making and be easi-

Prolonged breast-feeding In some developing countries, women breast-feed their children for several years. This ensures ongoing nutrition for the child and some degree of contraception.

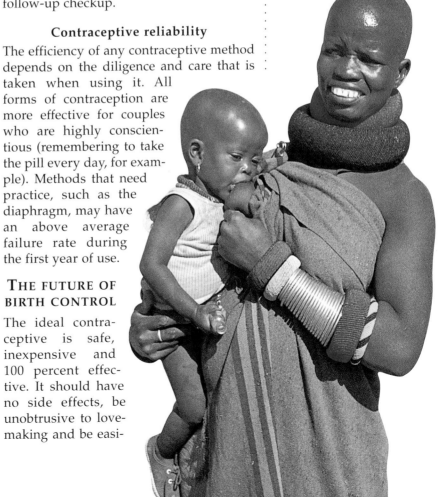

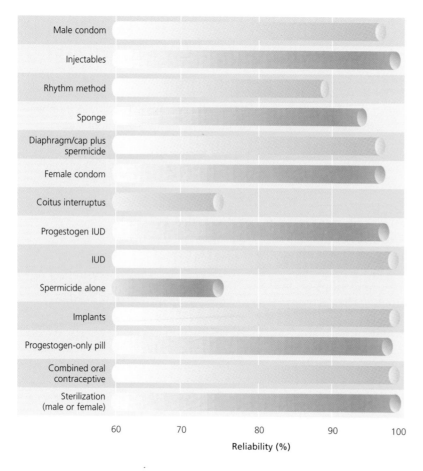

Male condom	
Injectables	
Rhythm method	
Sponge	
Diaphragm/cap plus spermicide	
Female condom	
Coitus interruptus	
Progestogen IUD	
IUD	
Spermicide alone	
Implants	
Progestogen-only pill	
Combined oral contraceptive	
Sterilization (male or female)	

60   70   80   90   100

Reliability (%)

Contraceptives compared The efficacy of a contraceptive is measured by how many women out of 100 using that method become pregnant in one year.

ly reversible. At the moment no single contraceptive meets all of these criteria, but researchers continue to look for one that does. The following methods of contraception for women are all being investigated.

The personal contraceptive system is a small handheld monitor that stores the results of urine tests and calculates the days on which a woman should avoid sex because she is ovulating.

Injectable microspheres and implanted microcapsules are placed under the skin, where they release hormones into the body at a constant daily rate. They cannot be removed, but they dissolve harmlessly and are designed to provide contraceptive protection for up to 18 months.

The vaginal ring is a soft plastic ring impregnated with progestogen. It is placed in the vagina and can be worn either continuously or for 21 days out of 28, during which time it releases a steady amount of the hormone into the body. The ring contains enough of the hormone for use up to

six months. A ring containing estrogen and progestogen is also being researched.

Patches would deliver contraceptive hormones transdermally (through the skin) in the same way that hormone replacement therapy (HRT) patches do.

Nasal sprays would contain contraceptive hormones that prevent ovulation.

Contraceptive vaccines are being researched. A vaccine could work by disrupting the implantation of a fertilized ovum, by causing a man to make antibodies to his own sperm, by causing a woman to be immune to a man's sperm or by preventing the sperm from fertilizing an ovum. All of these vaccines are thought to be a long way from actual use.

Copper fix is a copper IUD that would be inserted into the wall of the uterus and have fewer side effects than current IUDs.

The abortion pill is being tested as a once-a-month method of contraception.

STERILIZATION

When a couple have completed their family or are convinced that they will never want to have children, they may decide that sterilization is a sensible alternative to using contraception for their remaining fertile years. Sterilization involves surgery to the reproductive organs that will permanently prevent pregnancy. Couples may also opt for sterilization for health reasons—some medical conditions make pregnancy dangerous—or to prevent the genetic transmission of serious diseases. The decision to be

fact or fiction?

The older the woman, the more effective the contraceptive.

Fact. As women get older, especially as they approach menopause, they ovulate less frequently. This means that even women who use contraception carelessly are less likely to become pregnant.

sterilized should not be taken lightly, since although it is sometimes possible to have a reversal operation, this may be associated with complications.

Female sterilization

Sterilization is a popular method of contraception in women over age 35. It is extremely effective in preventing pregnancy, it does not stop the menstrual cycle, and it has no impact on sexual enjoyment.

Sterilization works by blocking or cutting the fallopian tubes so that sperm cannot reach the ova, and conception can no longer take place. Sterilized women continue to ovulate each month, but the ovum no longer passes into the uterus to be shed during menstruation. Instead, it moves as far along the fallopian tube as it can and then stops, dies and is reabsorbed. Menstruation occurs as usual. Although it is rare, pregnancy can sometimes occur if one of the fallopian tubes has not been successfully blocked by surgery.

A quarter of sterilized women complain of heavier periods and worse premenstrual symptoms after the operation. Studies measuring amount of blood loss and ovarian hormone levels before and after women have received surgery show no change.

The latest advance in sterilization procedures involves inserting a tiny tube into the fallopian tube via the cervix. The tube deposits a blocking device that prevents sperm from coming into contact with ova.

Male sterilization—vasectomy

Vasectomy is a minor surgical procedure that provides almost 100 percent contraception. It involves cutting and tying the vas deferens (the tubes that carry sperm). This means that men can still ejaculate, but there is no sperm present in the semen (the sperm are reabsorbed within the testicles).

Vasectomy is a safer surgical procedure than female sterilization, with fewer post-operative complications, and it is estimated that a third of North American men will eventually undergo one. Surgery takes a few minutes and is performed by a doctor on an out-patient basis under local anesthetic.

Two to three months after vasectomy men are asked to provide samples of semen produced by masturbation—this is to ensure that any sperm remaining in the vas deferens before surgery have cleared.

WHAT FEMALE STERILIZATION MEANS

Sterilization is usually performed under general anesthetic. There are various techniques for blocking or sealing the fallopian tubes so that sperm is prevented from meeting an ovum. Sterilization is rarely reversible, and should be considered a permanent step.

Cautery
A high-frequency electric current is directed at each fallopian tube via a surgical instrument. The current burns through and seals the tubes. This sterilization process is known as cautery.

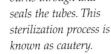

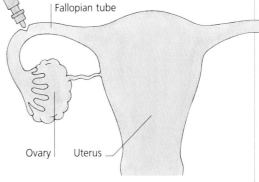

Fallopian tube

Ovary | Uterus

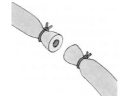

Cutting
A small section of each fallopian tube is cut away and the cut ends are tied and cauterized.

Constriction
The fallopian tubes are pulled up into a loop that is constricted with a tight band.

Clipping
A special clip made of plastic or metal is applied to each fallopian tube.

WHAT MALE STERILIZATION MEANS

A vasectomy does not impede ejaculation or orgasm, but it does mean that the fluid a man ejaculates is sperm-free. Since the tubes that need to be cut are just below the skin, they can be reached easily, making vasectomy a quick and straightforward procedure. The only problem men may experience is slight bruising or discomfort.

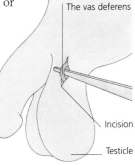

The vas deferens

Incision

Penis

Testicle

The cutting point
The ducts that carry sperm, the vas deferens, are cut just above the testicles on either side of the penis.

The vas deferens
When a man is about to ejaculate, sperm move up the vas deferens, which run from the testicles up toward the bladder.

Safer Sex

Wearing a condom during penetrative sex is the single most important measure that an individual can take to prevent the transmission of diseases such as gonorrhea, herpes, genital warts and, most important, HIV.

Safety first *Be careful not to damage the condom when tearing open the packet, and squeeze it out gently, rather than pulling it.*

The term "safe sex" became popular in the late 1980s to describe sexual practices thought to have a lower risk of transmitting HIV (see page 130). "Safer sex" has now replaced the earlier term, because no sexual practice involving body fluids can be completely free of risk. Safer sex practices offer protection not only from HIV but also from other sexually transmitted diseases and unplanned pregnancies.

CONDOMS

Using condoms during oral, vaginal and anal sex helps to protect against HIV as well as common STDs (see page 134), such as gonorrhea, herpes, genital warts and chlamydia. The condom provides a physical barrier to viruses and bacteria that may be carried in semen, vaginal secretions and other body fluids. Condoms should be used with nonoxynol-9, a substance that was developed as a spermicide but later found to kill some bacteria and viruses, among them HIV. A few people are allergic to nonoxynol-9, in which case condoms using alternative spermicides are available.

The amount of protection offered by a condom (from both disease and pregnancy) depends on how carefully it is used. Men who have not used a condom before should practice putting one on before they use one for sexual contact (see page 121). Likewise,

USING A CONDOM SAFELY

GUIDELINES	REASONS
Store condoms away from heat, light and damp.	Latex deteriorates in adverse conditions.
Check the expiration date before use.	Latex deteriorates over time.
Avoid any genital-to-genital contact until the condom is on.	Fluid is released from the penis during foreplay before ejaculation.
When putting the condom on, squeeze the tip between thumb and forefinger to expel air.	Air trapped in the tip during intercourse can cause the condom to split.
Use condoms only with water-based lubricants or jellies.	Oil-based products can damage latex. For example, baby oil destroys up to 95 percent of a condom's strength after only 15 minutes. Even substances such as suntan oil and lipstick can cause rubber to deteriorate.
Withdraw the penis and condom before the penis becomes flaccid after ejaculation.	If the penis becomes flaccid, there is more chance that the condom will slip off and semen will leak out.
Handle condoms carefully.	A tiny hole in the latex, caused by a ring for example, will allow semen to leak out.

women should familiarize themselves with the insertion technique for female condoms before they have intercourse (see page 122).

WHO IS MOST AT RISK FROM HIV?

When AIDS was first identified as an illness in the Western world, it predominantly affected young homosexual men. Today it affects heterosexuals and homosexuals in all cultures and from all walks of life. Nevertheless, it is still possible to identify groups who are considered to be high-risk.

Homosexual and bisexual people who have had casual sex or multiple partners are at risk, especially those who have had unprotected receptive anal intercourse. High-risk groups among heterosexuals include people who have or have had unprotected sex with multiple partners (or even just one infected partner) and men who have or have had unprotected sex with prostitutes (particularly in Africa, Asia and South America).

Drug users who share needles, snorting tubes (which can cause the nose to bleed) or other equipment that comes in contact with blood are a very high risk group.

HEMOPHILIACS who received blood products before products were tested for HIV are a risk group, as are people working or traveling in developing countries who received blood transfusions before blood was screened for HIV (some countries still do not screen blood). The sexual partners of people classified as high-risk are in danger themselves, and HIV-positive mothers can transmit the virus to their unborn babies.

CHANGES IN SEXUAL BEHAVIOR SINCE AIDS

Because no effective vaccines or cures for HIV exist, control of the virus has so far been limited to behavioral changes by individuals. Studies of the gay male population in the U.S. have shown a distinct change in sexual practices since HIV was first discovered in the 1980s. Most gay men have reduced the number of their sexual partners and in particular the number of unfamiliar sexual partners. Research carried out in San Francisco showed a decline in the number of newly infected individuals.

Trends in the heterosexual population have not been as encouraging. Because the transmission of HIV was first associated with homosexuality and intravenous drug

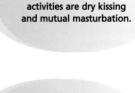

Highest-risk activities are unprotected anal, vaginal and oral sex or any activity that involves the exchange of blood.

Less risky activities are protected penetrative sex or protected oral sex (using a male or female condom).

RISKY ACTIVITIES Because HIV is carried in body fluids, levels of risk are determined by the chances of exchange or mingling of those body fluids.

Very low-risk activities are dry kissing and mutual masturbation.

Risk-free activities are solo masturbation; massage without genital contact; unshared sex toys; hugging; and holding hands.

Levels of risk Doctors now agree that some sexual practices are less risky than others. Although it is possible, in theory, for HIV to be transmitted through the exchange of saliva during kissing, this has not been found to be a common route of transmission. In contrast, unprotected anal sex is an established and common way for the virus to be transmitted.

use, many heterosexuals failed to perceive themselves as "at risk." According to the World Health Organization (mid-1996 estimates), 70 percent of HIV infections in adults worldwide are transmitted by heterosexual sexual contact. Male homosexual sexual contact accounts for between 5 and 10 percent of HIV cases.

Globally, teenagers and young adults between the ages of 15 and 24 are considered to be most affected by HIV/AIDS—more than 50 percent of new infections occur in this age group. At present rates, about 13 young people are infected every 5 minutes. An estimated 21 million people live with HIV/AIDS worldwide. Evidence that heterosexuals have not adjusted their behavior also comes from an increase in other STDs (see page 184) such as gonorrhea, syphilis, chlamydia and chancroid in urban areas of the U.S. In Canada, gonorrhea and chlamydia rates are disturbingly high among young women aged 15 to 19 years.

HIV and AIDS

The acronym HIV stands for human immunodeficiency virus. A person infected with HIV suffers progressive damage to the immune system until the body can no longer defend itself against infection.

Memorial quilt for AIDS victims *Since AIDS was first identified in 1981, thousands of people have died as a result of HIV infection in the U.S. alone. The AIDS memorial quilt, assembled at Washington, D.C., is part of the "Names Project," which aims to remember the victims of this devastating disease.*

The doctors in the U.S. who witnessed the first reported cases of AIDS in 1981 were stunned to see rare, life-threatening illnesses such as Kaposi's sarcoma repeatedly affecting young homosexual men. Such illnesses were previously limited to older men from Africa and the Mediterranean region, and to people with suppressed immune systems. Kaposi's sarcoma is a malignancy of the skin capillaries and connective tissue that causes disfiguring purple skin blotches.

Young homosexual men also began to show an increased incidence of another unusual condition—*PNEUMOCYSTIC PNEUMONIA*.

While doctors suspected immediately that a virus was responsible, it took them a couple of years to isolate and identify it. In the meantime arguments and accusations filled the media. The Soviet press accused the U.S. Army of genetically engineering the virus, while some members of the gay community accused the CIA of deliberately infecting the waters in New York City bathhouses.

In 1983 Dr. Luc Montaigner at the Institut Pasteur in Paris finally identified the virus. He named the virus "lymphadenopathy associated virus" (LAV). At the same time,

THE HISTORY OF HIV

When the first cases of AIDS were diagnosed in 1981, scientists believed that they were witnessing a completely new disease. Since then research has shown that HIV has been around much longer than originally thought. In fact, people arriving in Europe from West Africa in the early 1970s were becoming sick with AIDS-like symptoms, and evidence of HIV has been traced back to blood samples taken from Africans in 1959. Scientists hypothesize that the original source of the virus was the African green monkey. This species may have carried the virus—albeit in a different form—for thousands of years.

The origins of HIV Monkeys are thought to carry a virus known as simian immunodeficiency virus (SIV). It is only comparatively recently that SIV may have mutated to cause fatal illness in humans.

130

HIV CASES WORLDWIDE—THE MOST COMMON ROUTES OF INFECTION

Sexual intercourse
Penetrative sex is the most common route of transmission for HIV. It accounts for 70 to 85 percent of cases.

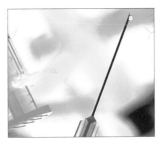

Needle sharing
Five to 10 percent of HIV infections result from contaminated injection equipment. Intravenous drug users are at high risk.

Blood transfusion
Blood or blood products (this includes organ donations) that are infected with HIV account for 5 to 10 percent of cases.

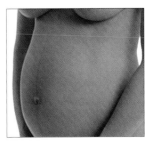

Mother to infant
Five to 10 percent of HIV cases are attributable to mothers passing the infection to their children.

another researcher, Dr. Robert Gallo, also identified the virus, naming it human T-lymphotropic virus (HTLV-III). A long dispute began between the two research teams over which had isolated the virus first.

Eventually, in 1986, the International Committee on Taxonomy of Viruses was called upon to decide the correct name for the virus. After much debate, the dispute was finally settled when U.S. president Ronald Reagan and Prime Minister Jacques Chirac of France announced that researchers had agreed that the official name for the virus would be human immunodeficiency virus-1 (HIV I) and that the royalties from tests developed for HIV I would be shared.

THE SPREAD OF AIDS

HIV spread very quickly through the gay community in the U.S. in the early 1980s. Experts blamed the speed of the spread on the promiscuity of gay men, and HIV and AIDS gained a reputation as the "gay plague." But the notion that linked the disease solely to the gay community had to be revised when people who exchanged blood in some way also became prone to infection. Such people included intravenous drug users and *HEMOPHILIACS* who received infected blood products. It was not long before non-drug-using heterosexuals began to test positive for HIV. Scientists, doctors and governments realized that anyone could become infected.

Unprotected sex, whether homosexual, heterosexual, anal or vaginal, is now the main method of HIV transmission worldwide. In Africa, Thailand and India, the large numbers of prostitutes and the high incidence of untreated sexually transmitted diseases have accelerated the rate of spread. The sores and inflamed membranes that characterize STDs such as *SYPHILIS* and *CHANCROID* make it easier to both transmit and become infected with HIV.

HOW HIV CAUSES AIDS

Despite controversy in the past, most scientists now believe that HIV is the cause of AIDS. Not everyone who is infected with HIV, however, goes on to develop AIDS. Some studies show that as many as 35 percent of people infected with HIV still have no symptoms after 10 years. Some of these people may never develop AIDS. This may be because they are protected in some way by their own genetic makeup or because the virus infecting them is flawed (has mutated) and is weaker than the usual HIV. Some children who were born with HIV have apparently succeeded in clearing the virus from their bodies.

HIV is known to enter the body through cuts, sores, tears and tiny breaks in the skin or mucous membranes. Sexual intercourse provides the usual route, and anal sex is particularly dangerous because of the abrasions and small tears that occur. The other main route of infection is needles that are contaminated with infected blood, then reused. Once inside the body, HIV begins its attack on the immune system by targeting T-helper cells, a crucial part of the body's immune defense.

HIV attaches itself to macrophages and T-helper cells—their surface receptors allow HIV to quite literally lock on to them—and then injects its core into the T-helper cell, incorporating its own genetic material into the cell's DNA. After HIV has entered the nucleus and changed the genetic structure of the T-helper cell, the virus can then start to replicate itself.

It is thought that as soon as T-helper cells become infected with HIV and the amount of virus circulating in the body—known as the viral load—starts to increase, the body's immune system mounts a massive response. From this moment on the immune system is locked in battle with the virus. Researchers estimate that HIV can multiply at the rate of a billion new viral particles every day, thereby overwhelming the immune system. HIV may also outwit the immune system and drug treatments by mutating into different forms.

The immune system sometimes successfully contains HIV for many years, but there usually comes a point when so many T-helper cells have been destroyed that the immune system can no longer function adequately and the person becomes ill. The combinations of infections that then afflict the body are traditionally referred to as AIDS and AIDS-related complex. Doctors are now trying to make this terminology simpler and increasingly refer to people as HIV symptomatic or HIV asymptomatic, and use the term "HIV disease" to cover all stages of the infection.

Stages of the infection

HIV infection progresses in stages. The first stage is the initial infection, when HIV enters the body—an undetectable process that leaves a person feeling well and without signs of any ill health. If a person has an HIV test too soon after becoming infected, no antibodies will be apparent and he or she will test negative. Antibodies are substances that appear in the blood in response to invaders such as bacteria or viruses; their role is to neutralize or destroy the invader.

It takes between 6 and 10 weeks (and occasionally longer) for the body to produce antibodies in sufficient numbers for an HIV antibody test to become accurate. Because of this period, known as the "viral window," doctors advise people to wait 12 weeks after possible exposure to HIV before being tested. The production of antibodies, known as seroconversion, goes unnoticed in many people, while in others it causes a short illness similar to flu or infectious mononucleosis. Symptoms include malaise, fever, swollen lymph glands and a rash over part or all of the body.

The second stage of HIV infection, called the asymptomatic carrier state or the dormant or latent stage, can last for years. Although HIV is busy replicating and mutating, the body's immune system keeps it in check, and the infected individual suf-

Infected T-cell T-cells infected with the HIV virus have a characteristic lumpy appearance, with irregular surface protrusions (seen here as white nodules). Budding out from the surface are thousands of tiny new HIV particles (colored green), ready to infect and destroy new T-cells.

Replication of HIV Viral particles use special proteins to lock on and gain entry to the target T-cell. Once inside, they incorporate their DNA into the host's genetic material, turning the infected T-cell into a virus factory, churning out millions of new HIV viruses.

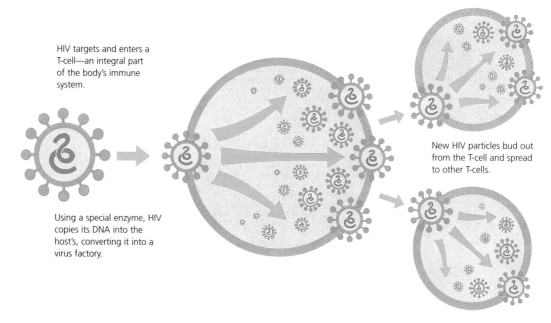

HIV targets and enters a T-cell—an integral part of the body's immune system.

Using a special enzyme, HIV copies its DNA into the host's, converting it into a virus factory.

New HIV particles bud out from the T-cell and spread to other T-cells.

HIV gets into bloodstream through:	Viral window	HIV negative	
	HIV asymptomatic	HIV asymptomatic (T-cell count can stay constant)	
		HIV symptomatic	
• unprotected sex • blood transfusion • sharing needles • the placenta	The viral window is the period between infection and the production of sufficient antibodies to detect that virus is present.	The immune system is keeping the virus in check, but the T-cells are gradually being depleted.	Some sufferers manage to clear the virus from blood; others keep it in check indefinitely.	In 90% of sufferers, the immune system loses its battle and the victim is susceptible to a range of infections.

1000	500	200	T-cell count per ml of blood

fers no symptoms of ill health. During this so-called healthy stage of the infection, the virus can be passed on unwittingly. The duration of the second stage varies from person to person. Some people succumb to the virus a few years after infection; others stay healthy for a decade or more.

To determine the stage of an infected individual, doctors measure numbers of T-helper cells in the blood. In a healthy person there will be an average of 1,000 such cells per milliliter of blood. In an HIV-infected person nearing the end of the asymptomatic stage, there will be approximately 500 T-helper cells per milliliter of blood. Although a person may remain asymptomatic with a T-helper cell count lower than 500, the next stage of HIV is considered to have begun.

A diagnosis of AIDS used to be made when the T-helper cell count dropped below 200. As doctors found more and more people who remained healthy despite a count below 200, they began to review this criterion for diagnosis. Now an apparently healthy person with a low T-helper cell count is more likely to be described as having asymptomatic HIV. Doctors are now able to measure the amount of HIV itself in the blood, and this is proving to be a better indicator of health and long-term prognosis than the T-helper cell count.

Apart from measuring T-helper cells or HIV levels, doctors can also interpret physical symptoms as signs that the infection is progressing. People with symptomatic HIV commonly experience fever, night sweats, diarrhea, weight loss, chronically swollen lymph glands, disturbance of vision and mental function, and a persistent cough (these symptoms can also be due to infections that are unrelated to HIV). Sufferers may become ill with atypical pneumonia, oral yeast infections, persistent HERPES SIMPLEX, fungal skin infection, hairy LEUKO-PLAKIA and Kaposi's sarcoma. These are typical in people with some kind of immunodeficiency or other underlying condition, but they are not always caused by HIV.

HIV progression
This chart shows the course of HIV and how the T-cell count can drop, weakening the immune system.

TREATING HIV INFECTION

Doctors treat HIV disease in a variety of ways. They use anti-HIV drugs to directly attack the virus's enzymes or its ability to attach to cells. These drugs block receptors on the host cell or deactivate the attachment mechanism of the virus. Treatment is also given to boost the immune system, specifically the T-helper cells. Lastly, treatment of individual infections is attempted.

A person with HIV disease may be given a cocktail of drugs designed to beat the virus's ability to mutate and become resistant. There are a large number of these drugs, and recommendations change monthly. On top of this, HIV-related infections—which can be bacterial, viral or fungal—must be treated, perhaps several at a time. With these drug cocktails people are remaining free of symptoms for more than 10 years after becoming HIV positive. So far an HIV vaccine has proved elusive; the best hope may be a drug that can attack the virus while it is in the lymph nodes.

Living with HIV
The likelihood of an HIV-infected person developing AIDS increases as time goes past. Many people keep the virus in check for 5 to 10 years; some indefinitely.

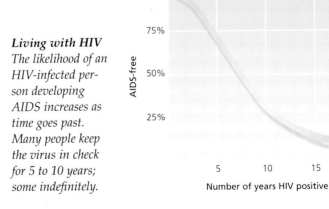

Other STDs

Sexually transmitted diseases are usually passed on by unprotected sex with an infected partner. While some diseases produce obvious symptoms, others, such as chlamydia, may be symptomless, meaning that they can be passed on unwittingly.

If a sexually transmitted disease (STD) is suspected, it is important to visit a physician or clinic immediately to get a professional diagnosis and receive prompt treatment. Many STDs are easily treated if they are detected at an early stage.

SYPHILIS

Syphilis can spread by vaginal or anal intercourse, oral sex, kissing, and skin-to-skin contact. It can also be passed on by infected blood transfusions and through the use of needles shared by drug abusers. Left untreated, it can be fatal.

Between 9 and 90 days after infection with syphilis, a small lump appears at the site of infection, usually on the genitals or around the anus, but sometimes inside the vagina or on the cervix. This lump develops into a firm sore or ulcer with raised borders, which is known as the primary chancre.

Several weeks after the chancre disappears, the disease moves into its second stage, in which lymph nodes all over the body may enlarge and dusky red spots appear on the skin, particularly on the hands and the feet. There may be sores on the hands and the feet; painless, wartlike growths on the genitals; headaches; low-grade fever; sore throat; and hair loss. Distinctive mucous patches known as snail-track ulcers may appear inside the mouth and throat. Complications, including a mild form of hepatitis, meningitis, kidney abnormalities and eye infections, may also occur.

Without treatment, these symptoms last about six weeks. Then syphilis enters a latent period in which the infected person feels healthy. Through some of the latent period syphilis continues to be infectious, and a woman can infect her unborn child for 8 to 10 years after becoming infected.

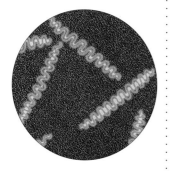

Treponema pallidum *Syphilis is caused by a bacterium that enters the body through mucous membranes and cuts in the skin.*

Neisseria gonorrhoeae *The bacterium responsible for gonorrhea can live in the vagina, cervix, urethra, rectum and eyes.*

VENEREAL DISEASES IN THE 19TH CENTURY

Treatment for STDs has advanced considerably in the last century. In the 19th century, doctors believed that syphilis and gonorrhea were the same disease at different stages. Patients were treated with mercury, which was painful and often ineffective. In 1909 doctors claimed that a derivative of arsenic was a cure for syphilis. Unfortunately, they would occasionally prescribe too much by accident, sometimes with fatal consequences. Today doctors rely on antibiotics to treat bacterial STDs.

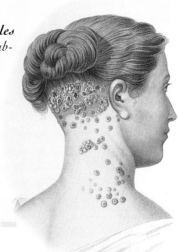

Syphilis pustules An engraving published in 1885 depicts chronic skin abscesses on the neck and base of the skull resulting from syphilis.

Some people are lucky enough not to enter the third stage of syphilis, but those who do suffer from brain damage, paralysis and cardiovascular problems, and finally die from the disease.

Syphilis can be diagnosed by microscopic examination of a smear from the primary chancre. In the later stages of syphilis, blood tests or spinal fluid examination is needed for diagnosis. High doses of antibiotics can cure syphilis, but any damage already done to the body cannot be reversed.

GONORRHEA

Neisseria gonorrhoeae is the bacterium responsible for gonorrhea. It can be passed on during unprotected anal or vaginal sex. Oral sex and deep kissing with an infected partner can cause throat infections.

Many people with gonorrhea have no symptoms and can pass on the infection unwittingly. Sometimes people discover they have gonorrhea only when they infect a partner who then experiences symptoms.

Typically, men infected with gonorrhea notice a discharge from the penis or anus and pain when urinating or defecating. The discharge is milky at first and becomes thick and yellow. Women are more likely than men to have symptomless gonorrhea. If there are symptoms, they may include a yellow vaginal or urethral discharge and frequent, urgent and painful urination. Unless gonorrhea is symptomless, signs of infection usually appear within two weeks of being exposed to the bacterium.

Untreated gonorrhea in men can lead to infection of the prostate gland, the epididymis and the seminal vesicles (see page 93). In extreme cases this can result in infertility, scarring of the urethra and problems with erections. In women untreated gonorrhea can spread through the cervix and uterus to the fallopian tubes, causing pelvic inflammatory disease (see page 144) and fertility problems.

In rare cases bacteria can spread into the abdominal cavity and cause inflammation of the membrane surrounding the liver. If bacteria enter the bloodstream, general illness, fever and arthritis may develop. Gonorrhea may also lead to eye infections, since an infected person can pass the bacteria from the genitals to the eyes on their hands. Babies born to infected mothers may develop serious illness or become blind.

Can We Talk About It?

DISCUSSING YOUR SEXUAL HEALTH

Most people find it hard to know where to start when broaching the subject of a sexually transmitted disease. Raise the subject before you become physically intimate, in a place where you can talk privately and without interruption. Presenting your partner with the facts about your STD and its method of transmission makes it easier for him or her to understand its implications. You may feel ashamed, confused and guilty, or you may worry that your relationship could end when you talk to your partner, but try to be strong minded. If you put off telling the truth, you will betray your partner and you may put his or her health at risk.

Your partner may respond with anger or shock, but both of you should try to avoid making hasty decisions until the information has sunk in. If your partner wants to ignore the dangers of an STD, don't be persuaded; if you have unprotected sexual intercourse you will face responsibility later for passing on the disease. In a relationship that is worth maintaining, sexual pleasure should be able to wait until you find out about the necessary precautions.

Doctors may take swabs from the vagina, urethra and anus (and sometimes the throat). The secretions are then cultured and examined microscopically. If the gonorrhea bacterium is present, antibiotics are prescribed. Some strains of gonorrhea have proved resistant to specific antibiotics. A strain of the infection known as Vietnam Rose, for instance, has evolved to produce an enzyme called penicillinase that inactivates penicillin. In such cases alternative antibiotics are prescribed.

NONSPECIFIC (NONGONOCOCCAL) URETHRITIS AND CHLAMYDIA

Nonspecific urethritis (NSU) is a condition that causes inflammation of the male urethra. It most commonly develops from a bacterium-like microorganism called *Chlamydia trachomatis* (other causes are shown on page 136). Chlamydia infections are transmitted by vaginal, anal and oral sex.

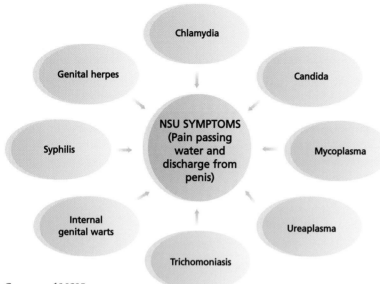

Causes of NSU
Nonspecific urethritis is very common. It can be caused by a wide range of the microorganisms responsible for STDs. Chlamydia is the usual cause.

In men the symptoms of chlamydial urethritis are burning pains when urinating and a urethral discharge that may be clear and watery or thick and yellow. Symptoms usually appear between one and three weeks after exposure to the infection. Some men may not have any symptoms.

Chlamydia in women is almost always symptomless, or the symptoms are so slight that they go unnoticed.

It is very important that chlamydia is treated promptly. In men it may lead to infections of the epididymis, prostate gland and rectum (see page 149). Occasionally it causes Reiter's syndrome, one of the main causes of arthritis in young men.

Because chlamydia is often symptomless in women, it may only be a complication of the infection that alerts a woman to the fact that something is wrong. As with gonorrhea, chlamydia can cause pelvic inflammatory disease (see page 144), which can result in blocked fallopian tubes and infertility. Chlamydia can be passed from mother to baby during childbirth.

The presence of a chlamydia/NSU infection in men is confirmed from swabs taken from the urethra. A slide is made from the swab and examined for pus cells. The specimen may also undergo special tests to try to distinguish chlamydia from the other causes of NSU. Samples of a man's urine are also examined for pus cells, and a rapid urine screening test can identify likely chlamydia infection. Female partners of men with NSU must always be screened and treated—they will rarely have symptoms of infection. Doctors will prescribe antibiotics to treat the disease.

CHANCROID

A common STD in tropical countries, chancroid is becoming more and more common in the U.S. and Europe. Caused by the bacterium *Hemophilus ducreyi*, chancroid should not be confused with a chancre, which is one of the main symptoms of the first stages of syphilis.

The infection usually starts with a small painful spot or pimple that develops into one or more ulcers. In men the ulcers appear on the foreskin or around the glans of the penis and in women around or inside the vagina. In both sexes there may be swollen, tender lymph nodes in the groin. Chancroid may appear around the anus if anal sex with an infected partner has taken place. The first signs of infection appear about a week after contact, and the ulcers can grow rapidly if not treated. If women have ulcers inside the vagina, they may not be aware that they are infected.

On rare occasions, the lymph nodes in the groin become large and swollen and rupture to release thick pus. Because chancroid causes large open sores, it may facilitate HIV transmission. Chancroid is diagnosed by physical examination and analysis of material from the ulcer under a microscope. Antibiotics are used to treat the disease.

TRICHOMONIASIS

Caused by a single-celled parasite called *Trichomonas vaginalis*, trichomoniasis is usually passed from person to person by sexual intercourse, although transmission is thought to be possible via moist objects

The Language of Sex

An old-fashioned term for sexually transmitted disease is venereal disease—in Latin "venereus" means "dedicated to Venus," the goddess of love and beauty. "The clap," a slang term for venereal disease, comes from the French word "clapoir," meaning "genital sore."

such as towels and washcloths. The parasite may be able to survive on damp or wet cloth for periods of up to 24 hours.

Men do not usually experience symptoms beyond mild urethral irritation. Women, in contrast, may have profound symptoms, such as a copious, foul-smelling, greenish yellow vaginal discharge. This can cause intense irritation and itching around the vaginal area. Intercourse may also become painful. Symptoms usually become apparent anywhere from a few days to a few weeks after contact with an infected person.

Trichomoniasis has been known to cause inflammation of the prostate gland in men. The infection can be passed from mother to baby during childbirth.

Trichomoniasis is diagnosed by identifying one of the parasites on a microscope slide, made when a swab is taken (see page 115) from the vagina or urethra. Treatment relies on antibiotics.

GENITAL WARTS

The virus responsible for causing genital warts is known as the human papillomavirus (HPV). More than 60 strains exist, a quarter of which cause warts that are sexually transmitted and appear only on the genitals. Genital warts are one of the most common STDs.

The wart virus can exist in a dormant or an active state. Warts can appear weeks or many months after initial exposure to infection—doctors do not know exactly what causes HPV to become active.

Genital warts start as tiny hard lumps on the penis, scrotum, vulva or anus that can be felt rather than seen (there may be one or several). They can also occur inside the vagina, urethra and rectum. Warts may stay the same size for weeks or months, or they may grow rapidly, becoming cauliflower-like in appearance. Rarely, they can grow large enough to block the vagina, urethra or anus.

Five types of the wart virus have been linked to cancerous growths of the genitals—particularly the cervix. A woman who has genital warts should have a Pap smear every six months to a year so that any abnormalities can be detected early. A test can confirm the presence of HPV on the cervix.

Warts on the external genitals can be diagnosed by physical examination. It takes a doctor experienced at recognizing genital warts to make a conclusive diagnosis, because there are other conditions, such as *Molluscum contagiosum* (a virus that causes small pearly lumps on the skin around the genitals and groin), that can resemble warts. Sometimes even normal lumps and bumps can be mistaken for genital warts. Wiping the potentially infected area with acetic acid (a vinegar-like liquid) can make the warts more easily visible.

The treatment for genital warts depends on how large they have grown, how persistent they are and whether they are internal or external. The first line of treatment for external warts is usually podophyllin solution applied directly to the warts and washed off later (podophyllin should never be applied to internal warts). Alternatively, a strong acid called trichloroacetic acid can be used. Large, internal or persistent warts

LYMPHATIC SYSTEM

The body's lymphatic system reacts to sexually transmitted disease in the same way as it does to other infections. Lymph nodes in the lymphatic system trap bacteria and viruses and then proceed to neutralize or destroy them. Sometimes the lymph nodes become enlarged in the process, which accounts for swollen glands.

Fighting infection
Lymphocytes attack and engulf foreign organisms that get past the body's outer defenses.

Lymphatics carry the protective fluid, lymph, around the body

Lymph capillaries carry lymph into larger vessels

Spleen produces antibodies and white blood cells that are carried around the body in the lymph

Lymph nodes become swollen when the body is fighting infection

SCABIES

Since it is not transmitted by sexual intercourse, scabies is not classified as an STD. However, most cases are acquired through skin-to-skin contact. Scabies is a microscopic mite that burrows under the skin, forming a small bump. It lays eggs and the new mites form thin, wavy burrow lines extending from the original site. The main symptom of the infection is intense itching. The preferred body areas of scabies mites include such warm, moist creases as in the armpits and on the genitals or the tops of the thighs. Scabies is treated with topical medications.

CAUSES AND TREATMENTS OF COMMON STDS

STD	CAUSE	TREATMENT
Syphilis	*Treponema pallidum**	Antibiotics
Gonorrhea	*Neisseria gonorrhoea**	Antibiotics
NSU/NGU	Multiple causes (see diagram page 136)	Antibiotics
Chancroid	*Hemophilus ducreyi**	Antibiotics
Trichomoniasis	*Trichomonas vaginalis***	Antibiotics
"Crabs"/pubic lice	*Pediculosis pubis***	Topical insecticide
Scabies	*Sarcoptes scabiei***	Topical insecticide
Genital warts	Human papillomavirus***	Podophyllin, trichloroacetic acid, electrocautery, cryotherapy, laser surgery
Genital herpes	Herpes simplex 1 and 2***	Antiviral drugs
Hepatitis B	Hepatitis B virus***	No specific treatment; bed rest, nutritious diet, preventive vaccine
Hepatitis C	Hepatitis C virus***	Interferon may prevent or slow progression of the disease.
HIV/AIDS	Human immunodeficiency virus***	Combinations of antiviral, immune-boosting and antibiotic drugs

*Bacterium **Parasite ***Virus

Pubic lice *Specially adapted claws allow the pubic louse to cling firmly to the hair of its host, where it feeds on the host's blood and lays its eggs.*

can be treated with cryotherapy (freezing), electrocautery (destroying tissue using an electric current) or laser surgery.

PUBIC LICE

Also known as "crabs," pubic lice are usually passed between people during sexual intimacy—not necessarily intercourse—but can also be caught from infested bedding, clothing, saunas and tanning beds.

Pubic lice feed on blood and can survive in a warm environment away from the body for up to 24 hours. Most people notice itching from lice bites between 5 and 14 days after infection. How quickly the infection is noticed depends on how many lice are present and how long it takes to become sensitized to the bites. People may also see small, brown, flat objects attached to their pubic hairs. The eggs are tiny and pale. Excessive scratching of the pubic area can lead to a secondary bacterial infection of the skin.

Pubic lice are easily recognizable under a microscope and can be treated with applications of prescription lotions or shampoos. Sexual partners should be treated, and bedding and clothes should be washed in very hot water or dry-cleaned.

GENITAL HERPES

There are two types of herpes virus, Herpes simplex 1 and Herpes simplex 2. Herpes simplex 1 typically causes cold sores around the mouth, and Herpes simplex 2 is usually responsible for the sexually transmitted herpes sores that affect the genitals. However, both types of virus can infect the lips and genitals.

Herpes viruses live in nerve cells, either lying dormant for the whole of a person's life or reactivating sporadically, causing new outbreaks of sores. Lowered immunity, stress, fatigue, strong sunlight and tanning beds can all cause the virus to reactivate.

The herpes virus is unpredictable. Some people become infected and never have symptoms, others experience an outbreak of sores within two days to two weeks of being infected, while still others suffer herpes attacks months or years after first becoming infected. It is generally accepted that the first attack of herpes is the worst and that subsequent attacks diminish in severity and occur further apart with time.

First symptoms include a tingling or itching sensation in the genital area, general malaise, a slight fever and swollen, tender lymph nodes. Sometimes there is discomfort on passing urine. Within hours, small painful blisters appear on the glans of the penis and the foreskin in men and the vagina, cervix or perineum in women. The blisters also appear on the anus and on the skin around the genitals. The blisters burst or are scratched open to reveal painful ulcers that can take between two days and three weeks to heal. Open blisters are highly infectious.

Genital herpes can spread to other parts of the sufferer's body—not just to the area around the lips and nose but to the eyes and throat as well. Women with herpes sores can pass the virus to their babies during delivery, and in the most serious cases this can cause brain infections and blindness.

A doctor can usually identify herpes sores by physical examination. The virus can be cultured from a swab taken from an ulcer.

Herpes is a chronic disease with no absolute cure. At the first signs of infection, doctors usually prescribe an antiviral drug such as acyclovir, which effectively limits the intensity and duration of symptoms and can be taken to prevent recurrence. If herpes attacks are linked to stress, relaxation therapies may help to prevent outbreaks.

HEPATITIS B

Like HIV, the hepatitis B virus lives in blood and body fluids and can be transmitted sexually, by sharing needles or by receiving an infected blood transfusion. It can also be transmitted on unsterilized needles used for acupuncture or tattoos. Hepatitis B is much more infectious than HIV, and researchers have isolated the virus in body secretions such as tears and sweat.

The hepatitis virus causes inflammation of the liver. Symptoms appear between six weeks and six months after infection (although the disease can sometimes be symptomless). Generalized aches and pains, mild fever, pain in the small joints of the hands and feet, tenderness in the liver area, nausea, loss of appetite, and jaundice may all be symptoms of hepatitis B.

Chronic forms of hepatitis B can lead to progressive liver damage and eventually cirrhosis (a condition in which the liver can no longer effectively remove toxic substances from the blood) and cancer of the liver. In places where hepatitis B is very common, such as Southeast Asia, tropical Africa and parts of China, it is estimated that 1 percent of those infected die from acute liver failure; 25 percent die from cirrhosis of the liver, and 5 percent die from cancer of the liver. There is an 80 percent chance that a woman carrying the hepatitis B virus will pass it on to her children at the time of their birth.

Hepatitis B can be diagnosed by a blood test. There is no cure, and treatment consists of bed rest and a nutritious diet. Doctors recommend vaccination for people who are at high risk, such as health-care workers, people who have multiple sexual partners and intravenous drug users.

HEPATITIS C

Hepatitis C is a highly aggressive strain of hepatitis. Like hepatitis B, it is transmitted in blood and semen, can stay in the body for life, and may cause liver damage. It does not, however, seem to be as easily transmitted sexually as hepatitis B or HIV. Twenty percent of hepatitis C sufferers develop cirrhosis, liver failure or cancer (10 percent die from these complications). There is no vaccine against hepatitis C. Worldwide, there may be 500 million hepatitis C carriers.

INFECTION WITH THE HEPATITIS B VIRUS

Hepatitis B can be symptomless, but an illness similar to influenza accompanied by jaundice and localized swelling is common. The virus may remain in the body and become chronic (persisting for a long time), so that the liver cannot function properly, and the risk of liver cancer is increased.

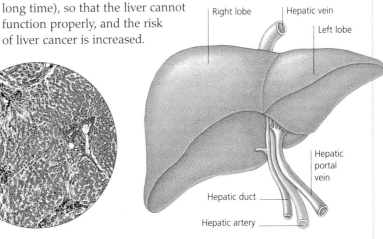

Damaged liver cells
Chronic hepatitis B can cause structural changes to the liver.

Inflammation of the liver
When inflamed the liver cannot fully perform its normal functions of regulating the levels of blood chemicals and removing toxins.

Female Disorders

Certain changes occur normally as part of a woman's reproductive life cycle: irregular bleeding around the time of puberty and menopause; amenorrhea during pregnancy; and premenstrual syndrome in the days leading up to menstruation.

If symptoms of female disorders do not coincide with certain stages of a woman's reproductive cycle, they may be signs of an underlying gynecological condition. Anything that is unusual or that does not have a straightforward explanation should be investigated by a doctor.

PREMENSTRUAL SYNDROME (PMS)

During the days leading up to menstruation, many women experience a combination of physical and emotional symptoms that have come to be known as premenstrual syndrome (PMS). For most women, the symptoms are minor, but in 10 percent of cases the symptoms are severe enough to disrupt normal life. PMS usually occurs between 5 and 12 days before a period and disappears within 24 hours before or after menstruation begins. The wide range of symptoms includes emotional instability, anxiety, depression, angry or tearful outbursts, bloating and swelling, constipation, headaches, breast tenderness, eating disturbances, changes in sexual desire, fatigue, and clumsiness.

Eating disturbances such as binge eating and craving sweet foods are typical PMS symptoms. These may be caused by low blood sugar that results from changes in the way the body processes carbohydrates.

Doctors have not identified exactly what causes PMS, but they believe it possible that high estrogen levels at the end of the menstrual cycle have a negative effect on the efficiency of the kidneys. This results in the retention of salt and water and the swelling of body tissues. Swollen tissues in the intestines may cause constipation and a bloated abdomen; swelling in the brain may cause headaches and emotional symptoms; breast swelling causes breast tenderness.

Some experts attribute PMS symptoms to an imbalance of progesterone and estrogen. Suppressing ovulation seems to cure PMS, which has led doctors to prescribe the contraceptive pill to sufferers. Another treatment is diuretic medication to eliminate excess fluid, but it has little effect.

Apart from prescription drugs, various natural remedies have proved effective for PMS symptoms. Many women report that homeopathy and yoga are helpful, as are high doses of vitamin B_6 (pyridoxine). High estrogen levels are thought to lead to reduced levels of vitamin B_6 in the body, which can cause low levels of certain brain chemicals, resulting in depressed mood and irritability. Gamma linoleic acid, found in evening primrose oil, is also recommended.

Easing breast discomfort Simple massage techniques can ease premenstrual breast pain. Using the backs of the fingers, make gentle circling movements between the breast and the armpit.

In addition to symptom relief, women suffering from PMS also need support and understanding from their partners and family.

MENORRHAGIA

Abnormally heavy menstrual loss of blood is known as menorrhagia. Blood loss can vary from woman to woman and even from one menstrual cycle to the next, but a woman suffering from menorrhagia loses more than 2.5 fluid ounces (80 ml) of blood per cycle. Heavy periods are not only uncomfortable, they can also cause iron deficiency anemia (in which the oxygen-carrying pigment in the blood falls below normal levels).

Menorrhagia is sometimes caused by the use of an intrauterine device (IUD) or by an imbalance of the hormones estrogen and progesterone (see page 101). Some women experience heavy bleeding around the time of menopause. Because heavy bleeding may also be caused by fibroids, polyps, endometriosis or malignancies, a doctor should always be consulted. Treatment for menorrhagia depends on the cause; doctors may recommend *DILATATION AND CURETTAGE (D&C)*, hormone treatment or, in severe cases, removal of the uterus.

DYSMENORRHEA

"Primary dysmenorrhea" is the term for the cramps that often accompany menstruation. It is common in teenage girls and young women and is thought to be due to a high level of the hormone prostaglandin, which is secreted by the uterine lining. Prostaglandin makes the muscular wall of the uterus contract, causing acute cramplike pains. Women who experience severe dysmenorrhea may secrete 15 times as much prostaglandin as women who do not suffer from period pain.

The pain of primary dysmenorrhea is usually centered in the lower abdomen and may radiate down the inner thighs and into the back. The standard treatment is painkilling medication. Aspirin, which acts directly on prostaglandin, is often more

fact or fiction?

PMS is a psychosomatic problem.

Fiction. In the past some doctors believed that PMS was a psychological condition and treated women with tranquilizers. Today PMS is recognized as a problem with a physiological cause: tranquilizers should never be prescribed as a treatment unless there are other disorders.

effective than much stronger painkillers. Other antiprostaglandin drugs, such as the fenamic acids and naproxen, are prescribed specifically for painful periods.

Suppressing ovulation with the contraceptive pill is another way to control period pain. Some women also find that self-help measures, such as exercise or calcium supplements, alleviate pain.

Secondary dysmenorrhea is menstrual pain that arises for the first time in an adult woman whose menstrual cycle is well established. A medical reason usually surfaces for the sudden onset of menstrual pain, and secondary dysmenorrhea should always be investigated by a doctor. Common causes of the condition include endometriosis, fibroids and pelvic inflammatory disease (PID).

Uterine cavity
Myometrium
Endometrium

Menstrual cramps The muscular wall of the uterus, the myometrium, contracts to cause cramping pains during a menstrual period.

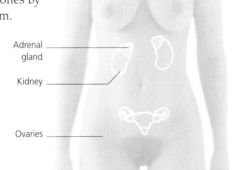

THE BODY'S HORMONE-PRODUCING SITES

The hormones responsible for sexual development and function are produced and secreted into the bloodstream by a number of different endocrine glands. The pituitary gland is known as the master gland, since it coordinates the activities of other endocrine glands.

Some menstrual disorders result from over- or underproduction of hormones by the endocrine system.

Menstrual control Hormones that can influence the menstrual cycle are released by the brain, the ovaries, and the adrenal and thyroid glands.

Hypothalamus
Pituitary gland
Thyroid gland
Thymus
Adrenal gland
Kidney
Ovaries

141

CYSTITIS—AN INFLAMMATION OF THE BLADDER

Cystitis is one of women's most common complaints. The main symptom is frequent, urgent urination—typically a small amount of urine is passed and there is stinging or burning pain in the urethra. Sometimes blood or pus may be visible in the urine. Pain in the lower abdomen and back, and fever and malaise, may indicate that the infection has spread to the kidneys.

The causes of cystitis include infection, allergies and physical trauma. The bacterium that is often responsible for cystitis lives naturally in the bowel and rectum, but it can easily be transferred to the vaginal area or the urethra. Some women suffer cystitis symptoms in response to highly perfumed products such as vaginal deodorants or soap. Cystitis may also be caused by trauma to the urethra. Sometimes during sexual intercourse the penis hits the opening of the urethra, causing tiny abrasions. This can happen when the vagina is insufficiently lubricated.

Cystitis can become recurrent, but symptoms are often moderated by drinking large amounts of water. Over-the-counter medications that make the urine more alkaline will reduce pain on urination and render the urine less hospitable to bacteria.

If self-help measures for cystitis fail, a doctor may prescribe antibiotics. A urine sample will be taken to confirm that cystitis is due to bacteria and, if it is, which bacterium is responsible.

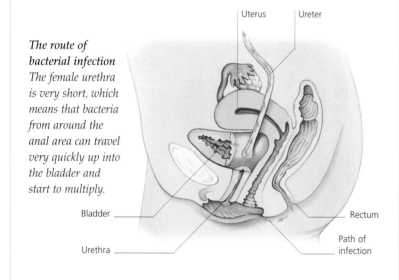

The route of bacterial infection
The female urethra is very short, which means that bacteria from around the anal area can travel very quickly up into the bladder and start to multiply.

Uterus | Ureter

Bladder

Urethra

Rectum

Path of infection

IRREGULAR BLEEDING

By their late teens, most girls have established a regular pattern of menstrual bleeding—they have a menstrual period at regular intervals and bleed for approximately the same number of days each month. If bleeding is erratic for three months or more, menstruation is termed irregular. During some stages of a woman's life, such as puberty and menopause, this is normal, but irregular menstruation at other times may be a sign of an underlying problem. Common causes of irregular menstruation include stress, hormonal imbalances and overweight or underweight. More serious causes include ectopic pregnancy, miscarriage, polycystic ovaries, cervical or uterine cancer, polyps, fibroids, thyroid gland problems, and endometriosis.

The treatment for irregular menstruation depends entirely on the cause. Unusual bleeding should always be investigated by a doctor, who may perform diagnostic techniques such as an endometrial biopsy or dilatation and curettage (D&C). These procedures will allow diagnosis of any abnormality or malignancy.

Contraceptives such as the pill and IUDs can cause some bleeding or spotting between periods. This is not true menstrual bleeding but a recognized side effect of these contraceptives. If bleeding is heavier than occasional spotting or persists for more than three months, a doctor should be consulted about the possibility of changing contraceptives.

AMENORRHEA

When a woman never menstruates, her condition is termed amenorrhea. There are two types of amenorrhea: primary amenorrhea, when menstruation has not started by age 16, and secondary amenorrhea, when a woman with an established menstrual cycle suddenly stops menstruating.

Primary amenorrhea may be caused by low body weight or a family tendency of late menarche (first menstruation). Rarely, primary amenorrhea is caused by a physical or hormonal abnormality.

Secondary amenorrhea is a normal result of pregnancy and a permanent result of hysterectomy and menopause unless hormone replacement therapy (HRT) is prescribed (see page 78). It can also signal problems such as endocrine or ovarian disorders, or *ANOREXIA NERVOSA*.

The contraceptive pill may cause temporary amenorrhea—when a woman stops taking the pill it can be months before her menstrual cycle returns to normal.

Amenorrhea should be investigated by a doctor. If no cause is apparent from either a woman's gynecological history or physical examination, then her thyroid, pituitary and ovarian hormone levels will be measured.

If a woman suffering from diagnosed amenorrhea wants to become pregnant, a doctor may need to prescribe a fertility drug that will induce ovulation.

CANDIDIASIS

This yeast infection occurs around the vulva and vagina and occasionally in the mouth. The symptoms of candidiasis are soreness around the vulva and vagina and a thick, white odorless vaginal discharge. There may be mild or severe vulval irritation.

Candidiasis occurs only when the normal, healthy environment of the vagina is disturbed. Taking antibiotics and using highly perfumed soaps on the genital area are two common ways of acquiring a yeast infection. An increase in the intake of dairy products has also been claimed to cause candidiasis. Rarely, candidiasis is a symptom of a serious illness, such as *DIABETES*.

Self-help techniques include gentle washing with warm water (never soap) and wearing loose cotton underwear. A tampon dipped in live yogurt and inserted into the vagina may be helpful, but some women say it is unlikely to help once the infection is established. Medical treatment for yeast infections consists of antifungal suppositories or creams or oral medication.

Candidiasis is not considered an STD, and can occur in women who are virgins. It can, however, be passed to a woman's sexual partner—a recurrent infection may mean that the couple is passing it back and forth.

FIBROIDS

Also known as myomas, fibroids are benign growths of the muscle tissue in or on the wall of the uterus. Fibroids may be symptomless, unless they have grown large enough to press on nearby organs, such as the bladder or the bowel, causing problems such as frequent urination or constipation. If a fibroid grows inward to the cavity of the uterus, it may result in heavy or irregular menstruation. Fibroids can develop to the size of a grapefruit or even larger, but they usually exist as small discrete lumps inside the wall of the uterus. Small fibroids should not have any effect on fertility or pregnancy. They should be monitored by a doctor, but do not normally require treatment.

The cause of fibroids is not known, but their growth seems to depend on estrogen stimulation. When estrogen levels fall at menopause, fibroids stop developing and typically decrease in size. Therefore, menopausal women with large fibroids may not be prescribed HRT.

Large fibroids that cause symptoms or present a danger during pregnancy because they obstruct the birth canal need medical attention. Occasionally fibroids can become infected or start to degenerate, causing pain. Rarely, fibroids can grow on stalks that can twist and cut off the fibroid's blood supply, causing acute pain. Severe fibroids may be treated by hysterectomy or by myomectomy (a surgical technique that removes the fibroids but leaves the uterus intact).

BACTERIAL VAGINOSIS

A vaginal infection known as bacterial vaginosis is caused by an overgrowth of the normal vaginal bacteria. The main symptom is a thin, gray discharge that has a fishy odor. Sometimes there may be vulval burning or itchiness, but the infection can also be symptomless.

Some women who use a diaphragm or condoms and spermicide (or women who have genital warts) experience repeated episodes of bacterial vaginosis—this suggests that the infection may occur more readily when there is a change in the acidity of the vagina.

Treating bacterial vaginosis with antibiotics usually eliminates the problem.

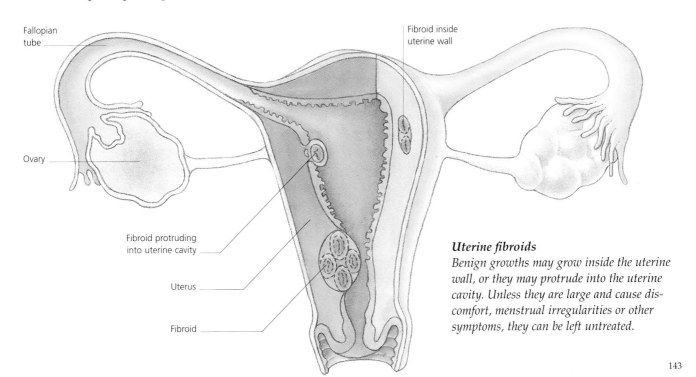

Fallopian tube

Fibroid inside uterine wall

Ovary

Fibroid protruding into uterine cavity

Uterus

Fibroid

Uterine fibroids
Benign growths may grow inside the uterine wall, or they may protrude into the uterine cavity. Unless they are large and cause discomfort, menstrual irregularities or other symptoms, they can be left untreated.

Bartholin's glands
Most women are not aware that they have Bartholin's glands unless these glands become infected and form a painful abscess that requires treatment. Situated on either side of the vagina, they secrete some of the lubrication produced during sexual arousal.

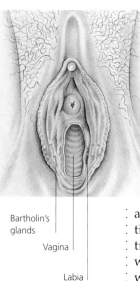

Bartholin's glands

Vagina

Labia

POLYCYSTIC OVARY

Also known as Stein-Leventhal syndrome, polycystic ovary is a condition in which the ovaries enlarge and contain multiple cysts. Sufferers experience scanty menstrual periods or do not menstruate and are often infertile. About 50 percent of women with polycystic ovary have excessive body and facial hair and a tendency to obesity. Typically, a girl with polycystic ovary disease menstruates normally for about two years after *MENARCHE*, then her periods become increasingly irregular and may cease completely.

Polycystic ovary is caused by an imbalance of the hormones that control ovulation. This imbalance prevents ovulation and causes excess production of testosterone. The condition is diagnosed from its symptoms and by physical examination, *ULTRASOUND* scans, *LAPAROSCOPY* and blood hormone tests.

Doctors usually prescribe hormone-based drugs to treat polycystic ovary—sometimes the contraceptive pill can effectively regulate a woman's menstrual cycle. Occasionally a wedge of ovarian tissue is removed surgically. The type of treatment depends on the severity of a woman's symptoms and whether or not she wishes to become pregnant in the future.

BARTHOLINITIS

There are two pea-sized glands on either side of the entrance to the vagina known as Bartholin's glands. Their normal function is to secrete lubricating fluid during sexual arousal. Occasionally they become infected, resulting in a condition called bartholinitis, which causes the glands to swell and become sore, sometimes to the extent that even walking becomes painful. If the duct from the gland becomes blocked as a result of infection and subsequent scarring, a Bartholin's cyst forms. This is a painless swelling of the gland, but the cyst is vulnerable to repeated infections.

Bartholinitis can be treated with antibiotics. In the case of a severe infection where an abscess forms, it may be necessary to drain the abscess surgically. If a Bartholin's cyst develops, it may be surgically removed or the duct leading to the gland may be turned into an open pouch. Even if both Bartholin's glands have to be removed, the vagina will still produce adequate lubrication during sexual intercourse.

CERVICAL AND UTERINE POLYPS

Polyps are small, fingerlike growths that occur on the mucous membrane of the uterine lining and the cervical canal. There may be one or many, and they are usually benign rather than malignant. Polyps may be symptomless, or they may cause bleeding between periods or bleeding after intercourse. If they ulcerate, they can become infected, causing a vaginal discharge.

Doctors treat polyps that cause troublesome symptoms with dilatation and curettage (D&C) or electrocautery (in which an electric current is used to destroy tissue), depending on whether they are in the uterus or the cervix. If a malignancy is suspected, the polyps will be removed and examined for evidence of cancer.

PELVIC INFLAMMATORY DISEASE (PID)

Infection or disease of the pelvic organs results from a variety of causes, most commonly sexually transmitted diseases (STDs; see page 134) such as chlamydia and gonorrhea. Less commonly, pelvic inflammatory disease (PID) may occur after miscarriage, abortion or childbirth. It is a serious infection that can permanently affect fertility. Infections can enter

OVARIAN CYSTS

Cysts in or on the ovaries are common and, in most cases, benign. They are usually fluid-filled sacs, although they can be solid growths. Many women who have ovarian cysts do not experience symptoms and may not know they have them. Most cysts need no evaluation or treatment. When symptoms occur, these are likely to be abdominal discomfort, pain during intercourse and irregular menstrual bleeding or amenorrhea. If a cyst twists or ruptures, there may be pain, nausea and fever. If a cyst causes discomfort or needs to be investigated for malignancy, it may be viewed or biopsied through a laparoscope or surgically removed.

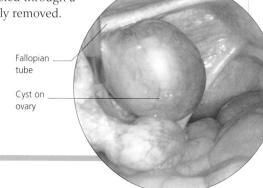

Treating large cysts
Occasionally, when a cyst is very large, the whole ovary may need to be surgically removed.

Fallopian tube

Cyst on ovary

the reproductive tract through the vaginal entrance and then travel up through the cervix and uterus to the fallopian tubes. The cervix is usually an effective barrier against any infection, but infecting organisms can enter when carried by sperm. Infection is also more likely during menstruation, when the cervical canal is not filled with protective mucus. Inserting objects into the uterus or the cervix (during abortion or the insertion of an intrauterine device, for example) increases the risk of PID. Occasionally PID can result from infection occurring elsewhere in the pelvis, such as the appendix.

PID should always receive medical attention. It can cause mild or intense abdominal pain, pain during intercourse, fever and vaginal discharge. Menstrual bleeding may be heavier, and spotting may appear between periods. Alternatively, there may be mild symptoms or none at all.

Treatment for PID consists of a course of antibiotics and bed rest. Taking time to rest and recover is important to minimize the possibility of scarring inside the fallopian tubes. In severe cases, a woman may need an operation to drain pus from the fallopian tubes, but this is unusual.

ENDOMETRIOSIS

The tissue lining the uterus is called the endometrium. Endometriosis is a painful gynecological condition in which fragments of endometrial tissue adhere to other parts of the body. Sites where this can happen include the fallopian tubes, the bladder, the ovaries, the lining of the abdominal cavity and even the intestines.

Displaced endometrial tissue is not malignant, but it does respond to a woman's menstrual cycle as if it were inside the uterus. This means it builds up and breaks down and bleeds in a monthly cycle. Because the blood cannot escape from abnormal sites, it may cause inflammation, pain and cyst formation. Scar tissue may form over the site of inflammation, causing adhesions in the abdomen.

Common symptoms of endometriosis are abnormal menstrual bleeding, abdominal pain and bloating, lower back pain, and pain during menstruation, intercourse and bowel movements. Endometriosis is also associated with infertility, and, as with other chronic painful conditions, sufferers may experience insomnia and depression.

The symptoms of endometriosis are relieved during pregnancy and frequently disappear permanently after a woman gives birth. Doctors often advise sufferers to try to conceive sooner rather than later if they know that they want children. Treating endometriosis with hormonal drugs can be successful, as can surgical treatments. Hysterectomy used to be recommended for women who did not want to become pregnant in the future, and many women have obtained relief in this way. If a surgeon removes the ovaries in addition to the uterus, a woman will go on to experience premature menopause (hormone replacement therapy is usually prescribed in such cases). Unfortunately, if the ovaries are not removed, any remaining endometrial tissue may still respond to the hormones they produce.

UTERINE PROLAPSE

The uterus normally rests in the abdomen, supported by muscle and connective tissue, and only the cervix projects down into the vagina. When the muscles and ligaments become weak, the uterus can sag, causing a condition called uterine prolapse.

Prolapse occurs in degrees. In a mild case of prolapse the uterus descends slightly, so that the cervix sits lower down in the vagina than usual. In more severe cases the

The complications of PID Infection can travel through the female reproductive tract, with consequences such as infertility.

Possible sites of endometriosis Endometrial growths may occur on any of the pelvic organs. One explanation of endometriosis is that menstrual fluid, containing fragments of endometrium, flows backward into the fallopian tubes and into the pelvic cavity.

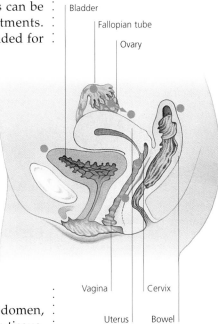

Bladder

Fallopian tube

Ovary

Vagina

Cervix

Uterus

Bowel

Blocked fallopian tubes, leading to ectopic pregnancy

Blocked fallopian tubes, leading to subfertility

Transmission of infection to baby at birth

Recurrent episodes of PID that do not respond to treatment

The complications of PID

Spread of infection to blood, leading to septicemia

cervix moves a long way down the vagina—this can be extremely uncomfortable and penetration during sexual intercourse can become difficult or impossible. In very severe cases the cervix and part of the uterus can actually protrude outside the vaginal opening. There may be no symptoms of prolapse or there may be a dragging sensation in the lower abdomen. Backache may occur, and sometimes stress incontinence (leaking small amounts of urine on sneezing, coughing or exertion).

Overstretched, weakened muscles can be caused by pregnancy and frequent births. Weak pelvic muscles can be further weakened by heavy lifting, obesity, constipation or a chronic cough (all of which increase intra-abdominal pressure). Uterine prolapse is more common in postmenopausal women, as this is when pelvic muscles and ligaments slacken.

In mild cases of prolapse, exercising the *PUBOCOCCYGEAL (PC) MUSCLES* by repeatedly contracting and relaxing them can help. Alternatively, a device called a ring pessary may be used to support the uterus, but this can erode the already thin urogenital tissues of postmenopausal women.

In severe cases surgery can repair the front and back walls of the vagina or repair defects in the muscles and connective tissue supporting the uterus. A hysterectomy may be advised for postmenopausal women.

CERVICAL CANCER

Early cervical cancer is symptomless and invisible to the naked eye. It is not until the cancer has progressed that symptoms such as bleeding between menstrual periods or after intercourse appear. Occasionally the malignant area becomes infected, causing a vaginal discharge. Pain is not a symptom until late into the disease, when the cancer has spread to other pelvic organs.

There are cell changes in the cervix, known as precancerous changes, that precede malignancy, and these can be easily detected by a Pap test. This involves collecting some cells from the cervix and examining them microscopically (see page 148). If more severe abnormalities are present, a colposcopy (a detailed examination using a magnifying device) may be recommended.

Treatment depends on the stage of the disease, whether it has spread and whether a woman is planning to have children in the future. Destruction of cancerous cells on the cervix can be carried out using heat (electrocautery and laser treatment) or cold treatment (cryosurgery). Hysterectomy is not usually performed unless the cancer has spread beyond the cervix.

TYPES OF HYSTERECTOMY

The surgical removal of the uterus is known as hysterectomy. It is carried out when the uterus is severely prolapsed, when conditions such as endometriosis have not responded to other treatments or when cancer is present. In some types of hysterectomy a woman's ovaries are removed. This brings about premature menopause (unless the woman is postmenopausal).

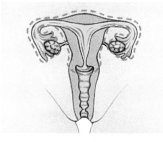

Hysterectomy and bilateral salpingo-oophorectomy
The fallopian tubes and ovaries are surgically removed as well as the uterus and the cervix.

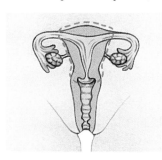

Hysterectomy
The uterus and cervix are removed, and the fallopian tubes and ovaries are left intact.

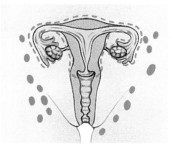

Radical hysterectomy
If a reproductive cancer has spread, the pelvic lymph nodes are removed as well.

ENDOMETRIAL CANCER

Cancer of the uterine lining, often referred to as uterine or endometrial cancer, is most common in postmenopausal women. Symptoms are irregular menstrual periods, spotting between periods or after sexual intercourse, and, if a woman is postmenopausal, a bloodstained discharge.

Endometrial cancer is diagnosed from a sample of endometrial tissue. It is often treated with a full hysterectomy (removing the ovaries, fallopian tubes and uterus). If the cancer has spread, *RADIATION THERAPY* and *CHEMOTHERAPY* may be given.

Breast Cancer

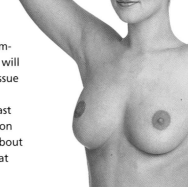

In its early stages breast cancer is usually detected as a small, painless lump found in the upper, outer quadrant of the breast (although it can be in any part of the breast). Occasionally the skin overlying the lump appears puckered or dimpled, and in advanced stages there may be ulceration. Other warning signs include a bloody discharge from the nipple or a nipple that is becoming inverted. Only one in five lumps is malignant, but regular breast self-examination is an important part of breast care and, if any unusual changes are noticed, immediate medical attention is critical.

The best time to conduct breast self-examination is just after the end of a menstrual period (the breasts are often lumpy in the days prior to menstruation). Women should look carefully at their breasts in a mirror as well as feeling them manually.

One way to detect breast cancer early is by mammography, which provides an X-ray image of the breasts. If a solid lump is detected, doctors will perform a biopsy, in which a piece of tissue is removed to establish whether it is malignant. If it is, a biopsy of the lymph nodes will reveal whether the cancer has spread this far.

Radiation, chemotherapy and hormonal treatment may be recommended, and surgery (see below) will aim to preserve as much breast tissue as possible. Women may also be offered cosmetic surgery and breast reconstruction. With early detection and treatment of breast cancer, about 85 percent of women survive for at least five years.

Looking at the breasts

Use a mirror to study the contours of each breast. Do this with the arms beside the body and then raised behind the head. Look for abnormalities.

Feeling the breasts

Pressing gently with the middle three fingers, trace large circles around each breast. Feel for unusual lumps. Check under the collarbone and armpits.

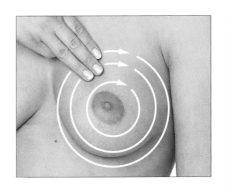

TYPES OF COMMON BREAST SURGERY

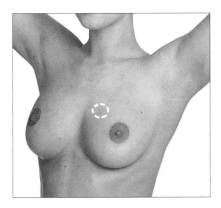

Lumpectomy

Removing a lump from the breast is a straightforward operation that leaves the whole of the nipple and most of the breast intact. As well as the lump, a surgeon will usually remove a small area of surrounding tissue.

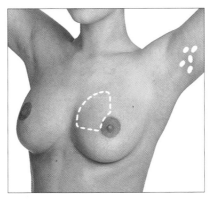

Partial mastectomy

When a cancerous area is not confined to a small discrete lump, a partial mastectomy is usually carried out. A sample of the lymph nodes in the armpit may also be taken. Alternatively, they may be removed.

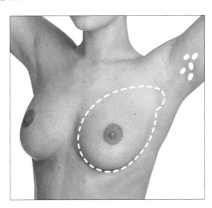

Total mastectomy

The whole breast, including the nipple and areola, and sometimes the lymph nodes, is removed. The only breast surgery that is more extensive than this is a radical mastectomy, involving the removal of muscles. This is rare.

THE PAP TEST—AN EARLY WARNING FOR CERVICAL CANCER

A Pap test is carried out in a doctor's office. The woman lies on her back or on her side with her knees bent, and an instrument called a speculum is inserted into the vagina. By opening the speculum inside the vagina, the doctor has a clear view of the cervix. A sample of cells is collected and transferred onto a glass slide for microscopic examination.

A woman should have her first Pap test when she turns 18 or after she starts to have intercourse. Women should discuss with their physicians how often the test should be done. Most physicians recommend annual tests to age 35 and, if there has been no abnormality, tests every two or three years until age 69.

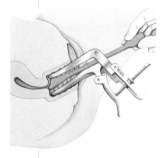

Having a Pap test
A small spatula or brush is used to collect cells from inside the cervical opening.

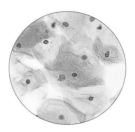

A healthy result
Cells taken from a healthy cervix are all roughly the same size and have small central nuclei.

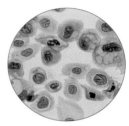

Signs of abnormality
Cancerous or precancerous changes include enlarged cell nuclei and coarse clumps and strands.

EARLY DIAGNOSIS

In the U.S., cancer of the genital organs accounts for approximately 250,000 deaths per year. It has been estimated that if women had Pap smears at least every two years and sought early medical advice about abnormal bleeding during and after menopause, around 100,000 lives could be saved over the next five years. Early diagnosis and prompt treatment are essential. Early diagnosis depends largely on women getting regular checkups and seeking early advice about unusual symptoms.

OVARIAN CANCER

Cancer of the ovaries is less prevalent than cervical or endometrial cancer, but it is responsible for more deaths each year than any other pelvic cancer. Although ovarian cancer can affect any age group, women aged 50 and over are most at risk. Ovarian cysts (see page 144) are not usually cancerous.

Ovarian cancer is often symptomless until it spreads elsewhere. Sometimes the first warning signs are digestive symptoms such as nausea. Alternatively, if the tumor spreads, fluid may collect in the abdomen, causing swelling.

A doctor will look for a diseased ovary using *LAPAROSCOPY*. He or she will examine ovarian tissue removed from an enlarged ovary to make a diagnosis. If malignancy is discovered, surgery involving the removal of the ovaries, fallopian tubes and uterus will probably be recommended. Radiation therapy and *CHEMOTHERAPY* are often recommended following surgery.

VAGINAL CANCER AND DES

Vaginal cancer was once almost unknown. Rarely was a woman diagnosed with the disease, and she was almost certainly in the 50-plus age range. When the incidence of vaginal cancer began to rise in the 20th century, especially in younger women, doctors realized that it was an iatrogenic disease (medically induced) caused by a synthetic hormone called diethylstilbestrol (DES).

DES was given to pregnant women by obstetricians to prevent miscarriage. Unfortunately, not only did it have no impact on rates of miscarriage, but it also became linked with an increased risk of a particularly rare form of vaginal cancer. The increased numbers of women who were being diagnosed with vaginal cancer more commonly had mothers who had been given DES during pregnancy.

The symptoms of vaginal cancer include a bloodstained vaginal discharge and spotting after intercourse. If the cancer has spread, other symptoms may include pain on intercourse, when urinating and when passing a bowel movement. Treatment depends on the extent of the disease, but hysterectomy and removal of the upper vagina and pelvic lymph nodes, followed by radiation therapy, is usually necessary.

OTHER FEMALE CANCERS

Two less common types of cancer affect the fallopian tubes and the vulva. Both affect postmenopausal women. Abnormal vaginal bleeding is the usual sign of cancer of the fallopian tubes. Persistent vulval itching or irritation can be a sign of cancer of the vulva. Sometimes there may also be a lump, an area of discoloration or an ulcer on the vulva. Some women delay seeking help about vulval irritation because of embarrassment, but if it is detected early, survival rates for vulval cancer are good.

Male Disorders

Although not susceptible to the same range of urogenital infections as women, men still need to be vigilant about genital health from a young age. While prostate cancer affects older men, testicular cancer is a young man's disease.

A combination of simple self-examination techniques and medical tests—particularly in relation to the testicles and prostate gland—should ensure that any disorders that threaten fertility or the health of the body are detected early.

PROSTATE PROBLEMS

The function of the prostate gland is to secrete a milky fluid just before ejaculation. This secretion helps to make semen liquid. The two most serious health problems that can affect the prostate gland are enlargement and prostate cancer (see page 152).

Enlarged prostate gland

The prostate gland begins to enlarge in men over the age of 50 and is a common source of problems in later life. When the prostate gland enlarges, it can put pressure on the urethra, making it harder for urine to flow from the bladder out of the body. A man may notice that it takes him a long time to begin urinating or that his stream of urine is very weak. The medical name for a normal enlarged prostate is benign prostatic hyperplasia (BPH). BPH is induced by a form of the hormone testosterone.

Other symptoms typical of BPH are frequent urination, especially in the middle of the night, and terminal dribbling: the flow of urine trickles out slowly at the end of urination rather than stopping abruptly. Men may experience abdominal discomfort and swelling if the bladder is not able to empty itself completely, and they may have difficulty in postponing urination. If the condition is more serious, bladder or kidney infections and kidney stones may develop, accompanied by fever, a burning sensation when urinating and blood in the urine.

A man complaining of urinary symptoms should be examined by a doctor, who will feel the prostate gland manually through the front wall of the rectum.

Treatment of BPH depends on the severity of symptoms. Although most older men have some degree of prostatic enlargement, the obstruction this causes to the urethra varies. Moderate symptoms may be treated with hormones or drugs that decrease the size of the prostate or relax muscles to increase urine flow. Men suffering from severe symptoms may need surgery to remove the prostate gland.

EXAMINING THE PROSTATE GLAND

Prostate examination
The walnut-sized prostate gland encircles the urethra just under the bladder. A doctor can examine the prostate manually through the front rectal wall.

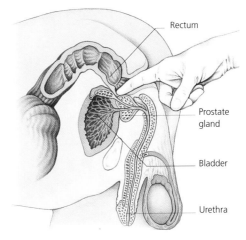

Rectum

Prostate gland

Bladder

Urethra

X-ray showing an enlarged prostate
The gold area in the center is the bladder. The violet circle in front of the bladder is the enlarged prostate gland.

TORSION OF THE TESTICLES

At puberty the testicles become more mobile and occasionally twist around on themselves, cutting off the blood supply. This is called torsion of the testicles and causes acute pain and sometimes discoloration and swelling in the scrotum. Urgent medical intervention is required to save the testicle and preserve fertility, as irreversible damage can be done in a matter of hours. If medical help is delayed, a doctor may have to surgically remove the damaged testicle. Fortunately, one testicle is sufficient for a man to remain fertile.

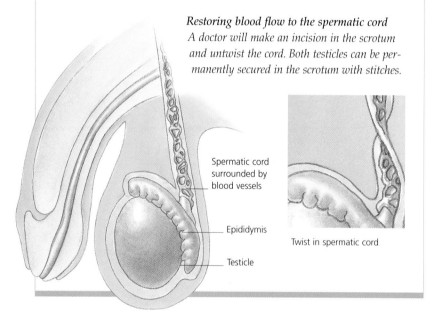

Restoring blood flow to the spermatic cord
A doctor will make an incision in the scrotum and untwist the cord. Both testicles can be permanently secured in the scrotum with stitches.

Spermatic cord surrounded by blood vessels

Epididymis

Testicle

Twist in spermatic cord

SWOLLEN TESTICLES

The testicles are two oval-shaped organs that hang in the scrotum behind the penis. They are fragile and highly sensitive and, due to their position, prone to injury. Swelling of the testicles or scrotum is usually harmless, but if caused by a bacterial or viral infection, it may lead to a lowered sperm count. Swellings should be investigated by a doctor whether large or small, uncomfortable or painless.

Prostatitis

Inflammation of the prostate gland, known as prostatitis, is usually caused by a bacterial infection that has spread from the urethra. It can affect men of any age. Bacteria from the rectum, and chlamydia (see page 135) are just some of the many organisms that can cause prostatitis.

The symptoms of prostatitis include pain when passing urine and increased frequency of urination. There may be fever, a discharge from the penis, and pain between the anus and the penis (the perineum) and in the lower back and genitals.

Prostatitis is diagnosed by physical examination of the prostate gland, analysis of urine, and milking of the prostate during digital rectal examination in order to push secretions into the urethra, where they can be collected on a swab. Prostatitis can take some time to clear up and tends to recur. Treatment for the condition includes long courses of antibiotics, bed rest and anti-inflammatory painkillers.

Prostatodynia is a relatively common problem characterized by the presence of prostatitis symptoms but the absence of any infection. Treatment is difficult, and painkillers may not help. The sufferer may find symptom relief by increasing the frequency of ejaculation, taking regular exercise, eating sufficient fiber to keep bowel movements regular, and avoiding cigarettes and alcohol. Hot baths and direct heat treatment to the prostate may also be soothing.

TESTICULAR PROBLEMS

The most serious problems include torsion of the testicles and cancer, both of which can necessitate surgical removal of the testicle. Other problems may cause subfertility.

Orchitis

Roughly 25 percent of men who have mumps as adults go on to develop orchitis—infection and inflammation of the testicles. The testicles become painful and swollen, and the man may run a fever. Orchitis sometimes leads to permanent damage of the testicle. If both testicles are affected, subfertility may result. Treatment of orchitis consists of painkilling drugs and ice packs to relieve pain. A physician should be consulted.

Inflammation of the testicle and epididymis—the network of tubes at the back of the testicles—is a separate condition called epididymo-orchitis, usually resulting from bacteria that have spread from an infection in the urethra. Doctors prescribe antibiotics to treat this condition.

Swellings

A painless swelling of the scrotum caused by fluid collecting in the tissues surrounding the testicles is known as a hydrocele. It usually occurs in men between age 45 and 60. A hydrocele can be small or large, sometimes growing to the size of a small melon.

Diagnosis involves physical examination and shining a light through the testicles to see if the swelling contains clear fluid. The hydrocele may be an abnormality that has existed from birth, or it may be due to an injury or an infection. On rare occasions, the cause is a tumor of the testicle.

If a hydrocele is large enough to cause discomfort, it can be drained using a needle and syringe. An irritant substance can then be introduced between the two layers to

fact or fiction?

Not ejaculating when sexually aroused causes pain and damage to the testicles.

Not ejaculating can cause temporary physical discomfort, but it does not cause damage. When men become extremely aroused but do not ejaculate, they may suffer from a harmless condition known as testicular ache or "blue balls." This occurs because of vasocongestion (increased blood supply to the genitals).

cause scarring where the hydrocele formed, which will prevent recurrence. If a hydrocele is found to be present at birth and does not disappear spontaneously, it may be surgically repaired by removing a small amount of tissue.

Another type of swelling in the scrotum is a hematocele. This results from an injury, such as a fall or blow to the testicles. The injury causes bleeding within the scrotum, and the subsequent buildup of blood causes the swelling. An operation is necessary to drain the blood.

Testicular swelling can also result from a varicocele—this is a collection of varicose veins, usually on the spermatic cord above the left testicle. It occurs when the blood cannot drain properly from the testicle. About 10 to 15 percent of all men suffer from this condition.

A varicocele may be painful, and it raises the overall temperature of the testicles, increasing the likelihood of male subfertility by lowering the sperm count. Doctors diagnose varicoceles through physical examination or from a heat-sensitive detector wrapped around the testicles. The latter can reveal a varicocele before it can be felt on clinical examination. In the presence of great discomfort, or if subfertility is a problem, surgical treatment may be carried out to remove the varicocele.

Sometimes painless swellings occur in the _EPIDIDYMIS_. The swelling, known as a spermatocele, is a harmless cyst filled with sperm and fluid. Spermatoceles need surgical removal only if they are very large or uncomfortable.

Undescended testicles

When a male baby is born, his testicles are examined by a pediatrician to see if they have descended into the scrotal sac. In about 3 percent of full-term and up to 30 percent of premature male babies, however, one or both testicles fail to fully descend—a condition known as cryptorchidism. Sometimes the condition resolves itself spontaneously after a few months. Hormone therapy may promote normal testicular descent. When hormone treatment fails, surgery may be recommended, usually before two years of age. The main risks associated with cryptorchidism are testicular cancer and possible subfertility later on during adulthood.

PENILE PROBLEMS

Although there are several sexually transmitted diseases (see page 134) that can cause a penile rash or discharge, everyday problems are relatively few.

Balanitis

Inflammation of the glans of the penis is called balanitis. The skin may feel sore and itchy and look red and moist.

There are several causes of balanitis. Yeast infections or trichomoniasis (see page 186) may infect the glans of the penis and, if not treated, can be passed back and forth between sexual partners. Allergic balanitis results from contact with a substance to which the skin is sensitive, such as spermicide, soap or laundry detergent. Other causes include poor hygiene and a tight foreskin that cannot be retracted to wash the glans. If the latter causes recurrent balanitis, circumcision may be necessary. Balanitis can also cause the foreskin to tighten by causing scarring within the foreskin.

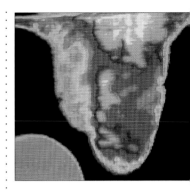

**Taking testicular temperature** A temperature map of a testicle containing a varicocele shows how this condition raises the temperature in and around the scrotum (orange and purple show hot areas). This can lower a man's sperm count.

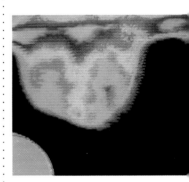

**Normal temperature** A healthy testicle shows a cool, even temperature pattern.

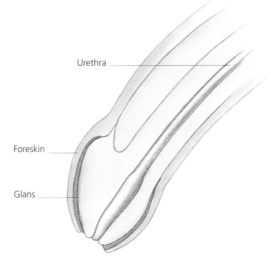

Urethra

Foreskin

Glans

**Inflammation of the glans** The area of the penis that is affected by balanitis is the glans. The glans is the smooth-skinned tip of the penis, which is covered by foreskin in uncircumcised men.

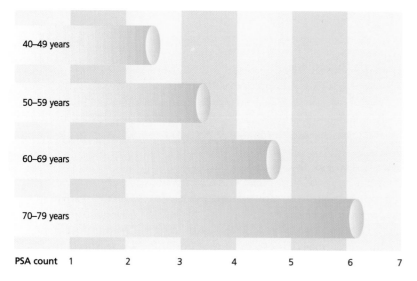

40–49 years

50–59 years

60–69 years

70–79 years

PSA count 1   2   3   4   5   6   7

Normal PSA levels
There is a substance in a man's blood known as prostate specific antigen (PSA). Although PSA levels increase naturally with age, there is a sudden jump if cancer develops in the prostate gland. By routinely measuring PSA levels in a man's bloodstream, a doctor can detect any malignancy early and take appropriate action. But many other things can elevate the PSA besides prostate cancer. Talk to your doctor about the pros and cons of PSA testing. Newer more specific prostate cancer tests are being developed.

Rarer, but more serious, causes of balanitis include diabetes (the excess sugar in the urine encourages bacteria to multiply, giving rise to infection) and malignant changes in the penis.

Diagnosis of balanitis is from physical examination and swabs (see page 115). The way a doctor treats balanitis depends on diagnosis. Yeast infections are treated with antifungal medications, and allergies are minimized by avoidance of the allergen. Symptoms can be relieved by bathing in a warm saltwater bath.

Doctors advise balanitis sufferers about personal hygiene. They recommend that men should clean the glans and foreskin regularly with plenty of warm water and gentle, non-perfumed soaps to avoid the possibility of future infection.

Phimosis

When the foreskin of the penis is so tight that it cannot be drawn back, the condition is referred to as phimosis. In very young, uncircumcised male babies, phimosis is quite normal. After six months, however, the foreskin should be able to be partially retracted. If it cannot, boys may experience difficulty urinating and recurrent infections such as balanitis. If phimosis persists into adulthood, it can make erections painful, and circumcision may be necessary to rectify the condition (see page 92).

MALE CANCERS

Malignant changes can affect the penis, the testicles, the scrotum or the prostate gland, but the latter type of cancer is the most common as men get older.

Prostate cancer

Cancer of the prostate gland is the most common type of malignancy in men. Screening for this type of cancer involves regular manual examination of the prostate. Blood tests and *ULTRASOUND* scans are controversial, and the pros and cons of these tests should be discussed with a physician. The blood test identifies a substance called prostate specific antigen (PSA). The presence of PSA in the blood can detect small cancerous changes before there are any symptoms, but it often gives a positive result in many men who do not need treatment. The risk of developing prostate cancer is three times greater than normal if an immediate relative has suffered from it.

Prostate cancer is slow-growing and does not normally produce symptoms until late in the disease. In fact, symptomless prostate cancer is often discovered during treatment for an enlarged prostate gland. If prostate cancer spreads, it usually moves to the lymph nodes and bones. Late symptoms are bone pain, *ANEMIA*, weight loss and blood in the urine or semen.

The treatments for prostate cancer include surgery, *RADIATION THERAPY, CHEMOTHERAPY* and hormone treatment to counter the action of testosterone.

Cancer of the testicles

Testicular cancer occurs most commonly in men between the ages of 20 and 35. Malignant tumors occur more frequently in the right rather than the left testicle, although in approximately 2 percent of cases tumors are present in both testicles.

The first sign of a problem is usually a firm, painless swelling in the testicle, although some men experience pain and inflammation. An undescended testicle that was not corrected before age two constitutes one of the main risk factors for testicular cancer. Another is having a brother with testicular cancer. The incidence of testicular cancer has risen dramatically over the last 30 years. It is the third leading cause of male deaths in the age group 20 to 40.

An ultrasound scan, which can usually discern a malignant tumor, is necessary for diagnosis. Blood tests are also used in diagnoses, since tumors may produce abnormally high levels of certain chemicals. A biopsy then confirms the diagnosis, and if there is cancer, the affected testicle is surgically removed. Radiation therapy and chemo-therapy may also be implemented, especially if the cancer has spread.

If only one testicle is removed because of malignancy, the other testicle will continue to produce sperm, so that fertility should be restored to normal some two years after treatment. When detected early, testicular cancer is curable in most men.

Cancer of the penis

Penile cancer is quite rare and seen mainly in men over 50 years old. The tumor can start anywhere on the head of the penis as a small painless lump, often rough and wart-like in appearance. Sometimes the tumor may appear on the foreskin as a painful ulcer. The tumor gradually develops into a cauliflower-like mass. A highly malignant tumor may spread quickly, affecting the lymphatic glands in the groin within a few months.

Circumcised men have a slightly lower risk of penile cancer. Smoking and poor per-sonal hygiene are risk factors for penile cancer. Other risk factors are thought to be phi-mosis and exposure to certain viruses and skin conditions.

Biopsy of the tumor will allow a doctor to diagnose penile cancer. Because penile cancer tends to spread slowly, small tumors require only removal of the tumor and radiation therapy. If the tumor is advanced, then more extensive surgery, involving removal of part or all of the penis, is required.

The worldwide incidence of cancer of the penis varies widely. In Europe and the U.S. it accounts for about 5 percent of all cancers, while in Asiatic countries it accounts for approximately 20 percent of cancers.

Cancer of the scrotal skin

Malignant changes in the scrotum have been directly linked with cancer-causing chemicals found in oil, soot and tar. Men, such as mechanics, who work with these materials are at risk if these substances repeatedly come in contact with the scro-tum. Such workers are advised to wear pro-tective clothing and to wash all residue off their hands before handling their genitals.

The cancer starts as a painless lump or ulcer on the scrotum. Lymph nodes in the groin may swell if the cancer spreads. Treatment includes surgery, radiation therapy and chemotherapy.

TESTICULAR SELF-EXAMINATION

Men should carry out monthly examinations of their testicles beginning at age 14 to 16. The exams enable them to detect lumps and swellings that may be signs of cancer. Testicular cancer, if diagnosed early, is one of the most easily cured forms of cancer.

During or after a bath or shower is the best time to examine the testicles, as the scrotal skin is relaxed. It should be loose and move freely over the testicles, making it easy to feel the normally smooth surface of the testicles between the thumb and the forefinger.

The epididymis should be identified as the small, soft, slightly lumpy area at the back of the testicles. Signs to look out for are lumps, areas of pain or discomfort, swelling in either testicle, or ulceration of the scrotal skin. All of these should be considered worthy of medical examination. All young men should be taught self-examination procedures, just as young women are taught to conduct a breast self-examination.

The site of a possible tumor
Tumors are most likely to be found in the right testicle. Cancerous lumps usually feel firm to the touch and are not tender when pressed.

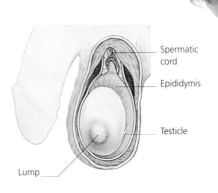

Spermatic cord

Epididymis

Testicle

Lump

The examination technique
Palpate each testicle in turn, with the index and middle finger below the testicle and the thumb on top. Gently rolling the testicle between fingers and thumb will reveal any abnormalities.

Abnormal Sex Organs

Rarely, something happens to a developing fetus that results in sexual abnormalities, such as the presence of both male testicles and female ovaries. Usually a defect in the chromosomes or a hormonal imbalance is responsible.

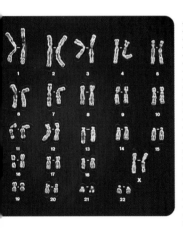

Chromosome pairs
Defects with chromosomes are rare: most people have the full complement of 23 pairs.

FETAL MASCULINIZATION

A rare condition known as congenital adrenal hyperplasia occurs in female fetuses with overactive adrenal glands (see page 141). Adrenal glands produce steroids, some of which have a similar effect to male sex hormones. Baby girls may be born with a penis and scrotum. Corrective surgery and hormone treatment ensure normal female development.

Sexual abnormalities may be obvious as soon as a child is born, but others may not be discovered until puberty. Surgery on the sex organs and hormonal treatment can often help assign a gender to people whose physical sex is ambiguous.

HERMAPHRODITISM

A person with both male and female genitals, or ambiguous gender, is known as a hermaphrodite. Hermaphroditism is present from birth and is caused by an imbalance of hormones in the mother's uterus during fetal development. The condition is treated with surgery and hormone therapy.

There are four general types of hermaphroditism. True hermaphrodites, a rarity, have ovaries and testicles, and also ambiguous external genitalia that seem to be both male and female. An affected child is usually raised as a boy.

In agonadal hermaphroditism the testes and ovaries are absent or underdeveloped. The genitals are clearly male or female, but the chromosomal sex of the individual is opposite to the genital sex.

Male pseudohermaphrodites have testicles and female genitals, whereas female pseudohermaphrodites have ovaries and male genitals. The most common cause of male pseudohermaphroditism is androgen insensitivity syndrome (AIS). This occurs when the fetus is insensitive to the male sex hormones that are produced by the developing testicles. Therefore no penis forms and the baby has the outward appearance of a girl. Surgery can remove the testicles and construct or lengthen the vagina. Menstruation and conception are impossible, but hormone therapy ensures an otherwise normal life as a woman.

TURNER'S SYNDROME

Girls with Turner's syndrome have only one female sex chromosome: X instead of XX. They are clearly female at birth but may have other physical abnormalities, such as webbed neck, short stature or congenital heart disease. At puberty, these girls do not menstruate or grow breasts. Female hormones may improve growth and breast development.

KLINEFELTER'S SYNDROME

Rarely a boy may have an extra sex chromosome: XXY instead of XY. Klinefelter's syndrome may pass unnoticed until puberty. Boys who are affected have small testicles that produce little or no sperm. They may also have a female body shape with wider than average hips and enlarged breasts. Surgery to remove breast tissue, combined with testosterone therapy, helps to enhance a masculine appearance.

The Language of Sex

The word "hermaphrodite" derives from the minor Greek god Hermaphroditus, the son of Hermes, messenger of the gods, and of Aphrodite, the goddess of love. The nymph Salmacis fell in love with him, and the gods answered her prayers by uniting them in one body with both male and female qualities.

OVERCOMING PROBLEMS IN LOVE & SEX

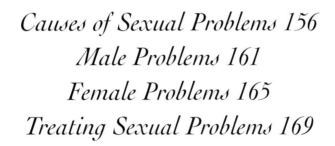

Causes of Sexual Problems 156
Male Problems 161
Female Problems 165
Treating Sexual Problems 169

Causes of Sexual Problems

Sexual problems can be caused by physical factors such as tiredness, illness or alcohol intake, or psychological factors such as anxiety or depression. Sometimes the physical and psychological causes of problems are intertwined.

Sex books There is a diverse range of sex books available. Some aim to be titillating; others take a self-help or educational approach. Looking at a sex book with a partner is one way to initiate a conversation about sex.

When a person is in poor or reduced physical health, his or her body cannot respond to sexual stimuli in the normal way. General fatigue and hormonal disorders can reduce sexual drive, and damaged nerves and fibrous tissues, or malfunctioning valves in blood vessels, can interfere with normal sexual response. Sex drive is also closely linked to an individual's psychological state.

SEX AND MEDICATION

A number of prescription and over-the-counter medications have side effects that can be detrimental to a person's sex life. Many of the medications that are prescribed for high blood pressure (hypertension) can reduce libido. Ten to 15 percent of men taking methyldopa, one of the most commonly used drugs for hypertension, have reduced libido and erection problems. High doses of methyldopa are known to cause orgasmic problems in women.

Medication for angina reportedly causes erection difficulties in about 10 percent of users. More everyday medications such as antihistamines, which dry up nasal secretions in cold and hayfever sufferers, can inhibit vaginal lubrication in women, making sex painful (see page 166). Diuretics, which are commonly prescribed for congestive heart failure, can decrease sexual desire and cause erection problems in 20 to 25 percent of male users. Medication for peptic ulcers (such as cimetidine) can reduce testosterone levels and cause impotency problems in about 12 percent of male users; and medication used to treat epilepsy can cause sexual dysfunction and reduce sexual desire in both men and women.

For people who experience sexual problems when taking a new prescription drug, a doctor may reduce the dosage or even change medications. Individuals react differently, and not everyone will experience the same side effects from the same medication. In most cases, a drug can be found to treat a particular illness that does not affect sexual behavior and response.

SEX AND ALCOHOL

Although alcohol consumption can decrease sexual inhibition in men and women, its negative effects on sexual performance have been widely documented. Alcohol depresses the nervous system, so men and women who have had several or more drinks have impaired sexual responses, making it difficult to achieve an orgasm. Alcohol also dilates small blood vessels all over the body, which means that there is less engorgement of blood in the penis and in the walls of the vagina. This can inhibit sustained erection in men and vaginal lubrication in women. Decreased vaginal lubrication is also caused by the dehydrating effect of alcohol consumption.

According to sex therapists Masters, Johnson and Kolodny, 40 to 50 percent of all male alcoholics have low or nonexistent sex drives. This is because the toxins in alcohol directly affect the male sex hormone testosterone; the testes shrink, and the production of testosterone is greatly decreased. In addition, these smaller amounts of testosterone are quickly broken down in the body by increased levels of liver enzymes, another side effect of alcoholism. In female alcoholics, 30 to 40 percent report that they have problems with sexual arousal, and about 15 percent report an inability to reach orgasm or a significant reduction in the intensity or frequency of orgasm.

LONG-TERM ILLNESSES

Multiple sclerosis, *DIABETES*, arthritis, heart disease and circulatory problems can all have adverse effects on sexual function and desire. Multiple sclerosis (MS), in particular, is a progressive, serious condition of the nervous system. About 25 percent of male MS sufferers experience problems in erection and orgasm, and about the same number of women suffer from reduced sensitivity in the genital area. Long-term illnesses do not necessarily prevent sexual intercourse, but patience, understanding and an ability to be flexible, especially by a sexual partner, are necessary.

PSYCHOLOGICAL PROBLEMS

Although some sexual problems, such as vaginismus (see page 166) or impotence, may seem to be physical in nature, they are often psychologically induced, with fear, anxiety or guilt at their root.

Sexual satisfaction is closely linked to an individual's state of mind. When a person is confident and happy, he or she is usually able to appreciate the positive and pleasurable aspects of life, including sex. To enjoy sex, an individual must be able to let go of inhibitions, be intimate with a partner and feel relaxed and confident about his or her body. However, when someone is unhappy,

Feelings of chronic stress or anxiety

Fear of sex resulting from past sexual trauma or abuse

Nervous disorders or depression

SEXUAL PROBLEMS
State of mind can have a profound effect on an individual's sexual responses. There are many psychological causes of low libido and other problems.

Relationship problems, including boredom

insecure or subconsciously distracted, his or her sexual behavior will be adversely affected. Worries about work or money may create feelings of anxiety, as may relationship problems—not getting along well with one's partner, doubting his or her faithfulness, or feeling guilty about being unfaithful oneself.

Problems may arise as well from low sexual self-esteem. A person who perceives himself or herself as unsexy, unattractive, inexperienced, too old or too overweight to give or receive sexual pleasure is likely to find that pleasure elusive.

Negative views about sex can also impede enjoyment. Parents, for example, may pass on the belief to their children that sex is immoral. Masters and Johnson, who say that men from strict religious backgrounds often have erection problems, stress that it is not the religious teachings that cause problems but the associated attitude that sexual pleasure is sinful.

rather than being an expression of that relationship. Alternatively, people who have had problematic childhoods may withdraw from sexual relationships completely.

Sex and depression

Doctors and psychologists make a distinction between depression and depressed mood. The former refers to a clinical illness, while the latter refers to the downcast feelings that most people temporarily experience in response to everyday bad news. Depressed mood does not have a profound effect on an individual's ability to function sexually in the way that clinical depression does. Clinical depression can be emotionally, socially and physically incapacitating and, in extreme cases, can lead to suicide. Often treated as a medical condition because of its physical symptoms and the feelings of malaise it produces, depression causes the disturbance of an individual's psychological well-being. Depression can develop as a response to certain life events, such as the breakup of an important relationship, bereavement or unemployment, or it can appear for no clear reason.

The feelings of melancholy, hopelessness and inadequacy that characterize depression can cause a sufferer to stay at home alone all day. A depressed person may lose interest in life to the extent that such previous desires as food, sleep, socializing and sex no longer hold any appeal.

Although having no interest in sex does not necessarily mean that someone is depressed, it is one of the hallmarks of depressive illness. A doctor suspecting that a patient suffers from clinical depression may well ask questions about the individual's libido.

Depression is an illness that can have a marked effect on a person's sense of self—how he or she values or feels about himself or herself. The ability to derive pleasure from sexual activity is closely linked to feel-

Childhood trauma
One of the most compelling reasons for sexual problems in adulthood is sexual violation in childhood. Children who have been abused need sensitive counseling from a specialist.

Some individuals may have unresolved feelings about childhood situations—parents divorcing, being unpopular or bullied at school, or simply feeling unloved by the people around them when they were growing up. Although these issues may not seem to be directly related to sex, they can have a profound effect on self-esteem and behavior during adulthood.

Men and women who felt unloved, abandoned or rejected during childhood, for example, may try to compensate for such loneliness by becoming sexually promiscuous. For them, many sexual partners may be required before they can feel desired, needed and loved, and even then the satisfaction may be only temporary. Promiscuity works as a defense against loneliness, but although the individual acts of sex might be enjoyable, an ongoing sexual relationship will be difficult to maintain when fueled by insecurity. Sex can become a way of convincing oneself that a relationship exists,

fact or fiction?

Good sex cannot be planned.

Fiction. Although sex is a natural human activity, sexual pleasure is not always as easy and spontaneous as people expect it to be. Good sex is often a result of knowledge and planning: knowledge about the way the body works sexually and about the sexual needs and responses of you and your partner; planning for sex by thinking about mood, setting and practical considerations as contraception.

ings of self-esteem and self-worth. Any kind of depressive illness is likely to have a negative effect on sexual behavior.

Although lack of sexual desire is a common symptom of depression, the situation may work in reverse, so that the sexual problem precipitates the depression. For example, a man who is suffering from impotence and whose sexual partner is unsympathetic can begin to doubt his masculinity. As his self-esteem falls, feelings of rejection and worthlessness increase, and depression may set in.

Past sexual trauma

Intimacy can make both men and women feel vulnerable. Successful sexual relationships depend on partners who feel relaxed, secure and trusting with each other. In healthy adult relationships, trust and security evolve over a period of time, but people who have had damaging sexual experiences in the past may find it difficult to relax enough to allow a normal sexual relationship to develop.

If a child is abused, his or her natural instinct to trust will be damaged, and later sexual development and adult relationships may be adversely affected. This is especially so when the childhood abuse includes sexual abuse.

Childhood sexual trauma can range from indecent physical exposure to experiences of violent adult sex. Although more girls than boys are known victims of childhood sexual abuse, boys may also be targets of adult sexual interests.

Children who have been involved in adult sexual activity of any kind frequently find themselves confused about sex and sexuality when they become adults. They may harbor great anxiety about sexual behavior, or they may suffer unresolved guilt and shame as a result of their past experiences. Either feeling can make normal sexual relationships difficult or impossible.

Sexual trauma also occurs during adulthood. Men and, more often, women may find themselves the subject of unwanted sexual attention—from verbal harassment to physical molestation or rape. Whether these events are psychologically or physically invasive, or both, the resulting sexual trauma can be extremely difficult to overcome. Rape victims commonly have a sense of acute violation and loss of control over their own bodies and lives. Sometimes sexual trauma can be so great that long-term psychological help is needed; even then the effects of abuse may last, causing depression and sexual and emotional problems.

Stress and sex

A certain amount of stress in life is normal. In order to face certain challenges, the body's chemical balance alters and a surge of adrenalin is released into the bloodstream. The body can cope with this altered chemical balance for a short period of time, but when everyday pressures build up without relief, stress becomes chronic. For men and women in such circumstances, life is so stressful that any sort of spontaneous enjoyment can become impossible.

Chronic stress especially damages good sexual relationships. Its effects are slow and insidious. Sexual interest, desire and activity may decrease to such an extent that a partner begins to doubt his or her attractiveness. Male sufferers often find themselves experiencing erection problems.

When the cause of stress is obvious—for example, the sudden loss of employment by the main earner in a household—a strong personal and sexual relationship may be a source of strength and reassurance. More often than not, however, sudden stress can expose the weaknesses in a relationship. Issues that have never been addressed or properly resolved, such as how to manage money or to cope with strained family relationships, become a focus of tension that inhibits sexual interest.

The stress scale
Different life events bring about different levels of stress. People who are experiencing extreme emotional stress should expect their libido to be adversely affected. The Holmes-Rahe stress scale (summarized below) is one attempt to quantify the amount of stress associated with different life events.

High
- Death of a husband or wife
- Death of a family member
- Divorce
- Marital separation
- Jail sentence or being institutionalized
- Illness or injury

Medium
- Marriage
- Loss of job
- Retirement
- Health problems of close member of family
- Major change at work
- Change of financial status

Low
- Child leaving home
- In-law problems
- Trouble with employer
- Change in working hours
- Change in social activities
- Holiday season

Sexual boredom

The ancient Greeks recognized boredom as a very dangerous state, one that created a desire to act impulsively in ways otherwise considered foolish, simply to escape from a mundane state of inactivity. An educated and thoughtful man prided himself on having enough interests to prevent him from sinking into boredom.

Can We Talk About It?

SEX IS BECOMING ROUTINE

Instead of blaming your partner for being no good in bed, discuss the routine nature of your lovemaking as a problem you both have. Start by acknowledging that you also contribute to the boredom by not introducing anything new. Then ask your partner to tell you specifically what he or she would like you to do to make sex more interesting. Remind each other of the early days of your relationship and what you then found erotic. Recall your early sexual encounters with each other, where they happened and who initiated them. Ask each other what you enjoyed most during that time. Be completely honest in your responses. Agree with your partner to give each other a pleasant sexual surprise in the coming week. This could be sharing a bath or finding a new place to enjoy a seduction. These experiences should appeal to you and your partner's senses of taste, smell, touch, sight and hearing. Anything unusual could arouse both partners' interest. At the end of the week, tell each other what you enjoyed about each other's surprises and why.

Many good books and videos exist on sexual behavior, with advice about specific sexual techniques and ways to keep romance and eroticism alive in your relationship. Ask your partner to buy one with you and look at it together, discussing what you like and don't like; then make a date to try out some new ideas.

Sexual boredom usually results from lovemaking that has become routine and predictable. If one or both partners lose interest, lovemaking soon becomes unimaginative and unfulfilling. Either partner may look elsewhere for sexual excitement and embark on an affair. The sexual excitement surrounding an illicit relationship very often forms its basis. When the relationship becomes more established or legitimate, the sexual excitement disappears, leading to boredom yet again.

The key to preventing boredom is to consciously maintain an interest in a sexual partner and exercise variety, fun and spontaneity in the relationship. Sexual excitement comes naturally at the beginning of a relationship but frequently declines when a couple stop making time for each other or start taking each other for granted. Initial sexual excitement may lead a couple into cohabitation and marriage, but if they do not devote time and energy to their relationship, sex may become a low priority.

Sexual ignorance

Masters and Johnson believe that there are two main causes of sexual problems—ignorance and fear. Their published works have done a great deal to dispel both, but many people remain ignorant on both an emotional and a physical level.

People do not necessarily find sex naturally easy or instantly fulfilling. Lack of knowledge about the sexual anatomy or physical response of a sexual partner can provoke intense anxiety, which can hinder spontaneous sexual expression.

Sexual ignorance is common—and virtually inevitable—in people who are having sexual relations for the first time; but lack of sexual knowledge can cause problems at other times of life as well. Many men and women are ill informed about the sexual changes associated with aging. Men may not realize that slower and weaker erectile responses coupled with a decreased urgency to ejaculate are entirely normal. Similarly, women may be unaware that they will produce less vaginal lubrication as they get older. If men and women respond to these changes with anxiety, they may exacerbate or even create sexual problems.

Individuals may also feel reticent about having sex if they are ignorant about such issues as contraception or STDs.

Male Problems

At some time in their lives, most men will experience some anxiety about their sexual performance, or temporarily lose interest in sex. Two common sexual problems are an inability to maintain an erection and premature ejaculation.

Some sexual problems can be a short-lived response to nervousness or an overconsumption of alcohol. Others may prove to be long-term or chronic and need to be diagnosed and treated by a professional, such as a doctor or sex therapist.

LOW SEX DRIVE

Men vary greatly in the frequency of their sexual activity. Some men claim to think about or desire sex almost all the time; others feel satisfied by making love every other week. Throughout a man's life, sexual desire increases and decreases, depending on his age, his life situation, his stress levels, his relationships and many other interconnected factors. In terms of age, a man's sexual peak usually occurs around his late teens and early twenties.

Male sexual drive is determined by both physiological and psychological factors. Sexual desire can be suppressed with drugs that inhibit the production of sex hormones—this treatment has been used for male sex offenders. Similarly, people with disorders such as Klinefelter's syndrome (see page 154), which causes low levels of sex hormones, have low libidos.

Occasionally men have sexual phobias that inhibit their libidos. Such phobias can result from past unpleasant sexual experiences (including sexual abuse), low self-esteem, a fear of physical intimacy, or the entrenched belief that sex is wrong or dirty.

In many cases men simply have a naturally low sex drive that cannot be linked to a hormonal disorder or a sexual phobia. This need not be treated as a problem unless the man's partner has a significantly higher sex drive and their different sexual needs give rise to tension and disagreement.

The treatment for low sex drive depends on whether the underlying cause is physical or psychological. If a man and his partner are happy with relatively infrequent intercourse and do not perceive lack of libido as a problem, no treatment is necessary.

Reduced sex drive

Although low sex drive is not necessarily a problem, reduced sex drive may be. Reduced sex drive indicates that a man's libido was once satisfactory to him and his partner but has now dropped to a dissatisfying level. This drop can be precipitated by such factors as relationship difficulties, a new baby in the family, work or financial worries, fatigue, or grief. Ill health and poor diet can also reduce sex drive.

A good counselor or sex therapist can help to restore sexual desire by identifying the underlying causes of reduced sex drive and working through them with a client.

ERECTION PROBLEMS

An inability to have or maintain an erection is known as erectile insufficiency, but the term "impotence" is still the most widely used when erection problems are described. Although an erection may not be an

Sources of stress
Men who are stressed may find they become less interested in sex. Such multiple commitments as meeting work deadlines and childcare can have a detrimental effect on an individual's personal life.

Treating Erection Problems

Many treatments are available for men who cannot achieve a natural erection for physical reasons. Some doctors recommend injecting the penis with such drugs as papaverine. Drugs like this dilate the penile arteries, causing a sudden increase in blood flow to the penis and, therefore, an erection. Men are taught to inject themselves at home, and the resulting erection typically lasts between one and two hours. Penile injections do not work in all cases of erection problems, however, and they sometimes cause pain and scarring.

One alternative is an implant, which is surgically installed by a urologist. Some implants can be inflated with air when an erection is desired. Others consist of flexible rods that leave the penis in a perpetual state of semi-erection. The most sophisticated (and expensive) implant consists of three pieces: a squeeze pump in the scrotum, a reservoir of liquid stored under the abdominal skin and an implant in the penis. A less invasive method is the penile splint, a sheath reinforced with plastic "ribs" that covers the penile shaft but not the glans.

USING A PUMP DEVICE

A common device that men with erectile problems can use to induce an erection is a vacuum pump. The penis is lubricated with a water-soluble jelly and then inserted into the pump. The air is drawn out of the pump, and the resulting vacuum causes blood to rush into the penile vessels, making the penis erect. A penile ring placed on the end of the pump is then slipped onto the penis to maintain the erection. The ring should not be left on for more than 30 minutes at a time.

The vacuum pump
This device can enable lovemaking by producing an erection (ejaculation may not occur as heavily as usual). It is used in conjunction with a penile ring that stops blood from flowing out of the penis.

Penis is inserted here.

Ring to be slipped onto base of penis

Pump handle to draw out air

Penile tube

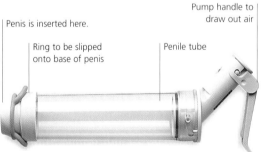

Side loops help positioning and removal of ring.

Penile rings
Rubber rings can be used independently of vacuum-pump devices by men who can gain but not maintain erections. They come in various sizes.

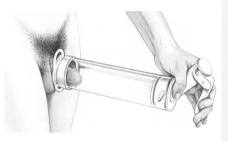

1 The penis is inserted into the cylinder, which should be held tightly against the body to make an airtight seal. The cylinder handle is pumped up and down.

2 Once an erection has been achieved, the penile ring is eased off the plastic sleeve and onto the base of the penis. This prevents the penis from becoming flaccid.

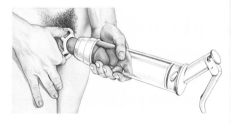

3 A release valve is pressed to allow air to fill the vacuum so that the cylinder can be removed. After sexual intercourse, the ring is removed from the penis.

absolute requirement to prove a man's potency, it is considered by many men and women as the clearest sign of a man's strength, virility and sexual identity. This is why difficulty in attaining an erection evokes feelings of embarrassment, shame, anxiety and inadequacy in a man.

An erection occurs when blood flow increases and swells the spongy tissues of the penis (see page 91). The increase in blood flow is triggered by physical or psychological stimulation. A man's inability to achieve or maintain an erection can occur as a result of such physical factors as impeded blood flow (as in the case of diabetes), overconsumption of alcohol, acute fatigue or a drug side effect.

Erections generally decline in frequency and firmness as a man ages, but, depending on his lifestyle, a 70-year-old man may still be able to achieve an erection regularly. Heavy smoking, eating and drinking, however, all have adverse effects on the erectile tissues in the penis.

Psychological causes of erection problems can range from boredom and lack of interest in a partner to feelings of guilt and anxiety. Any activity, such as putting on a condom, that draws attention to the firmness of an erection can lead to self-consciousness and *DETUMESCENCE*. Sometimes a physical cause can develop into a psychological one. For example, a man who on one occasion fails to achieve an erection because he has drunk too much alcohol may feel that he has failed sexually and be anxious on subsequent occasions when he tries to perform.

As with other sexual difficulties, diagnosing the cause of erectile insufficiency requires knowledge of both physical and psychological causes and their interdependency. An erection that subsides on penetration, for example, may have a different cause from an erection that is lost after penetration or an erection that was never full in the first place. A man who has erections in his sleep is unlikely to be suffering from an underlying physical problem. A man can find out whether he has erections during his sleep by placing a paper ring around the base of the penis—if he finds the ring broken when he awakes, he has probably had an erection during the night.

It is not known how widespread erection problems are. It is generally agreed that most men experience unwanted loss of or

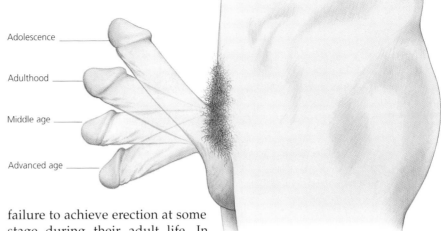

Adolescence

Adulthood

Middle age

Advanced age

failure to achieve erection at some stage during their adult life. In 1992, the U.S. National Consensus Conference on Erectile Dysfunction estimated that over 10 percent of adult men may suffer from serious erection problems.

PREMATURE EJACULATION

Ejaculating before or quickly after sexual penetration is described as premature ejaculation. Like low sex drive, it may be a problem only if a couple perceive it as such. Some couples cope easily with early ejaculation, especially if a woman reaches orgasm quickly or reaches orgasm before or after intercourse via masturbation.

Angle of erection
Although penile length and girth determines the angle of a man's erection, age also has a big impact. In men of advanced age, the erect penis is more likely to point downward than upward. This is not a sign of erection problems.

TREATING PREMATURE EJACULATION

Premature ejaculation can be treated using two types of squeeze technique. When a man is feeling highly aroused and close to ejaculation, pressure applied to the top or the bottom of the penis will temporarily diminish his erection.

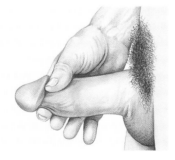

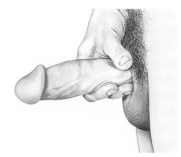

The "top" squeeze
The thumb and fingers are used to squeeze the penis just below the glans. Either the man or his partner can apply pressure until the feeling of intense arousal passes.

The "bottom" squeeze
The man or his partner should apply firm pressure around the base of his penis. This variation of the squeeze technique is useful when the man's penis is inside the vagina.

The more highly arousing a sexual situation is, the more easily ejaculation is triggered. Sometimes prolonged foreplay that includes manual or oral penile stimulation can result in hyperarousal, so that a man ejaculates soon after penetration. Young men who are just becoming sexually active often suffer from premature ejaculation, as do men with new sexual partners or men who are having sex for the first time in a long while. Anxiety about being able to perform adequately also hastens ejaculation.

Ejaculation occurs in the late stages of sexual arousal, when rhythmic contractions occur in the muscles of the pelvic floor and at the base of the penis. To treat premature ejaculation, contractions need to be controlled so that ejaculation is delayed.

Many men suffer from premature ejaculation, but it is one of the most successfully treated problems.

Arousal patterns

Arousal patterns
Normal sexual arousal (see top graph) is a joint sequence of excitement, plateau, orgasm and resolution. When a man ejaculates prematurely, however, his arousal and orgasm (see bottom graph) takes place very quickly and his partner's level of arousal can remain slight for the duration of the sexual encounter.

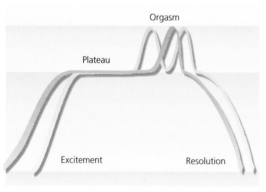

Normal sexual arousal

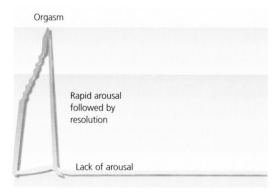

Premature ejaculation

Female arousal
Male arousal

Treating premature ejaculation

Some drugs delay ejaculation and help give men a feeling of ejaculatory control. However, a more common treatment for premature ejaculation is the squeeze technique.

The squeeze technique requires a partner's cooperation. She has to manually stimulate her partner to erection. As she continues stimulating him, her partner must recognize the feelings of imminent ejaculation—this is called ejaculatory demand—and ask her to stop. She then places her thumb on the frenulum and her forefinger around the coronal ridge (see page 92) and applies strong pressure to this area for four to five seconds. The man should lose the sensation of ejaculatory demand and his erection may wane. The woman can then continue manual stimulation.

The exercise should be repeated five times a day for a few weeks or until it is possible for the man to have longer periods of stimulation where his ejaculatory sensation is under control. Some men may ejaculate the first or second time the squeeze technique is being performed. This is quite common and should stop after a few sessions.

A similar method is the stop-start technique (sometimes called the stop-and-go technique), which does not require a partner's participation. A man masturbates until he gets an erection, then simply stops stimulation. He continues with this exercise until he can gradually stimulate himself for longer periods, stopping when he recognizes he is close to ejaculatory demand.

When a man feels confident that he has gained sufficient ejaculatory control, the woman should guide his penis into her vagina and let it lie there without any thrusting movements for 10 seconds or so. This is called the "quiet vagina" technique, and the side-by-side or woman-on-top position is best for this.

If ejaculatory feelings are still under control using the quiet vagina technique, then thrusting movements can gradually commence. If ejaculatory demand builds up so much that the man feels he cannot control it on a stop-start basis, he should withdraw his penis and he or his partner should apply the squeeze technique.

RETARDED EJACULATION

When a man has an erection but fails to ejaculate or ejaculates only after a considerable length of time (between 30 minutes and one hour of repeated thrusting), this is known as retarded or inhibited ejaculation. This can become a source of frustration and physical pain for both him and his partner.

The causes of retarded ejaculation are uncertain. The problem tends to occur in high-achieving men who strive for perfection. It may also occur in men who fear their own sexual power and unconsciously try to inhibit it, in men who dislike the messiness of ejaculation and in men who are afraid of making their partners pregnant. If any of these is the underlying cause, sex therapy may be necessary.

Heavy alcohol consumption or taking tranquilizers, antidepressants or medication used to treat high blood pressure may also delay ejaculation in some men.

Female Problems

Before the sexual revolution of the 1960s, women's sexuality was not widely discussed. Today people have a greater understanding of female sexual response and problems related to female libido and orgasm.

Whereas ejaculation is a reflex response in men, the female orgasm is far more elusive. The inability to reach orgasm (anorgasmia) is just one sexual problem that many women experience and seek help for.

LOW AND DECREASED SEX DRIVE

A woman's sex drive depends on her emotional and physical health, and changes in these will affect her libido. Libido can also be affected by the menstrual cycle, most typically increasing around ovulation or before menstruation.

Sex drive, however, can decrease during times of stress or fatigue, or when there is frustration, anger or poor communication in a relationship. Sex drive is usually at its height at the beginning of a relationship and gradually decreases as the initial excitement wears off.

A woman's sexual desire reaches its peak later in life than a man's; this is believed to result from women taking longer to learn about their sexual response patterns (see page 100). Sex drive is more complicated in women than men because orgasm is not so closely linked to intercourse.

Pregnancy almost certainly affects a woman's sex drive. Desire may be increased by the rise in circulating hormones, while debilitating symptoms such as morning sickness and fatigue may reduce it. After childbirth, many women find that their libido diminishes. This may be due to the fatigue and extra effort involved in caring for a newborn baby, or to tears and stitches resulting from the birth, which make sexual intercourse temporarily painful. A fear of pregnancy can likewise have a negative effect on a woman's libido.

The onset of menopause, with its decrease in the body's production of estrogen, can also reduce sex drive. Taking hormone replacement therapy (HRT) can boost it, but some menopausal women experience a natural revival of sexual interest and energy without HRT. This may be because sex is no longer associated with reproductive responsibilities and can be enjoyed without the inconvenience of contraception. The same is often true after a hysterectomy (see page 146).

A woman concerned about a lack of, or decrease in, sexual desire should consult her doctor. Treatment for lack of libido will depend on the underlying cause. If the problem is physical, hormone replacement therapy may be appropriate. If low sex drive has a psychosexual cause, or is linked to emotional or relationship difficulties, counseling or sex therapy may help.

The impact of stress Working long hours in a stressful job can cause emotional and physical problems, including diminished sex drive.

Self-image Women often report that their sexual desire is affected by how they feel about themselves physically. If a woman feels attractive, she is more likely to feel sexy.

CAUSES OF PAINFUL SEX

CAUSE	TREATMENT
Penis bumping the cervix or an ovary through the vaginal wall	Change in sexual position
Vaginal dryness	Artificial lubricant (as a temporary measure) or HRT for postmenopausal women (not all women can take HRT)
Gynecological infection (such as bartholinitis)	Appropriate treatment from a doctor
Recently performed episiotomy	Healing time before having intercourse
STD (such as herpes)	Appropriate treatment from a doctor (herpes treatment may not always involve medication)
Unstretched hymen	Gently encouraging hymen to stretch or seeking medical help if penetration is impossible
Allergic reactions to spermicide or latex	Change in spermicide, condom or diaphragm, or, if problem persists, change in method of contraception
Irritation due to prolonged intercourse	Avoiding intercourse until soreness goes away
Vaginismus	Counseling and sex therapy

THE IMPACT OF VAGINISMUS

Vaginismus is a female problem, but it can also affect male partners. If the pain of vaginismus forces a woman to avoid penetrative sex, her partner may see this as emotional rejection and, in extreme cases, begin to suffer erectile problems. The woman may try to satisfy her partner in other ways, and the couple become accustomed to sex that does not include penetration. As a result, the man suffers from "conditioned erectile dysfunction."

VAGINAL DRYNESS

One of the first signs of female sexual arousal is vaginal and vulval wetness. As a woman becomes aroused, the vaginal walls respond by secreting moisture, which aids penetration and prevents penile thrusting from causing abrasions to the vaginal wall. In terms of arousal, vaginal lubrication is the female equivalent of the male erection.

If a woman does not produce enough lubrication before intercourse, penetration can be uncomfortable or painful. The simplest reason for lack of lubrication is that the woman is not sufficiently aroused. This may be because foreplay has been short or nonexistent or because she does not want sexual intercourse at that particular time.

Vaginal dryness can also be due to low estrogen levels—a common occurrence after childbirth (especially if a woman is breast-feeding) and at menopause (see page 76). Hormone replacement therapy (HRT) helps to restore the estrogen balance after menopause. Heavy alcohol consumption can cause vaginal dryness as a direct result of the dehydration produced by alcohol.

Short-term remedies for vaginal dryness include artificial lubricants in the form of water-based lubricating jellies (oil-based products should not be used with condoms because they destroy rubber) and saliva. When the problem persists, a doctor or sex therapist may be able to diagnose and treat an underlying cause.

PAINFUL INTERCOURSE

Pain during sexual intercourse may have a physical cause that should be diagnosed and treated by a doctor. It helps if a woman can describe the location and type of pain and the stage of sexual intercourse at which it occurs: on penetration, during thrusting or during orgasm. One cause of extreme pain during intercourse is a gynecological condition called bartholinitis, an inflammation of the Bartholin's glands on either side of the vaginal entrance (see page 144).

VAGINISMUS

Occasionally, women cannot have sexual intercourse because their vaginal muscles go into spasm whenever penetration is attempted. This condition, known as vaginismus, not only makes penetration difficult or impossible but also causes pain from the muscle spasm and extreme pain when penetration is attempted.

Vaginismus is a psychological condition involving deep-rooted fears or anxieties about sex. It can result from a past traumatic sexual experience, such as rape; a careless first vaginal examination; or a subconscious fear of sex, pregnancy and childbirth. Some postmenopausal women whose vaginal tissue has shrunk and does not lubricate sufficiently develop vaginismus because they learn to associate sex with pain.

When penetration is attempted, a woman with vaginismus has an expectation of pain, and her body automatically tenses in anticipation. At first this reaction may be a protective mechanism, but it later becomes an automatic reflex after the source of pain or trauma is removed.

If sensitively managed, treatment for vaginismus is highly successful. A therapist will discuss a woman's attitudes toward sex and try to unravel any deep-seated fears she may have. The therapist will also teach the woman about her body's sexual responses and how to relax her pelvic-floor muscles. The woman is encouraged to use a mirror to explore her genitals with her fingers and, when she is ready, to practice dilating the vagina with a series of "vaginal trainers." A woman continues using vaginal trainers until she feels comfortable and relaxed enough for sexual penetration. She should then attempt intercourse in a woman-on-top position, which will give her control over the depth and speed of penetration.

INABILITY TO REACH ORGASM

To reach orgasm, a woman needs to be relaxed and free of distractions. This means feeling comfortable about her surroundings and her partner and relaxed about her body and sexual responses. Any sort of inhibition, whether psychological or physical, can make orgasm difficult. For many women, losing control is not an easy thing to do, especially in the presence of another person, when they feel at their most vulnerable.

Women are orgasmic to different degrees. Some women reach orgasm easily during intercourse. Others reach orgasm only in specific sexual positions. Others can reach orgasm through masturbation only, not through intercourse. Still others never reach orgasm under any circumstances. The latter problem is true anorgasmia. Orgasmic responses—or lack of them—constitute a problem only if a woman or her partner perceives them as such.

Lack of orgasm does not necessarily indicate that there is anything physically or psychologically wrong with a woman, or that she cannot enjoy sex. Many women have learned to put other people's needs and pleasures before their own; since reaching orgasm requires that a woman exclude all other stimuli and focus on her own sexual pleasure, she may feel selfish. In other words, she may worry that by concentrating on herself, she is denying her partner sexual pleasure. If a woman believes that she has

SELF-HELP FOR VAGINISMUS

A woman can treat vaginismus under the guidance of a sex therapist using her fingers or vaginal trainers. Vaginal trainers are plastic devices that come in graded sizes. The woman practices inserting the smallest trainer first; when she has mastered this, she moves on to larger-sized trainers.

Vaginal trainers
Different-sized trainers designed for insertion into the vagina can help women to overcome the problem of vaginismus.

Self-examination
By using a mirror to explore her body, a woman can learn to relax her genital muscles and so overcome vaginismus.

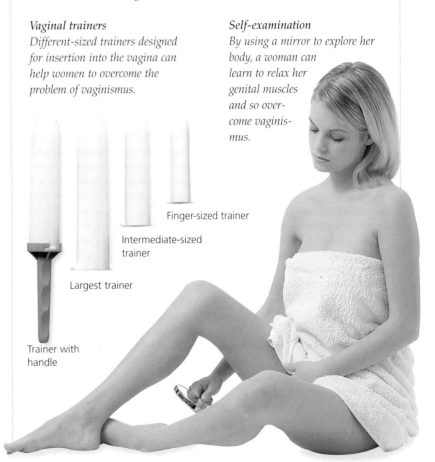

Finger-sized trainer

Intermediate-sized trainer

Largest trainer

Trainer with handle

SEX ADDICTION

Affecting both men and women, sexual addiction is uncommon and defined as a compulsive dependence on frequent, ritualized sexual activity. The addict is preoccupied with sexual matters and carries out special rituals to intensify sexual arousal and excitement. Addicts engage in sexual activity irrespective of the risks, but their desire for sex is marked afterward by dissatisfaction and hopelessness as the compulsion interferes with everyday life. Sex addicts are thought to be motivated by low self-worth or a fear of loneliness. They gain a sense of power from sexual conquests, even though the feeling is short-lived. They may crave an intimate relationship but not know how to achieve it.

no rights to sexual pleasure, or lesser rights than her partner, she will be prevented from learning about her own sexual needs and responses. She will lack necessary knowledge about the way her body works. Alternatively, a woman may know how to reach orgasm by masturbation but feel too inhibited to tell her partner how to incorporate this into their lovemaking.

If a woman has never experienced an orgasm, she should start by exploring her own body to discover what type of touch or other sexual stimulation feels good. Time alone, unhurried and without any pressure to perform, is a vital factor for this task. Some women find a relaxing bath an ideal setting. Sexual aids such as vibrators are helpful for stimulating orgasm, and fantasizing or reading an erotic book can enhance arousal and help to eliminate distracting thoughts. Sex therapists believe that nearly all women who suffer from anorgasmia can be taught to achieve an orgasm through masturbation.

A significant number of women can reach orgasm on their own or when their partner uses manual or oral stimulation but find it difficult to climax during intercourse. If this is the case, the bridge technique may be helpful. In this technique, clitoral stimulation is provided by the woman's partner—or by the woman herself—up to the point of orgasm, then it is stopped and penile thrusting is used to trigger orgasm. The side-by-

Can We Talk About It?

NOT REACHING ORGASM

Start by telling each other how important orgasm is to you. Do you feel that it is an essential part of intercourse; that it is sometimes important, but not always; or that sex is a fulfilling experience without orgasm? Tell your partner whether you want to change your joint expectations of intercourse or change the way you have sex so that orgasm becomes more likely. If you take the latter approach, tell your partner how he can help you reach orgasm. If you do not know, suggest to your partner that seeing a sex therapist would help you to learn more about your sexual responses.

If you have been faking orgasm, make clear your reasons for doing so: perhaps you wanted to live up to your partner's expectations. Explain that you never intended to deceive him and that now you are being honest because you want to find new ways of interacting sexually with him.

side and woman-on-top sexual positions are recommended for the bridge technique because they allow easy access to the clitoris. A vibrator can be used to provide clitoral stimulation.

The bridge technique
For women who find it difficult to reach orgasm during intercourse, the bridge technique can help by providing extra stimulation.

STAGE 1 Woman or her partner stimulates her clitoris manually or using a vibrator.

STAGE 2 Stimulation continues until the woman feels that she is close to orgasm.

STAGE 3 Penetration occurs and penile thrusting provides the bridge to orgasm.

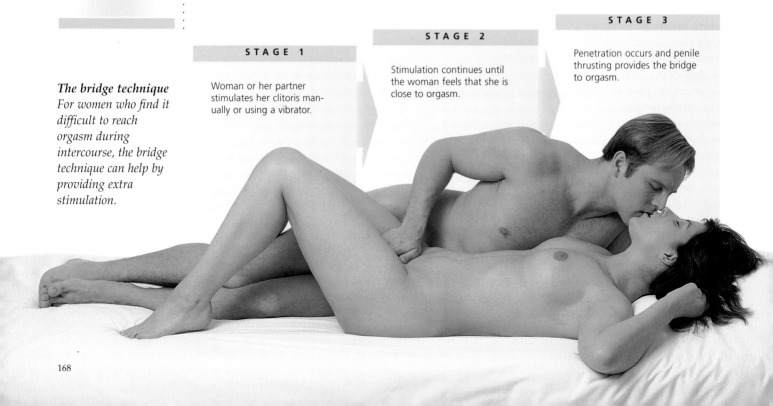

Treating Sexual Problems

A bewildering array of therapies exist to treat sexual and emotional problems, but not all practicing therapists have received recognized training and accreditation. Seeking a doctor's advice about sexual problems is always advisable.

When deciding on a treatment for a sexual problem, it is important to understand its cause. Does the sexual problem have a psychological cause, or could it have a physical basis, in which case it should be treated by a doctor? If the problem is definitely a psychosexual one, is it due to emotional or relationship difficulties that would be treated best by a relationship counselor? Or is it a long-standing anxiety about sexual technique or performance that sex therapy could address? Sometimes people manage to treat minor sexual problems at home with self-help techniques and a supportive partner.

Anyone offering treatment for sexual problems must have a knowledge of both the physical and psychological aspects of sexual behavior or be part of a team covering all aspects of treatment. In approximately one-third of people seeking help for what seem to be psychological difficulties in their sex lives, an underlying physical disorder is present. The possible physical causes of sexual problems should always be eliminated first of all.

In most large communities, there are professional therapists, clinics and programs that specialize in treating sexual dysfunctions and deviations, gender identity problems, sexual addic-

tions, and the effects of sexual abuse. For more information, contact the American Association of Sex Educators, Counselors and Therapists (AASECT) or the Sex Information and Education Council of Canada (SIECCAN).

SEX THERAPY

A sex therapist treats problems in three main areas of the sexual response cycle: desire, arousal and orgasm. Therapists can also treat problems of sexual technique or phobic responses such as vaginismus (see page 166).

Sex therapists aim to help an individual or couple discover how to enjoy their sexuality free of difficulties and inhibitions. Some single people approach sex therapists because a sexual problem is preventing them from entering a relationship. Others go into sex therapy as couples because their sex life is no longer satisfactory (or has never been satisfactory).

Virtually everyone has the natural ability to be sexual. Yet as people grow up they may develop inhibitions that prevent the natural or spontaneous expression of sexuality in adulthood. Even simple reprimands made by an adult to a young child about touch-

fact or fiction?

Sex therapists recommend masturbation for sexual problems.

Fact. Masturbation is a good way to gain sexual self-knowledge. Women can build up their sexual confidence by using self-stimulation—a woman who knows that she is capable of reaching orgasm on her own will feel more confident about reaching orgasm with a partner. Sex therapists suggest using masturbation as a type of self-directed sensate focus (see page 170). Specific masturbation exercises can also help men overcome premature ejaculation.

Dr. Ruth *Well known for her candid no-nonsense advice, Dr. Ruth Westheimer is a famous television and radio personality as well as a trained psychotherapist specializing in sexual dysfunctions.*

169

THE ORIGIN OF SEX THERAPY

The principles of sex therapy were first explained by Masters and Johnson in their groundbreaking 1969 book *Human Sexual Inadequacy*. Their work was extended by Helen Singer Kaplan, who, in *The New Sex Therapy* (1974), moved the subject into the mainstream of good psychiatric and medical practice. Treatments have, except for some minor modifications in practice, remained largely unchanged, although knowledge about the chemistry of sexual function has increased.

ing his or her genitals may instill in the child the belief that there is something forbidden or naughty about this body part. People may feel great pressure to be sexually attractive and to perform sexually. As a result, women feel inadequate if they do not have coital orgasms, and men feel inferior if they cannot sustain repeated erections.

Sex therapy helps redirect people's thoughts from those that obstruct or inhibit sexual arousal and pleasure. A sex therapist encourages clients to stop judging and evaluating their sexual experiences, and instead to concentrate on the physical sensations and sensual aspects of sex.

A good sex therapist will compile a complete picture of a sexual problem. What were the initial triggers? In what context did symptoms first arise? How did the client's sexual partner respond? Does the problem occur only in specific circumstances? What impact does the sexual problem have on a client's relationships?

When to see a sex therapist

Deciding when to seek professional help for a sexual problem can be difficult, especially since problems such as erectile difficulties

can often be treated at home with self-help programs. Sex therapists Masters, Johnson and Kolodny suggest that if any of the following are present, a person should consider sex therapy rather than home treatment.

- Sex drive is absent or little thought is ever given to sex.
- A relationship is characterized by anger, bitterness and conflict.
- Ejaculation occurs through a flaccid penis more than 10 percent of the time.
- Feelings of sexual guilt are having a negative effect on sexual behavior.
- Either partner is uptight about sex.
- Sexual abuse that took place in childhood is having a negative impact on adult sexual behavior.
- Either partner is uncomfortable about touching the other's genitals.
- Obsessive and troubling sex urges are occurring.

Surrogate partners

Sex surrogacy is a branch of sex therapy first suggested and adopted in the 1970s by Masters and Johnson in the treatment of men and women with sexual problems. The

TREATING SEXUAL PROBLEMS WITH SENSATE FOCUS

A sequence of exercises known as sensate focus is used to help couples learn or relearn how to interact sexually. Before a couple embark on sensate focus, a sex therapist will conduct detailed interviews with both partners about their sexual histories and their

responses and attitudes toward sex. Sensate focus aims to restore the sensual pleasure of sex by teaching individuals to concentrate on pleasurable sensations instead of anticipating and worrying about intercourse. It is helpful for orgasmic problems and reduced sex drive.

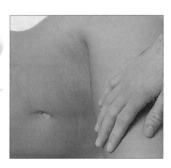

1 Touch your partner's skin but omit sexual parts of the body. Ask your partner to tell you what he or she enjoys.

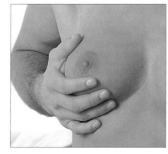

2 Experiment with touching sexual areas of the body, such as the breasts, nipples and genital area.

3 A therapist will advise you about the next stage, suiting it to the particular needs of you and your partner.

surrogate partner is trained in the principles of sex therapy and attempts to treat a client's problems by having sexual intercourse or being sexually intimate with him or her. Surrogate partners are also known as body work therapists. Sex surrogacy was surrounded by controversy from its outset and was soon abandoned by Masters and Johnson. Today it is largely discredited and its use confined mainly to work with young, physically impaired clients.

There are numerous practical and ethical problems associated with surrogacy, including the risk of HIV infection. Sex surrogates by definition must have multiple partners, and even practicing safer sex (see page 128) cannot eliminate the risk of infection. Also, it may be difficult for clients and surrogate partners to maintain a professional relationship with each other: sexual intimacy can have a profound emotional impact, and it may become difficult for sex surrogates and their clients to distinguish successfully between sex and emotional involvement, which can lead to further problems.

Sensate focus

One of the basic principles of sensate focus is that individuals with sexual problems become "self-spectators" during sex. For example, both a woman who has problems reaching orgasm and a man who tries to stop himself from ejaculating too soon will be so preoccupied with assessing their own performance that the sensual pleasure of sex will be lost.

Through conversation, a sex therapist builds up a picture of a couple's sexual problems. He or she will then give the couple an assignment to do at home. In many cases this begins with partners learning to touch themselves while alone to discover their own sensitive areas. The initial assignment together requires the couple to undress and simply take turns touching each other. The partner who is "giving" the

The Language of Sex

Sex therapy, like other types of therapy, rarely produces instant results. Sex therapists respond to this fact by using "repetition," "insight" or "bypass." Repetition involves frequently practicing a task; insight is understanding the emotional issues that can block therapy; bypass means changing the type of task that the clients do.

touch is forbidden to touch the breasts, nipples and genital area (sexual arousal and intercourse are not the aims at this stage), and the partner who is "receiving" the touch must try to relax and enjoy the experience (he or she should report anything that feels distracting or uncomfortable). This type of assignment gives couples the opportunity to touch each other in an enjoyable way without the pressure or anxiety that sexual intercourse can provoke.

After reporting to the sex therapist about the success of the first assignment, a couple will be given a second assignment. This time they extend the touching to the entire body, including the breasts, nipples and genitals. The receiving partner gives specific feedback about what he or she enjoys most. He or she can also give specific instructions or place his or her hand on top of the giving partner's hand to offer guidance about the speed and pressure of touch. Sex and orgasm are still forbidden.

The cycle of sexual problems When treating sexual problems, sex therapists aim to break down the sequence of negative thoughts that turn sex into a chore and make individuals feel as though they are failing.

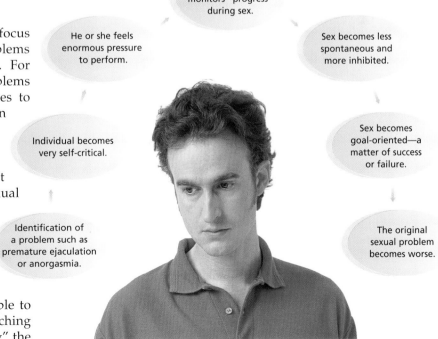

He or she obsessively monitors "progress" during sex.

He or she feels enormous pressure to perform.

Sex becomes less spontaneous and more inhibited.

Individual becomes very self-critical.

Sex becomes goal-oriented—a matter of success or failure.

Identification of a problem such as premature ejaculation or anorgasmia.

The original sexual problem becomes worse.

COUNSELING

Whereas sex therapy usually involves sexual exercises that people practice on their own at home, counseling is based on conversations with a trained person in an office context. In a counseling session the counselor listens to the emotional problems of a client and helps the client to resolve his or her current difficulties and find better ways to cope in the future.

Counseling is typically recommended when sexual problems are coupled with deep-rooted emotional anxieties. For example, erectile difficulties that have come about because a man has lost his sense of sexual confidence may respond well to sensate focus, but erectile difficulties that are caused by a lifelong conviction that sex is wrong or dirty may be better treated by counseling.

Using fantasies ▶
Many people are aroused by dressing-up or role-playing games, especially when dominant and submissive roles are involved.

After a couple have completed the first two stages of sensate focus, they move on to the third. This varies according to the sexual problem that the couple are experiencing. For example, if the woman has difficulty reaching orgasm, her partner will spend the next stage concentrating on her genital area. The aim is not for her to reach orgasm but to experiment with different forms of touch without feeling pressured. The woman should make clear what feels good and what does not. Further exercises then help a couple to apply the knowledge they have gained to full penetrative sex.

The third stage of sensate focus for a couple suffering from erectile problems involves the basic touching—in turn—of the second stage but requires the man to gain an erection and then lose it. Masters and Johnson say: "Tell your partner to deliberately stop touching the penis once an erection occurs and to move her touch elsewhere on your body. The reason behind this maneuver is simple: you need to discover for yourself that it's not a tragedy when an erection peters out, because erections come and go pretty much by their own volition."

Once a man has discovered the different sensory inputs that he needs to gain an erection, a sex therapist will recommend further sensate focus exercises to transfer this knowledge to mutual touching and, eventually, to full sexual intercourse.

Sensate focus encourages people to open up all their sensory channels—touch, taste, smell, sight and hearing—so that sex becomes a sensual and erotic experience.

Fantasy as therapy

Erotic fantasies (see page 51) are often viewed as self-indulgent or confined to arousal during solitary masturbation. In fact, sexual fantasies can be used therapeutically in all kinds of sexual situations, including inter-course with a partner. Fantasies can be especially useful in overcoming problems of sexual arousal or reaching orgasm, and sex therapists who employ sensate focus techniques frequently recommend that their clients fantasize.

Sexual fantasies are unique to the individual, although as Nancy Friday demonstrated through her collections of sexual fantasies, *My Secret Garden* and *Men in Love*, there are common themes. Many people fantasize about previous sexual experiences that they found particularly erotic. These fantasies may involve a person's current partner or an old lover and consist of reliving the encounter or sometimes embellishing it. Other fantasies involve imaginary settings or imaginary lovers. Sometimes fantasies include elements beyond the experience of the individual (such as homosexual sex). Or they may include elements that a person would never want to experience in real life (such as sex involving force or strangers, or being watched having sex).

Fantasy may be particularly helpful for women who have difficulty reaching orgasm. It can boost arousal levels, and women who feel inhibited, self-conscious or easily distracted during intercourse may find that it helps them concentrate on their own sexual pleasure.

Some women worry that fantasizing during intercourse is disloyal to their partners. They may be accustomed to fantasizing during masturbation but are reluctant to do so during intercourse because they feel guilty or inadequate. Sex therapists reassure clients about the value of fantasy. Indeed, the brain is often described as the single most important organ of sexual pleasure. Therapists characterize fantasies as the equivalent of daydreams or "private aphrodisiacs" that are a useful aid to arousal. Without them, women could be putting themselves at a sexual disadvantage. Fantasies can be private or shared. For some partners, acting out fantasies together can heighten arousal and increase openness and intimacy.

GLOSSARY
INDEX
ACKNOWLEDGMENTS

Glossary

A

ABORTION
The termination of a pregnancy by any means before the fetus has developed sufficiently to survive outside the uterus. An abortion may be spontaneous (miscarriage); therapeutic (when the mother's health is at risk); or elective (done at the mother's request). Elective abortion may be induced with drugs or performed surgically. It is rarely performed after the 26th week.

ACQUIRED IMMUNODEFICIENCY SYNDROME (AIDS)
An infection with either human immunodeficiency virus (HIV) I or HIV II causing a deficiency of the immune system.

ACROSOME
A small area on the head of the sperm containing enzymes essential for fertilization.

ADRENAL GLANDS
A pair of small glands located on top of the kidneys. They produce many hormones, some of which influence sexual characteristics such as body shape and hair.

ADULTERY
Voluntary sexual intercourse between a married partner and someone other than their lawful spouse.

AMENORRHEA
The absence of menstrual periods.

AMINO ACIDS
A group of chemical compounds that form the building blocks of proteins.

AMNIOTIC FLUID
The clear fluid that surrounds the fetus throughout pregnancy.

ANAL SEX
The penetration of the man's penis into his partner's anus and rectum.

ANAPHRODISIAC
A substance, usually a food or drink, that inhibits sexual arousal.

ANDROGENS
The general term for male sex hormones. They are produced by the testes and adrenal glands and in very small amounts by the ovaries.

ANEMIA
A condition in which the blood cells contain abnormally low hemoglobin, the chemical responsible for carrying oxygen around the body.

ANOREXIA NERVOSA
A medical condition characterized by lack of appetite and inadequate nutritional intake. The person usually has a very distorted body image, believing they are fat. Some people die from self-starvation. The condition is seen most often in adolescent girls.

ANORGASMIA
The absence of or inability to achieve orgasm.

ANOVULATION
The condition in which the ovaries fail to produce mature ova, or eggs.

ANTIBODIES
Proteins produced by certain white blood cells. They neutralize invading microorganisms. Also known as immunoglobulins.

ANUS
The opening at the end of the digestive tract through which feces are expelled.

APHRODISIAC
A substance, usually a food or drink, thought to be able to induce an increased state of sexual arousal.

APOCRINE GLANDS
Sweat glands located in the armpits and genital region that do not become active until puberty.

AREOLA
A circular area of darker skin surrounding the nipple.

AROUSAL (SEXUAL)
A mental and physical state of awareness and stimulation; the stage in the sexual response cycle in which the body prepares itself for intercourse.

ARTIFICIAL INSEMINATION
The introduction of semen into the vagina or uterus by means other than sexual intercourse for the purpose of achieving pregnancy.

ASSISTED CONCEPTION
A term covering various methods by which a couple who are having difficulty conceiving naturally may be helped to have a child. This includes artificial insemination and IVF.

ATROPHY
The wasting away of a tissue or organ.

AZOOSPERMIA
An absence of sperm in the semen that results in male infertility.

B

BACTERIAL VAGINOSIS
An infection in the vagina caused by an overgrowth of bacterial organisms normally found there and resulting in an offensive, fishy-smelling discharge.

BALANITIS
An inflammation and irritation of the glans and foreskin of the penis, caused by bacteria, fungi or viruses; a tight foreskin; poor hygiene; or an allergy. Balanitis may be sexually transmitted.

BARTHOLINITIS
An inflammation of the Bartholin's glands causing intercourse to become very painful.

BARTHOLIN'S GLANDS
Small glands situated on either side of the vaginal opening that secrete lubricating fluid during sexual arousal. Also called vestibular glands.

BENIGN PROSTATIC HYPERPLASIA (BPH)
A nonmalignant enlargement of the prostate gland. The condition is normal in men over 50 years old.

BIRTH CONTROL
Natural or artificial methods of totally preventing or lessening the frequency of pregnancy.

BLADDER (URINARY)
A hollow organ for storing urine. It is situated near the sexual organs.

BLASTOCYST
The rapidly subdividing mass of cells resulting from the fertilization of the ovum by the sperm.

BONDAGE SEX
Sexual activity that involves being tied up.

BULBOURETHRAL GLANDS
Glands that secrete clear fluid during sexual arousal in men. They are situated below the prostate gland. Also known as Cowper's glands.

C

CANDIDIASIS
An infection of the sexual-genital system, rectum or mouth with a yeastlike fungus. Also known as "thrush."

CANTHARIDES
A very potent aphrodisiac that can prove fatal. It is made from the crushed bodies of a beetle.

CAP (OR CERVICAL CAP)
A barrier contraceptive made from plastic or rubber and placed over the entrance to the uterus, thus preventing sperm from entering.

CAPACITATION
The process involving changes to the enzymes in the sperm acrosome making it possible for the sperm to penetrate and fertilize the ovum. This process starts as the sperm comes into contact with secretions in the vagina and uterus.

CAPILLARY
A vessel that carries blood between the smallest arteries and the smallest veins.

CASTRATION
The removal of the testes or ovaries; usually performed due to disease or as a treatment for prostate or breast cancer.

CELIBACY
Complete voluntary abstinence from sexual relationships, often because of religious or moral beliefs.

CELLS OF LEYDIG
Cells within the testes that are almost exclusively responsible for the production of testosterone.

CERVICAL CANCER
Malignant growth affecting the cervix.

CERVICAL INCOMPETENCE
A weakness of the cervix that prevents full-term pregnancy of nine months. As the fetus increases in weight, pressure on the weak cervix causes it to open prematurely. Treatment involves temporarily closing the cervix with a stitch.

CERVICAL (OR UTERINE) POLYPS
Benign growths on the cervix (or uterus).

CERVIX
The medical term for the neck of an organ. Usually refers to the neck of the uterus, separating the uterus from the vagina and making a passageway for menstrual blood flow and sperm. The cervix dilates during labor, allowing the baby to enter the vagina.

CHAKRAS
According to the doctrine of Tantra, the seven major nerve centers through which sexual energy is mediated.

CHANCROID
An STD, common in tropical countries, that is characterized by genital ulcers and swollen lymph nodes in the groin.

CHEMOTHERAPY
Treatment of cancer or infection using drugs that act selectively on cells responsible for the disorder.

CHLAMYDIA
A bacterial infection that is the most common cause of the STD nonspecific urethritis (NSU). It may affect fertility.

CHROMOSOMES
Threadlike structures made up of DNA carrying inherited genetic information that influences physical and mental characteristics.

CILIA
Hairlike projections found in many organs of the body, including the fallopian tubes, where they transport the ova to the uterus by moving rhythmically.

CIRCUMCISION, MALE
Removal of the foreskin of the penis.

CIRCUMCISION, FEMALE
Removal of all or parts of the clitoris and labia.

CLITORIS
Part of the female genitalia; a small external, erectile organ located just below the pubic bone. It is the focal organ of female sexual arousal.

CLOMIPHENE
A drug used to treat infertility in women. It stimulates ovulation and may lead to multiple births.

COHABITATION
Living together as a sexually active heterosexual or homosexual couple.

COITUS INTERRUPTUS
The withdrawal of the penis from the vagina before ejaculation. It is unreliable as a method of contraception.

COLOSTRUM
The thin, yellowish fluid produced by the breasts just before and after childbirth. The proteins and antibodies in colostrum help the immune system of the newborn.

COLPOSCOPY
A visual examination of the vagina and cervix, usually using illuminated magnification.

CONCEPTION
The fertilization of an ovum by a sperm, followed by implantation of the resulting zygote in the wall of the uterus.

CONDOM
A barrier method of contraception, usually made of latex. The male condom is in the form of a sheath that is placed over the erect penis before intercourse. The female condom is inserted into the vagina and the penis enters inside the condom. Also used as protection from STDs.

CONTRACEPTION
The process of preventing conception by preventing ovulation, fertilization or implantation of the fertilized ovum.

CONTRACEPTIVE PILL
A method of female contraception in which hormones are taken in pill form to prevent ovulation, change the consistency of cervical mucus to hinder the passage of sperm and make the uterine lining inhospitable to implantation.

CORONAL SULCUS
The ridge where the glans joins the shaft of the penis, to which the foreskin is attached during infancy.

CORPUS CAVERNOSA
Columns of spongy tissue in the shaft of the penis that give it its erectile ability. The two corpus cavernosa run parallel along the length of the penis.

CORPUS LUTEUM
The remains of the Graafian follicle after ovulation. Secretory cells grow in this empty follicle and produce progesterone and estrogen in early pregnancy until the placenta takes over. If conception does not occur, then the corpus luteum stops hormone production, regresses and is overgrown by scar tissue.

CORPUS SPONGIOSUM
The smallest column of tissue in the shaft of the penis, surrounding and protecting the urethra and expanding at the tip of the penis to form the glans.

CUNNILINGUS
Sexual stimulation of the vulva area with the tongue by a partner.

CYSTITIS
An inflammation of the inner lining of the bladder caused by infection, injury or irritation.

D

DNA (DEOXYRIBONUCLEIC ACID)
The principal carrier of genetic information in almost all organisms.

DETUMESCENCE
The process by which the penis becomes flaccid after orgasm when blood flows away from the genitals.

DIABETES
A condition in which the pancreas cannot produce sufficient insulin. Sufferers take pills or inject insulin in order to process glucose. Sufferers may experience sexual problems.

DIAPHRAGM
The most commonly used female barrier contraceptive. Made of plastic and rubber and available in different sizes, it fits inside the vagina to cover the cervix and prevent sperm from entering. Used with a spermicide.

DIETHYLSTILBESTROL (DES)
A synthetic hormone currently used as a "morning-after pill." It was previously given to women to prevent miscarriage but was found to raise the incidence of genital cancers in the female children of these pregnancies.

DILATATION AND CURETTAGE (D&C)
Widening of the cervical opening to enable scraping of the uterine lining. Used for termination of pregnancy, to prevent infection after miscarriage, to diagnose uterine problems or to remove uterine tumors.

DOUCHE
A cleansing liquid introduced into the vagina for hygienic or therapeutic reasons. Now believed to increase the chances of infection. Ineffective as a method of contraception.

DYSMENORRHEA
Pain or discomfort during or just before a menstrual period.

DYSPAREUNIA
Painful sexual intercourse.

E

ECTOPIC PREGNANCY
A life-threatening condition in which an embryo develops outside the uterus, most commonly in the fallopian tubes.

EJACULATION
The expulsion of semen from the penis, usually at orgasm—a reflex action that occurs when the penis is physically stimulated during intercourse or masturbation. May occur spontaneously during sleep.

ELECTRA COMPLEX
The psychological state in the Freudian model of psychoanalysis in which a girl "falls in love" with her father and emotionally rejects her mother.

EMBRYO
The term for the fetus between the second and eighth week after conception.

ENDOMETRIAL CANCER
Cancer of the uterine lining.

ENDOMETRIOSIS
A painful condition in which parts of the uterine lining attach to other parts of the body, perhaps inside the fallopian tubes, on the ovaries or on the outer surface of the bladder. The fragments of tissue are subject to hormonal control and bleed in response to the menstrual cycle, causing pain.

ENDOMETRITIS
An inflammation of the lining of the uterus due to infection, incomplete abortion, irritation from an IUD or fibroids. May also be part of menopausal changes.

ENDOMETRIUM
The inner lining of the uterus.

ENDORPHINS
A group of chemicals produced by the pituitary gland. Similar in structure to morphine, they help to control pain and are involved in orgasm.

ENZYMES
Proteins that catalyze chemical reactions in the body.

EPIDIDYMIS
A tiny tube about 18 feet long coiled inside the testes; the place where sperm are transported, are stored and mature.

EPIDIDYMITIS
An inflammation of the epididymis due to an infection, cyst, spermatocele or tumor.

EPISIOTOMY
A surgical cut made from the edge of the vagina toward the anus to prevent tearing during delivery of a baby.

Performed during a breech birth, a forceps-assisted birth or when the baby is large.

ERECTILE INSUFFICIENCY (DYSFUNCTION)
The inability to achieve or maintain an erection adequately for intercourse.

ERECTION
The enlargement and stiffening of the penis or clitoris during sexual arousal due to the tissues filling with blood. The penis elevates during erection.

EROGENOUS AREAS
Parts of the body that lead to some degree of sexual arousal when touched.

EROTIC
Anything associated with or causing feelings of sexual arousal.

EROTICA
Material of a sexual nature that portrays sexual activity in a more sensitive and often less graphic manner than pornography. The term can also refer to anything that triggers or increases sexual desire, such as erotic clothing, aphrodisiacs, sexual fantasies or sex toys.

ESTRADIOL, ESTRIOL AND ESTRONE
Types of estrogen.

ESTROGEN
A group of hormones produced in the ovaries and placenta, in the adrenal glands in both sexes, and in the testes. The most common forms are estradiol, estriol and estrone. They control female sexual development and the functioning of the reproductive system. Their function in men is to inhibit male secondary sexual traits.

ESTROGEN DRUGS
A group of drugs that synthetically replicate the estrogen hormones found naturally in the body. They are used in conjunction with progesterone drugs in the contraceptive pill; to treat infertility caused by underdeveloped ovaries; and in the treatment of menopausal disorders, prostate and breast cancer, and abnormal vaginal bleeding.

F

FALLOPIAN TUBES
A pair of tubes in which fertilization takes place. Cilia in these tubes transport the ovum to the uterus.

FAMILY PLANNING
Limitation of family size and regulation of the period of time between pregnancies by the use of contraception or abortion.

FELLATIO
Oral sex performed on a man's penis by a partner.

FEMININITY
Gender characteristics and performance associated with the female sex; the quality of femaleness.

FERTILITY
The ability to reproduce.

FERTILIZATION
The moment when a sperm penetrates a mature ovum in the fallopian tube. This is usually after sexual intercourse but may also be the result of artificial insemination or take place outside the body (see *In vitro fertilization*).

FETAL MASCULINIZATION
A rare condition that occurs in female fetuses with overactive adrenal glands. The hormones produced by the adrenal glands have an effect similar to that of male hormones, and baby girls may be born with a penis and scrotum. Corrective surgery and hormone treatment ensure normal female sexual development.

FIBROID (OR MYOMA)
A benign tumor developing in the wall of the uterus, whose growth depends on estrogen stimulation.

FIMBRIAE
The fingerlike projections that line the end of the fallopian tubes and meet the ovaries. At ovulation, the fimbriae wave in unison to sweep the ovum into the tube.

FLACCID
The relaxed state of the penis when it is not erect. Intercourse is impossible when the penis is flaccid.

FOLLICLE-STIMULATING HORMONE (FSH)
A hormone produced by the pituitary glands of both sexes that stimulates the gonads to produce sperm and ova.

FOREPLAY
The period of sexual play (touching and kissing) preceding intercourse in which both partners become aroused.

FORESKIN
The loose piece of skin that covers the glans of the penis in uncircumcised men.

FRENULUM
A small, triangular fold of highly sensitive skin on the underside of the penis where the foreskin is attached to the glans.

G

GAMETE
A male or female sex cell—sperm or ovum. Gametes contain half the normal number of chromosomes.

GENDER
A person's social or legal role as a sexual person, as opposed to their genital anatomy.

GENES
Units of hereditary information contained within chromosomes; they pass on an inherited developmental blueprint and determine the physical and mental differences between people. Half come from the mother and half from the father via the union of the ovum and sperm.

GENITALS
The male and female external reproductive organs.

GENITAL TUBERCLE
The fetal structure that goes on to develop into either the glans or the clitoris.

GENITAL WARTS
Warts that grow around the vagina, anus or penis. They can be sexually transmitted and increase the risk of cervical cancer.

GESTATION
The length of pregnancy—from conception to birth—in which the developing fetus is carried in the uterus. In humans this is nine months.

GLANS
The head of the penis.

GONADOTROPIN
Any hormone that influences the functioning of the ovaries or testes. Two are produced by the pituitary in males and females (follicle-stimulating hormone and luteinizing hormone), and a third (human chorionic gonadotropin) by the placenta in early pregnancy.

GONADOTROPIN-RELEASING HORMONE (GRH)
The hormone produced in the hypothalamus that controls the release of male and female sex hormones from the pituitary gland.

GONADS
Reproductive organs—testes in men that produce sperm, and ovaries in women that produce ova.

GONORRHEA
A sexually transmitted disease caused by bacterial infection. If left untreated, it can have far-reaching effects and complications on various parts of the body and may lead to infertility in both men and women. The disease may also be passed to the newborn baby during delivery.

GRAAFIAN FOLLICLE
The fluid-filled structure in the ovary that releases the ovum into the pelvic cavity at ovulation.

G-SPOT
Theoretically, a highly erogenous area located on the front wall of the vagina, between the back of the pubic bone and the front of the cervix.

GYNECOLOGIST
A doctor who specializes in diagnosing and treating problems related to the female reproductive system.

GYNECOMASTIA
An enlargement of one or both breasts in men due to the presence of excessive amounts of the female hormone estrogen. Slight gynecomastia is quite common at puberty.

H

HEMATOCELE
A swelling due to collection of blood in the scrotum, usually secondary to an injury. Similar to a bruise.

HEMOPHILIA
A hereditary blood disorder that almost exclusively affects men. The blood lacks clotting factor VIII. Hemophiliacs may suffer recurrent external and internal bleeding.

HEMOPHILIAC
A person suffering from hemophilia.

HEPATITIS (VIRAL)
An inflammation of the liver caused by one of many viruses. Hepatitis A is spread by contact with food or water contaminated with infected feces. Hepatitis B and C are spread mainly through sexual contact or infected blood.

HERMAPHRODITISM
An extremely rare congenital disorder in which both male and female

gonads are present and the external genitalia are not clearly male or female. Sufferers are infertile.

HERPES SIMPLEX
A family of two viruses responsible for "cold sores" around the lips, mouth and genitals. Both viruses can infect either area and are sexually transmissable through direct contact with sores. The main symptom of herpes is small, itchy fluid-filled blisters that burst and form scabs.

HOMOSEXUALITY, FEMALE
Sexual attraction between women; also known as lesbianism.

HOMOSEXUALITY, MALE
Sexual attraction between men.

HORMONES
Chemicals produced by various organs that affect physical and emotional changes in the body.

HORMONE REPLACEMENT THERAPY (HRT)
The use of any synthetic or natural hormone to treat a condition caused by deficiency in a particular hormone; usually refers to the use of estrogen hormones taken with progestogen to treat menopausal symptoms.

HOT FLASHES
A symptom of menopause that causes a rush of heat to the upper body and head, accompanied by sweating and sometimes dizziness.

HUMAN CHORIONIC GONADOTROPIN (HCG)
A hormone produced by the placenta during pregnancy. It maintains the corpus luteum and its production of estrogen and progesterone. Its detection in urine is the basis of most pregnancy tests.

HIV (HUMAN IMMUNODEFICIENCY VIRUS)
The virus that is the cause of AIDS and AIDS-related complex. Transmitted via blood transfusions, other blood-to-blood contact, the sharing of nonsterile needles and sexual intercourse. A fetus may also contract the virus from its mother. HIV attacks the T-lymphocytes, which are a part of the immune system, and may destroy their normal functioning.

HUMAN PAPILLOMAVIRUS (HPV)
A virus that causes genital warts. Infection with some forms of HPV increases the risk for cervical cancer.

HYDROCELE
A painless swelling of the scrotum, common in middle-aged men, that is caused by a buildup of excess fluid. It may be attributable to a number of causes, including infection, injury to the testes or a tumor.

HYMEN
A thin membrane that partially covers or occasionally surrounds the entrance to the vagina; usually broken during physical exercise or initial sexual intercourse.

HYPOGONADISM
Underactivity of the gonads caused by disorders of the pituitary gland, ovaries or testes that results in deficient production of gonadotropin hormones.

HYPOTHALAMUS
A region of the brain that controls much of the nervous system and hormonal functions. It is involved in regulating sexual response and activity, most of which takes place via the pituitary gland, to which it is connected.

HYSTERECTOMY
A surgical procedure to remove the uterus, usually performed for gynecological reasons. Sometimes surgery involves removal of the ovaries too.

I

IATROGENIC DISEASE
A disease that is induced by a drug or other medical treatment.

IMPERFORATE HYMEN
A congenital condition in which the hymen has no perforation through which menstrual blood can pass. The condition is generally not discovered until the onset of menstruation, when the buildup of blood behind the hymen causes severe abdominal pain. The condition can be remedied by a simple operation.

IMPLANT
Any material inserted into the body to replace a diseased structure, to deliver hormones or drugs at a steady rate, or for cosmetic reasons (for example, silicone implants to increase the size of the breasts).

IMPOTENCE
The inability to achieve or maintain an erection. This may be caused by a variety of psychological or physical prob-

lems or by the use of certain drugs. It becomes more common with age.

INFANTICIDE
The intentional killing of a baby or infant. Sometimes practiced in cultures where male offspring are valued over female offspring.

INFERTILITY
The inability to conceive and carry a fetus to term and delivery.

INTERCOURSE (SEXUAL)
Sexual activity involving penetrative sex.

INTRAUTERINE DEVICE (IUD)
A contraceptive device, usually made of plastic (with or without copper), that is placed in the uterus to prevent implantation of the fertilized ovum. It remains in place constantly and is replaced every two to five years.

INVERTED NIPPLE
A nipple that is turned inward rather than protruding. The condition does not normally interfere with breast-feeding. In older women, it may be a sign of breast cancer.

IN VITRO FERTILIZATION (IVF)
A method of treating infertility in which ova are removed from the ovary and fertilized outside the body.

IN VIVO FERTILIZATION
The natural fertilization of an ovum in the reproductive tract by artificial insemination or sexual intercourse.

K

KAMA SUTRA
An ancient Hindu text, written by Vatsyayana, that celebrates sex as a means of harmony between men and women and gives advice about sex and lovemaking.

KAPOSI'S SARCOMA
A malignant growth of the capillaries and connective tissue, previously considered rare and slow-growing but now seen frequently in an aggressive form affecting the skin and gastrointestinal and respiratory tracts of those suffering from AIDS.

KLINEFELTER'S SYNDROME
A chromosomal abnormality in which male infants are born with an extra X chromosome. The presence of any abnormality may go unnoticed until external symptoms become evident at puberty, the most notable being

enlarged breasts and failure of testes to grow. Affected males are infertile.

L

LABIA
The lips of the vulva that protect the entrance to the vagina and urethra. There are two sets of labia. The external pair, the labia majora, are fleshy, with pubic hair and sweat glands, and stretch from the perineum to the mons pubis. They cover the internal labia minora, which are smaller and hairless and meet to form the hood of the clitoris.

LABIOSCROTAL SWELLING
The fetal structure that goes on to form the scrotum in boys and the labia majora in girls.

LABOR
Childbirth, the process by which a child is delivered from the uterus into the outside world. It starts with the dilatation of the cervix and ends with the delivery of the placenta.

LAPAROSCOPY
The examination of the abdominal organs using a laparoscope, a viewing tube with a light attached, which is passed through a small incision in the abdomen. The abdominal cavity is filled with gas to separate the contents and make viewing easier. Useful to diagnose pelvic pain, infertility or other gynecological problems.

LESBIANISM
Female homosexuality.

LEUKOPLAKIA
Raised white patches on the mucous membranes of the mouth, vulva or glans of the penis. They are usually harmless but must be distinguished from similar premalignant changes in these areas.

LIBIDO
Sexual desire. Low libido can have psychological or physiological causes.

LUMPECTOMY
A surgical procedure to remove a benign or malignant lump from the breast. If this completely removes a cancer, the rest of the breast can be left intact.

LUTEINIZING HORMONE (LH)
A gonadotropin hormone produced by the pituitary gland.

M

MAMMOGRAPHY
A special X-ray examination sometimes using injected dye to detect abnormal growths in the breast. It cannot always distinguish between benign and malignant growths.

MANUAL STIMULATION
Rubbing or applying pressure to the penis or clitoris with the hands to produce arousal or orgasm.

MASCULINITY
Gender characteristics and performance associated with the male sex; the quality of maleness.

MASTECTOMY
A surgical procedure to remove all or part of the breast as a treatment for breast cancer. The amount of breast tissue that is removed depends on the progression of the cancer and the age and health of the woman.

MASTURBATION
Sexual self-stimulation usually by massaging the penis or clitoris with the hand to achieve arousal or orgasm.

MENARCHE
The onset of menstruation. This usually occurs in girls 2 to 3 years after the onset of puberty but may start anytime between the ages of 9 and 17.

MENOPAUSE
The point at which hormonal changes cause the cessation of menstruation. It typically occurs between ages 45 and 60 and is associated with various physical and psychological symptoms. Also called "the change of life."

MENORRHAGIA
An excessive loss of blood during menstruation due to benign or malignant growth in the uterus, blood disorders, or occasionally an IUD or hormonal imbalance.

MENSTRUAL CYCLE
The complex chain of hormonal reactions that trigger ovulation and menstruation. The average menstrual cycle is 28 days long.

MENSTRUATION
The periodic shedding of the uterine lining that occurs at the end of the menstrual cycle in ovulating women who are not pregnant. Menstrual blood flow lasts from three to eight days in each cycle.

MISCARRIAGE
The spontaneous loss of a fetus before it is able to survive outside the woman's body without artificial support. Ten to 15 percent of all pregnancies end in miscarriage.

MISSIONARY POSITION
A face-to-face sexual position in which the woman lies on her back and the man lies on top of her.

MITOCHONDRIA
The energy-generating units of most cells in the body. Mitochondria in sperm convert the nutrients found in semen to energy used to swim toward the ovum.

MITTELSCHMERZ
Lower abdominal pain, occurring on one side, suffered by some women during ovulation. Pain is not usually severe and lasts only a few hours.

MOLLUSCUM CONTAGIOSUM
A harmless viral infection affecting both children and, less commonly, adults. Symptoms are small, shiny, white lumps that release a cheesy substance if squeezed. They appear on the genitals, the inside of the thighs and the face, in groups or alone. The infection is transmitted by direct skin contact or sexually.

MONOGAMY
Marriage or cohabitation with only one person at a time, usually involving a sexual relationship.

MONONUCLEOSIS
A viral infection that causes a high temperature, sore throat, and swollen lymph glands and tonsils. Occasionally mild liver damage may occur. The disease usually occurs in adolescence, when the immune system is most likely to respond to contact with the virus.

MORNING-AFTER PILL
A form of postcoital contraception consisting of a high-dosage, combined pill that must be taken within 72 hours of unprotected sexual intercourse. The initial dose is repeated 12 hours later.

MORULA
The stage in the development of the embryo that occurs after the zygote has been through a process of three or four cell divisions and has become a solid cluster of cells. The morula continues to divide until it forms what is known as the blastocyst.

MOTILE
A term referring to the ability to move. For example, a sperm must have good motility in order to reach the ovum and fertilize it.

MULLERIAN DUCT
A paired set of ducts that is present in both male and female fetuses but goes on to develop into fimbriae, fallopian tubes and uterus in the female fetus.

MULTIPLE ORGASMS
The potential of some women to have several orgasms in quick succession if sexual stimulation is continued. Men are able to have multiple orgasms if they can learn to reach orgasm without ejaculating.

MUTUAL MASTURBATION
Masturbation engaged in with a partner before or as a part of sexual intercourse. Both partners stimulate each other simultaneously, possibly to orgasm.

MYOMAS (FIBROIDS)
Noncancerous muscle tumors, most commonly found in the intestine, uterus and stomach.

MYOMETRIUM
The layer of muscle in the uterus that lies beneath the mucous membrane of the endometrium. It is this muscle that contracts to expel the baby during childbirth.

N

NIPPLE
The small prominence at the tip of each breast that, in women, contains the openings from which the milk ducts emerge. Muscle tissue in the nipple allows it to become erect, which helps during breast-feeding.

NOCTURNAL EMISSION
Commonly referred to as a "wet dream"; ejaculation that occurs during sleep. It is normal in adolescent boys, and may occur in older men who are not sexually active.

NONOXYNOL-9
An active ingredient in some spermicides (some condoms are impregnated with nonoxynol-9). Also provides increased protection against certain sexually transmitted diseases and has been shown to kill the HIV I virus—impregnated condoms form part of a safer-sex routine.

NONPENETRATIVE SEX
Making love without the penis entering the vagina. For example, mutual masturbation or oral sex.

NYMPHOMANIA
A term used in the past to refer to women who were judged to have an abnormal sexual appetite. Nowadays used only in cases of sexual obsession arising as a result of mental illness.

O

OBESITY
A condition in which excess body fat exceeds by more than 20 percent the recommended amount for a person's height and age.

OEDIPUS COMPLEX
The psychological state proposed by Freud in which a boy is thought to "fall in love" with his mother and emotionally reject his father.

OLIGOSPERMIA
A sperm count below the level considered necessary for fertility; currently set at 20 million sperm per milliliter of semen. Low sperm count may be temporary.

OOPHORITIS
An inflammation of the ovaries that may be caused by infection with the virus that causes mumps or by a sexually transmitted disease.

ORAL STIMULATION
The action by which a man or woman brings their sexual partner to arousal or orgasm by stimulating the genitals with the mouth.

ORCHITIS
An inflammation of the testis commonly caused by an infection such as the virus that causes mumps. It causes swelling, severe pain and fever. This may result in a shrunken testis after the infection has subsided and can cause fertility problems.

ORGASM
Intense physical sensations caused by muscular spasms that occur at the peak of sexual arousal. In men, contractions of the inner pelvic muscles cause ejaculation of semen. Female orgasm is associated with contractions of the walls of the vagina and uterus. Orgasm can last up to a minute, although a duration of between 3 and 10 seconds is more usual.

ORGY
Group sex, often associated with the feasting of Roman times, that for many people carries connotations of debauchery.

OSTEOPOROSIS
A condition, commonly called "brittle bones," caused by a decrease in bone density. It is most common in postmenopausal women, whose ovaries have ceased producing estrogen, which helps maintain bone mass.

OVA
Female sex cells, or eggs. Women are born with a full complement of ova that mature and are released after puberty, usually at a rate of one per menstrual cycle.

OVARIAN CYSTS
Abnormal fluid-filled swellings of the ovary. Only rarely is a cyst caused by cancer of the ovary.

OVARIES
The paired female reproductive organs, situated at either side of the uterus, close to the opening of the fallopian tubes. The ovaries contain follicles in which ova are produced. The ovaries also produce the female sex hormones estrogen and progesterone.

OVULATION
The maturation and release of an ovum from a follicle within the ovary. It occurs midway through the menstrual cycle and is regulated by follicle-stimulating hormone. If a woman is not ovulating, she cannot conceive.

OXYTOCIN
A hormone produced by the pituitary gland that causes the contractions of the uterus during labor and stimulates the flow of milk in nursing women. Synthetic forms of the chemical are used to induce labor, to empty the uterus after an incomplete miscarriage or death of the fetus, and sometimes to stimulate the flow of milk.

P

PARAMETRIUM
The outer layer of the uterus that consists of tough fibrous tissue.

PELVIC CAVITY
The area in the lower part of the body trunk containing the genitourinary systems in both sexes, including the reproductive organs.

PELVIC INFLAMMATORY DISEASE (PID)
An infection affecting the internal female reproductive organs. PID often occurs as a result of a sexually transmitted disease such as chlamydia. It occurs mostly among young, sexually active women or those using IUDs. It may cause infertility or increase the risk of ectopic pregnancy due to the scarring of the fallopian tubes.

PENETRATIVE SEX
A sexual act involving the penetration of the vagina or the anus by the penis.

PENILE RINGS
Rubber rings that are placed around the shaft of the penis to allow an erection to be maintained; used to treat erectile insufficiency. Some penile rings are designed as sex toys to stimulate the woman's clitoris during intercourse.

PENIS
The male sex organ, through which urine and semen pass.

PERIMENOPAUSE
From the Greek "peri," meaning "around," the years and months leading up to and immediately following menopause.

PERINEUM
The area between the thighs in both sexes that lies behind the genitals and in front of the anus.

PESSARY
A device placed in the vagina to correct the position of a prolapsed uterus.

PHALLUS
Any pointed or upright object that resembles or symbolizes the erect penis.

PHEROMONES
Chemical substances, related to hormones, that are secreted by the body possibly to send signals of sexual readiness. The smell of these substances may trigger an instinctive sexual response in potential mates.

PHIMOSIS
Tightness of the foreskin that prevents it from being drawn back over the glans of the penis. Phimosis is normal in babies up to six months but is problematic if it persists.

PITUITARY GLAND
An important gland located at the base of the brain beneath the optic nerves and the hypothalamus. The pituitary gland produces a number of hormones affecting vital functions of the body, including growth, sexual activity and reproduction.

PLACEBO EFFECT
A psychological phenomenon in which a substance taken to achieve a certain physical or mental state is effective not because of any actual properties it possesses but because the user believes in its effectiveness. For example, most aphrodisiacs.

PLACENTA
The organ that develops during pregnancy to allow fetal respiration, feeding and excretion via the mother. The placenta also produces hormones that alter the woman's body and help maintain the pregnancy.

PLATEAU STAGE
A stage in the sexual response cycle that follows excitement. The culmination of the plateau stage may be orgasm or a slow resolution.

PNEUMOCYSTIC PNEUMONIA
An infection of the lungs caused by a microorganism that is dangerous only to individuals with an impaired immune system. It is a major cause of death in people suffering from AIDS.

POLYCYSTIC OVARY
Also known as Stein-Leventhal syndrome, a condition in which there is development of multiple cysts in the ovaries triggered by increased levels of testosterone. The condition results in a lack of menstruation, excessive body hair and infertility.

PORNOGRAPHY
Sexually arousing material, such as literature, films or magazines, that is usually simpler and more explicit than erotica. Pornography often has less artistic pretension than erotica.

POSTCOITAL
A term referring to the period after sexual intercourse and orgasm.

POSTCOITAL FATIGUE
A relaxed and drowsy feeling following sexual intercourse and orgasm.

POSTMENOPAUSAL
A term used to describe a woman who has been through menopause, ceased to ovulate and so come to the end of her reproductive life.

PREGNANCY
The time during which a new individual develops in the uterus, starting with conception and continuing until delivery of the baby. In humans, pregnancy lasts an average of 266 days from conception.

PREMARITAL SEX
Sexual intercourse or activity engaged in before marriage.

PREMATURE EJACULATION
Ejaculation that occurs before penetration or very rapidly afterward. It is a problem that is especially common in adolescent boys.

PREMENSTRUAL SYNDROME (PMS)
A condition affecting 90 percent of ovulating women at some time in their lives, characterized by a combination of emotional and physical symptoms, including irritability, depressed mood, fatigue, breast tenderness, head- and backache, and abdominal pain.

PREPUCE
The foreskin of the penis.

PRIMORDIAL FOLLICLES
Groups of cells in the ovaries that contain potential ova. Primordial follicles develop in the ovaries of a developing fetus 4 to 5 months after conception. They are activated at puberty by follicle-stimulating hormone, when some of them mature to release mature ova.

PROGESTERONE
The sex hormone secreted by the ovaries and by the placenta during pregnancy. It is essential for the normal function of the female reproductive system.

PROGESTERONE DRUGS
A group of drugs replicating the hormone progesterone that are used in birth control pills, either on their own or in conjunction with estrogen. They are also used with estrogen to treat menstrual problems and in HRT (reducing the risk of uterine cancer).

PROLACTIN
The pituitary gland hormone that stimulates breast enlargement during pregnancy and initiates milk production after delivery.

PROLAPSE
The displacement of part or all of an organ from its normal position. A structure that commonly prolapses is the uterus, which drops down into the vagina.

PROSTAGLANDIN
A fatty acid that acts in similar ways to a hormone. Prostaglandins occur in

various body tissues and are found in semen. They have several functions, including stimulating contractions during labor. Overproduction of prostaglandin causes abdominal pain and may contribute to PMS.

PROSTATE GLAND

A walnut-sized glandular structure surrounding the neck of the bladder and the urethra in men. It secretes substances into the semen as the fluid passes through ducts leading from the seminal vesicles into the urethra. Enlargement and cancer of the prostate gland become more common in men over 50.

PROSTATITIS

An inflammation of the prostate gland that normally affects men between the ages of 30 and 50 and is usually caused by a bacterial infection, which may be sexually transmitted.

PROSTATODYNIA

A relatively common male problem characterized by the presence of prostatitis symptoms but the absence of any infection.

PSEUDOHERMAPHRODITISM

A condition in which the individual possesses male testes and female genitalia or female ovaries and male genitalia. See also *Hermaphroditism.*

PSYCHOANALYSIS

Treatment for mental illness or psychological problems based on psychoanalytic theory, delving deeply into the patient's past. Psychoanalysis can help neurosis and personality disorders and has also been used to treat psychosis.

PSYCHOSEXUAL

A term that refers to a sexual problem or condition that, although the effects may be physical, has a psychological basis. For example, vaginismus resulting from the psychological impact of a previous traumatic sexual experience.

PUBERTY

The period, usually in the early teens, when an individual approaches sexual maturity and develops secondary sexual characteristics, such as pubic hair, breasts (in girls) and facial hair (in boys). The sex organs mature, making reproduction possible. Puberty usually occurs between ages 10 and 15 in both sexes, although it tends to occur earlier in girls.

PUBIC HAIR

Hair that grows around the genitals in males and females and that appears at the onset of puberty.

PUBIC LICE ("CRABS")

Small insects that can attach themselves with crablike claws to the pubic hair. They can be sexually transmitted or caught from infested bed linen and towels.

PUBOCOCCYGEAL (PC) MUSCLES

Muscles of the pelvic floor that support the internal sex organs.

R

RADIATION THERAPY (RADIOTHERAPY)

The use of a source of radiation, such as X rays, to treat certain kinds of cancer, including cervical and uterine cancer. It is also used to destroy remaining tumor cells after surgery in the treatment of breast cancer.

RECTUM

A short muscular tube forming the last section of the large intestine and continuing to the anus. Feces collect here, causing it to distend, creating the urge to defecate.

REFRACTORY PERIOD

A period of sexual unresponsiveness after male orgasm in which the body recovers. The man may become sleepy, and further sexual stimulation will fail to produce an erection. The length of the refractory period can be minutes or hours and depends on age.

RESOLUTION STAGE

A period after orgasm in which the body returns to its prearoused state. The breasts and genitals decrease in size, muscles all over the body relax, and blood flows away from the pelvic region so that the penis becomes flaccid. The heart rate and breathing return to normal.

RETROGRADE EJACULATION

A disorder in which the semen is forced back into the bladder (due to the valve at its base failing to close) during ejaculation. This may be due to disease or the result of invasive surgery in the pelvic region. Having intercourse while the bladder is full may sometimes lead to normal ejaculation, but there is no permanent cure.

RETROVERTED UTERUS

Sometimes called "tipped uterus," a condition in which the uterus is inclined backward toward the intestine instead of forward. Retroversion is a harmless variation from the norm and should not cause gynecological problems.

RHYTHM METHOD

A type of contraception using periodic abstinence from sexual intercourse during times when the woman is fertile and able to conceive. It works by attempting to predict ovulation. The method is unreliable and has a high failure rate.

RUBELLA

Also known as German measles, a viral infection that causes minor illness in children and usually only slightly more problematic illness in adults. If contracted by a woman in the early months of her pregnancy, however, it can lead to a number of severe birth defects. Rubella vaccination of infants and of women approaching childbearing age has significantly reduced the incidence of congenital rubella.

S

SAFER SEX

A term used to describe preventive measures taken to reduce the risk of acquiring or passing on an STD, including HIV.

SANITARY NAPKIN

A disposable pad of material designed to absorb menstrual flow while attached to a special belt or to underwear.

SCABIES

A highly contagious skin infestation caused by a mite that burrows into the skin and lays eggs. Scabies is passed on by close physical contact such as sexual intercourse or even holding hands. The condition causes severe itching, especially at night, and scratching results in scabs and sores.

SCROTUM

The pouch that hangs below the penis and contains the testes, epididymis and parts of the spermatic cords. The scrotum has an outer layer of thin, wrinkled skin with scattered hairs and oil-secreting glands on its surface.

SEBACEOUS GLANDS

Small glands in the skin that open

either into hair follicles or directly onto the surface of the skin, releasing an oily, lubricating substance called sebum. They are abundant on the scalp, labia minora and penile glands.

SEBUM
A secretion of the sebaceous glands that is composed of fats and waxes; it lubricates the skin, keeps it supple, makes it waterproof and protects it from cracking when exposed to a dry atmosphere. It also provides some protection from bacterial and fungal infections. Oversecretion causes overly greasy skin and may lead to acne or dermatitis.

SECONDARY SEXUAL CHARACTERISTICS
Sexually defining features that develop after the onset of puberty. In males they include facial and body hair, a heavier musculature, and deeper voice; in females they include breast development, broadening of the hips and thighs, pubic hair, and a generally more curved body shape.

SEMEN
The sperm-containing fluid produced by the man on ejaculation.

SEMINAL VESICLES
A pair of small glandular sacs that secrete most of the nutrient fluid in which sperm is transported in semen.

SEMINIFEROUS TUBULES
Tiny tubes inside the testes, in which the sperm are produced.

SENSATE FOCUS
A technique used in sex therapy, involving reawakening sensual responses using specific touch and massage exercises.

SEROCONVERSION
The production of antibodies after infection with HIV. It usually takes between 6 and 10 weeks for the body to produce enough antibodies for an HIV test to be accurate.

SERTOLI CELLS
Cells supporting the developing sperm, situated in the coils of the seminiferous tubules.

SEX ADDICTION
An uncommon condition, affecting both men and women, that is defined as a compulsive dependence on frequent, ritualized sexual activity. Such activity may be a substitute for an intimate relationship, which the sufferer is incapable of.

SEX SURROGACY
A branch of sex therapy, first adopted in the 1970s, in which the therapist attempts to treat a patient for sexual problems by having intercourse or being sexually intimate with him or her. A procedure that was always controversial and that carries great risks to emotional and physical health, it is now largely discredited.

SEXUAL AIDS
Also called "sex toys," a number of products available that are designed to increase sexual excitement and arousal, with or without a partner. Some of the most common are vibrators and dildos.

SEXUAL INTERCOURSE
The act of making love. The term is usually used to refer to penetrative sex, although it is sometimes used to describe other forms of sexual activity, such as oral sex, intimate touching or mutual masturbation.

SEXUAL POSITIONS
The positions adopted by a couple engaged in sexual intercourse. These range from man- or woman-on-top positions to side-by-side positions and rear-entry positions.

SEXUALLY TRANSMITTED DISEASES (STDS)
Infections transmitted primarily by sexual contact. Also known as venereal diseases.

SHALLOW THRUSTING
A technique used to help a man delay ejaculation. As he feels himself coming close to orgasm, the man resists the instinct to thrust deeper and instead slows down and makes his thrust more shallow. This helps to prolong intercourse.

SIXTY-NINE POSITION
Also called "soixante-neuf," a sexual position that allows a man and a woman to give oral sex to each other simultaneously. The position gets its name from the fact that the couple, one kneeling on top of the other, may be likened to the numerals 6 and 9 in close proximity.

SKENE'S GLANDS
Thought to be equivalent to the male prostate gland, female glands that are thought by some to be involved in female ejaculation following stimulation of the G-spot.

SMEGMA
An accumulation of sebaceous gland secretions beneath the foreskin of the penis, usually due to poor personal hygiene.

SOFT-ENTRY SEX
A technique that allows intercourse to continue if a man partially loses his erection during sex or if a couple wish to continue having sex after the man has had an orgasm. The man uses his fingers to gently guide the end of his penis into his partner's vagina.

SOMATOTROPIN
Also known as "growth hormone," a hormone secreted by the pituitary gland to stimulate tissue and bone growth.

SPERM
The male sex cell that fertilizes the female ovum. Sperm are produced within the testes in a process dependent on the production of testosterone and gonadotropin hormones commencing at puberty. Each sperm consists of a head that contains the genetic material and a tail that propels the sperm to the ovum.

SPERMARCHE
The onset of the male's ability to produce sperm in early adolescence.

SPERMATIDS
Cells in the last stage in the development of the sperm before they break free of the Sertoli cells, in which the final process of cell division and specialization takes place.

SPERMATOCELE
A cyst containing fluid and sperm that occurs in the epididymis.

SPERMATOCYTES
Cells in the second stage of the development of the sperm cells, which divide in such a way as to contain only half of the chromosomes contained in a normal human cell. The potential sperm are by this stage becoming increasingly specialized.

SPERMATOGENESIS
The process of sperm production that takes place in the seminiferous tubules of the testes.

SPERMATOGONIA
The first stage in the development of the mature sperm cell; simple germ cells are capable of becoming highly specialized spermatocytes and ultimately sperm.

SPERMICIDE

A contraceptive substance that kills sperm, normally used in conjunction with barrier method devices to increase effectiveness. Some spermicides may also help protect against STDs.

SPHINCTER

A ring of muscle around an orifice or internal passage that regulates inflow and outflow. For example, the sphincters that form the anus.

SPONGE, CONTRACEPTIVE

A method of contraception consisting of a disposable circular piece of polyurethane foam injected with spermicide. The sponge is moistened with water to activate the spermicide and is inserted in the vagina before sex.

STEIN-LEVENTHAL SYNDROME

See *Polycystic ovary.*

STERILIZATION

A procedure that renders a person infertile. In women, sterilization involves cutting, clipping, tying or otherwise obstructing the fallopian tubes. Male sterilization, known as vasectomy, is a surgical procedure in which the vas deferens are cut or tied.

STEROID HORMONES

A group of hormones that includes the male and female sex hormones: androgens, estrogens and progesterone as well as hormones from the adrenal glands. All steroid hormones are synthesized in the body from cholesterol.

SUBFERTILITY

A condition affecting a couple who are having difficulty conceiving. It may be due to physical causes such as low sperm count or mental causes such as high stress levels.

SURROGACY

A contractual agreement entered into for a woman to become pregnant and give birth for another woman (sometimes using the ovum of the latter woman with the sperm of her partner), with the understanding that the birth mother will surrender the child, after birth, to the contractual parents.

SYPHILIS

A sexually transmitted or, less commonly, congenital bacterial disease that if untreated passes through a number of distinct stages, usually over several years. The primary and secondary stages are characterized by a primary genital sore or chancre, and a rash and lymph node enlargement. The disease is highly infectious and may be contracted by kissing and other sexual contact.

T

TAMPON

Sanitary protection consisting of a "plug" of absorbent material, usually cotton, that is inserted into the vagina to absorb menstrual blood and is removed by an attached string.

TANTRIC AND TAOIST SEX

Two techniques for prolonging sexual intercourse. Tantra is an ancient Indian doctrine based on the Hindu ideas of balance and unity. Its principle is that sexual energy can unite male and female to achieve spiritual enlightenment. Taoism is an older, Chinese doctrine that teaches, among other things, that longevity and tranquillity can be achieved by sexual harmony in which the male uses self-control to ensure female sexual satisfaction.

TENTING

A feature of the plateau stage of the sexual response cycle in which the uterus rises from the pelvic cavity into the abdominal cavity. This results in the expansion of the vaginal cavity, creating an area where semen can pool after the man has ejaculated into the vagina.

TERATOGEN

An external agent, such as a disease, drug or environmental factor, that causes the development of physical abnormalities in the embryo or fetus.

TESTICLES (TESTES)

The paired male reproductive organs that produce sperm and the male sex hormone testosterone. They are located within the scrotum and connected to the penis via the spermatic cords.

TESTOSTERONE

The most important of the male sex hormones; it stimulates sexual development and controls reproductive functions. It is produced by the testes in men, and in lesser amounts by the female ovaries.

T-HELPER CELL

Also called T-lymphocyte, a type of white blood cell that is an essential part of the immune system, the normal function of which is affected by infection with HIV.

THROMBOSIS

The formation of a blood clot within any blood vessel. When in an artery it can block the blood supply and is a common cause of heart attack or stroke (a form of brain damage). The risk of thrombosis is increased in women taking the contraceptive pill who smoke.

THRUSH

See *Candidiasis.*

THYROID HORMONES

Hormones that regulate metabolism and in children are also essential in normal physical growth and mental development. They are produced in the thyroid gland, and their secretion is regulated by the hypothalamus and pituitary gland.

TORSION OF THE TESTICLES

Twisting of a spermatic cord that causes severe pain and swelling of the testes and if untreated leads to permanent damage. If performed in time, a simple operation can save the fertility of the testicle.

TOXIC SHOCK SYNDROME

A rare condition caused by an overgrowth of a toxin-producing bacterium in the vagina that may be triggered by the use of tampons. Symptoms occur suddenly and include high fever, vomiting, diarrhea, dizziness and muscular aches. This is followed by a rash and a sudden drop in blood pressure that causes shock.

TRICHOMONIASIS

A common infection of the vagina, often producing no symptoms. It is caused by a microorganism and is usually sexually transmitted. The infection may also be passed to men, in whom it affects the urethra. It may cause an offensive vaginal discharge.

TRIMESTER

A period making up one-third of a specified length of time. Pregnancy is divided into three trimesters, characterized by different developmental stages, both of the mother and of the fetus. The first trimester corresponds to weeks 1 through 13, the second to weeks 14 through 27 and the third to weeks 28 through 40.

TUMOR
A mass of tissue that forms when cells in a specific area reproduce at an abnormally increased rate. Tumors may be benign or malignant. All malignant tumors are classified under the general term "cancer."

TURNER'S SYNDROME
A rare chromosomal abnormality, affecting only females, in which one of the X chromosomes is absent or damaged. The syndrome causes a variety of physical and mental abnormalities, retarded development of secondary sexual characteristics, and infertility.

U

ULTRASOUND
Scanning with high-frequency sound waves to produce images of internal cavities without performing invasive procedures. It is commonly used to check on the development of the unborn child.

URETHRA
The tube by which urine is excreted from the bladder.

URETHRAL BULB
The portion of the urethra that expands like a balloon to hold semen just before ejaculation.

UROGENITAL FOLDS
The fetal structure that closes up to form part of the penile shaft in males and stays separate to form the inner labia minora in females.

UROGENITAL TRACT
The urinary, genital and reproductive organs in both sexes.

UTERINE CAVITY
The hollow inside the uterus that is lined by the endometrium and where the fetus develops during pregnancy.

UTERINE PROLAPSE
Displacement of the uterus from its normal position down into the vagina. This may be slight or, in the most severe cases, can result in a condition in which the uterus protrudes outside the vagina.

UTERUS
The hollow muscular organ of the female reproductive system, situated behind the bladder and in front of the bowel. At the narrow, lower end, it opens into the vagina via the cervix; the upper part opens into the fallopian tubes. During pregnancy the uterus expands to accommodate the growing fetus.

V

VACUUM ASPIRATION
A common method of surgically aborting a fetus.

VACUUM PUMP DEVICE
A piece of equipment that can be used by men suffering from impotence in order to achieve an erection.

VAGINA
The muscular passage that links the cervix to the external genitalia. The vagina has three functions: as a receptacle for the penis during intercourse, as an exit channel for menstrual fluid and as a birth canal.

VAGINAL TRAINERS
Devices used in the treatment for vaginismus. Increasingly larger, penis-shaped trainers are inserted into the vagina to gradually relax the muscles there and ultimately allow intercourse.

VAGINISMUS
Painful, involuntary spasms occurring when intercourse is attempted, making penetration impossible. The condition may be the result of a past traumatic sexual experience.

VAGINITIS
General medical term for vaginal inflammation and infection. Vaginitis may be due to bacteria, yeasts or a virus. It is sometimes called vaginosis.

VARICOCELE
A varicose enlargement of the veins surrounding the testes. The condition is common and is usually painless, requiring no treatment, although it is a possible cause of low sperm count.

VAS DEFERENS
Ducts that carry sperm from the testes to the seminal vesicles, where they are stored until ejaculation.

VASECTOMY
See *Sterilization*.

VASOCONGESTION
An increase in the amount of blood in body tissues, especially the penis, clitoris and labia during sexual arousal.

VENEREAL DISEASES
See *Sexually transmitted diseases*.

VESTIBULAR GLANDS
See *Bartholin's glands*.

VESTIBULE
The space at the opening of a tube or canal. The vulva is a vestibule receiving the urethral and vaginal openings.

VESTIBULITIS
An inflammation of the vestibular glands on either side of the vaginal entrance, causing severe pain during sexual intercourse.

VIBRATOR
An electrically powered device that when held against the genitals brings about arousal or orgasm through its vibrating action.

VIRGINITY
The physical state of not having experienced sexual intercourse.

VULCANIZATION
A process in the manufacture of rubber that made possible the production of condoms.

VULVA
The external female genitalia. The vulva includes the clitoris, labia majora and labia minora.

W

WITHDRAWAL METHOD
See *Coitus interruptus*.

WOLFFIAN DUCTS
The paired set of ducts found in both male and female fetuses that go on to develop into the epididymis, vas deferens, seminal vesicles and prostate gland in the male fetus.

Y

YOHIMBINE
An aphrodisiac made from the bark of a central African tree. It causes erections in men and arousal in women but causes a dangerous drop in blood pressure.

Z

ZYGOTE
The cell produced when a sperm fertilizes an ovum. It contains all the genetic material necessary to produce a new individual—half from the father's sperm and half from the mother's ovum.

Index

A

Abortion 119
Abstinence 116
Abuse see Child abuse;
    Domestic violence
Acquired immunodeficiency
    syndrome see AIDS
Acrosome 94
Adrenal glands 21–22, 88, 95,
    101, 141
Advanced age 80–84
    grandparenthood and 83
    illness and 83–84
    love in 82–83
    masturbation and 82
    sexual health and 82
    society and 80–81
Affairs 72–73
    casual 36
    gender differences and
    72–73
    male menopause and 79
    partner's reaction to 73
    sexual boredom and 160
AIDS 130–133
    bisexuality and 129
    blood transfusions and 129
    casual sex and 129
    drug users and 129
    hemophilia and 129
    high-risk groups 129
    history of 130
    HIV and 131–133
    homosexuality and 129, 131
    Kaposi's sarcoma 130
    prostitution 129
    related diseases 133
    spread of 131
Alcohol
    low sex drive and 163
    retarded ejaculation and 164
    sexual performance 156–157
Amenorrhea 142–143
    ovarian cysts and 144
    primary 90
    progesterone-only pill (POP)
    and 120
Amyl nitrate 49
Anal sex 66
    chlamydia 135
    condoms 128
    dangers of 66

health risks of 66
hepatitis 66
HIV/AIDS and 129
sexually transmitted
    diseases 66, 126, 128
Androgens 95
    sexuality and 29
Anorexia nervosa
    late menarche and 90
Aphrodisiacs 23, 48–49
Areola 103
Aromatherapy oils 44, 50
Arousal 40–43, 104–105, 108
    alcohol and 156–157
    brain contribution to 87
    female 38, 70, 86, 87, 104–105
    G-spot and 98, 107
    male 38–39, 107–110
    medication and 156
    rate 40
    reflex 87
    see also Foreplay;
    Masturbation
Arthritis 84
Attraction 12–13
    dress and 17
    opposites 15
    physiology of 21–23

B

Babies
Bacterial vaginosis 143
Balanitis 151–152
    symptoms of 152
    treatment of 151–152
Bartholinitis 144
    see also Vestibular glands
Beauty
    perceptions of 16
    stereotypes of 12–13
Benign prostatic hyperplasia
    149–150
Beta-enkephalins 87
Bilateral salpingo-
    oophorectomy 146
Biphasic pill 120
Birth control see Contraception
Bisexuality 17, 31
    HIV/AIDS and 129
Blind dates 24, 26
Blood transfusions 129
Bondage 37

Bone and muscle growth 88
Brain
    arousal 87
    function in love 21–23
    gay 29
    limbic system 21
Breast cancer 78, 147
    hormone replacement
    therapy (HRT) 78
    mammography 147
    mastectomy 103
    self-examination 147
    treatment of 147
Breasts
    breast-feeding 101, 102–103
    girls 88, 89
    male 89
    milk 102–103
    nipples 103
    prolactin 101
    self-examination 147
    structure of 102–103
    uneven development of 90
Bulbourethral glands 93

C

Cancer
    breast 78, 103, 147
    cervical 137, 146
    endometrial 78, 120, 146
    fallopian tube 148
    genital warts link 137
    liver 139
    ovarian 120, 148
    penile 153
    prostate 152
    scrotal 153
    testicular 152–153
    vaginal 148
    vulval 148
Candidiasis
    diabetes and 143
    symptoms of 143
    treatment of 143
Cantharides 49
Cap 122–123
    cervical 122
    sanitary protection and 113
    spermicide and 122
    toxic shock syndrome and
    123
    vault 122

vimule 122
Caressing 42
Casual sex 129
Celibacy 75, 116
Cells of Leydig 93
Cervical cancer 146
    genital warts and 137
    Pap test for 98, 146, 148
    symptoms of 146
    treatment of 146
Cervix 98
    os 98
    prostaglandins and 94
Chakras 56
Chancroid 136
    lymph node swelling 136
    symptoms of 136
    treatment of 136
Children
    grandparents and 83
    trauma and 208, 292
Chlamydia 135–136
Circumcision
    male 92–93
Clitoris 96
    excitement and 104
    glans 96
    masturbation and 38, 96
    oral sex and 64
    orgasm and 107
    sexual intercourse and
    105–107
    stimulators 50–51, 53
Cohabitation 74–75
    marriage deferral and 74
    personal values and 75
    sexual satisfaction and 74
    trial marriage and 74
Coitus interruptus 117
Colostrum 102
Combined pill 120
Communication
    sex life and 54
Condoms 121–123, 128–129
    anal sex and 66
    female 122, 129
    first-time use of 121, 128
    history of 117
    HIV and 117, 121
    sex toys and 50–51
    sexually transmitted
    diseases and 117, 121–122,
    128, 129

using 121
Contraception 116–127
  abortion 119
  abstinence 116
  ancient methods of 116–117
  caps 122–123
  coitus interruptus 116
  condoms 117, 121–122, 129
  diaphragm 117, 122–123
  emergency 125
  future 125–126
  hormone injections 121
  implants 120, 121
  intrauterine device
    (IUD) 78, 118, 123–124
  male pill 124
  menopause and 78
  natural methods of 124–125
  oral contraceptive pill 101,
    118–119
  reliability of 126
  rhythm method 116
  spermicide 124
  sponge 118
  sterilization 126–127
Coronal sulcus 92
Corpus cavernosa 91
Corpus luteum 101
Corpus spongiosum 91
Counseling 172
Courtship feeding 20
Cowper's glands 93
Cramps, menstrual
  see Dysmenorrhea
Cross-dressing 17, 30, 32
Cunnilingus 64, 82
Cystitis 142

D

D&C (dilatation and curettage)
  menorrhagia and 141
Dates
  blind 24, 26
  coworkers and 25
  safety on 25
  sex on first 35
Dating agencies 26
Depression 158
DES, and vaginal cancer 148
Diabetes 84
Diaphragm 117, 122–123
  sanitary protection and 113
  spermicide and 122–123
  toxic shock syndrome
    and 123
Dilatation and curettage see
  D&C

Dildos 38, 39, 50
Disabilities, and sexual
  intercourse 43
Discharge, vaginal 114, 135,
  137, 143, 145, 146, 148
Divorce 72
  adultery and 72–73
  causes of 72
  remarriage and 72
Doggie position 39, 53, 54
Dysmenorrhea 141
  prostaglandins and 141
  symptoms of 141
  treatment of 141

E

Eating disorders
  anorexia nervosa 90
Effleurage 45
Ejaculation 108
  changes with age 79, 81
  delaying 56–57
  first 89–90
  inevitability of 108
  masturbation and 38–39
  nocturnal 90
  orgasm and 35, 108–109
  premature 39, 43, 71
  reflex 87
  sexual intercourse and
    108–110
Emergency contraception 125
Emotions
  gender differences in 35
Endometrial cancer 146
  combined pill and 120
  progestogen and 78
Endometriosis 141
  combined pill protection 120
  symptoms of 145
  treatment of 145
Endometrium 99
Endorphins 21
Epididymis 93, 95
Epinephrine 21–22
Erections 108–110
  assisted 162
  changes with age 78, 81
  foreplay and 40
  length of 91
  masturbation and 38–39
  physiology of 91
  problems with 161, 162,
    171–172
  refractory periods and 56,
    70–71
  soft-entry sex and 57

treatment for insufficiency
    162
  vasocongestion 87
  see also Arousal; Ejaculation;
    Foreplay; Penis
Erogenous zones 41–42
  clitoris 38, 96, 104–107
  glans 92
  nipples 103
Erotica 47–51
  clothing 74
  food 49
  literature 36–37, 47–48
  videos 47–48
Estrogens 101
  menopause 76–77, 101
  menstrual cycle 86, 99
  oral contraceptive pill 101,
    119–121
  puberty 86, 90, 101
Extramarital sex see Affairs;
  Infidelity

F

Fallopian tubes 99
  cancer of 148
  fimbriae 99
  sterilization and 126
Family planning see
  Contraception
Fantasies 36, 51, 172
  masturbation and 38, 51
  sexual 36–37, 51
  sharing 51
  as therapy 172
Father/child bonding 74
Fellatio 64–65
Female disorders 140–148
  amenorrhea 142–143
  bacterial vaginosis 143
  candidiasis 143
  cervical polyps 144
  cystitis 142
  dysmenorrhea 141
  fibroids 143
  irregular menstruation 142
  menorrhagia 141
  ovarian cysts 144
  pelvic inflammatory disease
    120, 135, 136, 141, 144–145
  polycystic ovaries 144
  premenstrual syndrome
    140–141
  uterine polyps 144
  uterine prolapse 145-146
  vaginismus 43, 157, 166–167
  see also Cancer;

Hysterectomy;
    Mastectomy
Female sex organs 96–99
  cervix 98
  clitoris 96
  fallopian tubes 99
  fourchette 97
  G-spot 98
  hymen 97
  labia majora 96–97
  labia minora 97
  ovaries 99–101
  uterus 99
  vagina 96–97
  vestibular glands 98
Fetishism 35
Fibroids 143
Fight or flight response 21
Fimbriae 99
Finding a partner 24–26
First sexual experience
  adolescents 43, 97, 98
Flirting 18–19
Follicle-stimulating hormone
  (FSH) 88–89, 90, 100
Food
  sensual 48–49
Foreplay 40–46, 70–71,
  104–105, 108
  age changes and 81
  fantasies and 51
  masturbation and 39
  oral sex and 65
Foreskin 92–93
  frenulum 92
  hygiene 114, 151
  smegma 92, 114
Forward Bend 60
Fourchette 97
French kissing 42
French letters see Condoms
Frenulum 92
Freud, Sigmund
  on incest 16
  on orgasms 107
  on sexual orientation 30
Friction massage 44
Friendship
  love and 24
Front Kneeling 59
Frustration, sexual 43
FSH see Follicle-stimulating
  hormone

G

G-spot 98, 107
Gay gene 28–29

Gay men
  monogamy 75
  outing 27–28
  secrecy 27
  social network 27
Gay rights 27–28
Gender
  affairs and 72–73
  attitudes 35
  differences 35–37
  orientation 30, 31
  reassignment surgery 32
Genital hygiene 112–114
  female 112–114
  male 114
  male cancers 112
  sanitary protection 113
  vaginal deodorants 112
Genital warts (HPV) 137–138
  cancer link 137
  condoms and 128
  Pap tests and 137
  symptoms of 137
  treatment of 137–138
Genitals
  development in boys 88
  itchiness and 77
  oral sex and 64
  scented wipes and 112
  touching in childhood 38
Girls
  puberty in 88, 90
Glans (clitoris) 96
Glans (penis) 92
  balanitis and 152
  coronal sulcus 92
  sexual intercourse and 108
Gonadotropin-releasing
  hormones (GRH) 89
Gonorrhea 135
  symptoms of 135
  treatment of 135
Graafian follicle 100–101
Grandparenthood 83
GRH see Gonadotropin-
  releasing hormone
Gynecomastia 8–9

H

Hacking massage 45
Hair 13
  facial 89
  pubic 86, 89, 96
Heart disease 83–84
Heavy periods see
  Menorrhagia
Hematocele 151

Hemophilia 129
Hepatitis B 139
  anal sex and 66
Hepatitis C 139
Hermaphroditism 154
Herpes 138–139
Hite reports 35, 36, 64, 78, 80
HIV (human immuno-
  deficiency virus) 130–133
  asymptomatic stage 132-133
  bisexuality and 129
  blood transfusions and 129
  casual sex and 129
  changing sexual behavior
    and 129
  condoms and 114, 121–122
  drug users and 129
  genetic defense against 131
  hemophilia and 129, 131
  heterosexuals and 129
  high-risk groups for 129
  history of 130
  homosexuality and 129, 131
  infection, stages of 132–133
  prevention of 126
  prostitution and 129
  spread of 131
  transmission of 131–133
  treatment for 133
Homophobia 27–28
Homosexuality 13, 27–32
  HIV/AIDS and 129, 131
  marriage and 75
  sexually transmitted
    diseases and 75
  see also Gay men; Gay rights;
    Homophobia; Lesbianism
Hormone replacement therapy
  (HRT) 77–78, 79, 81, 101
  libido and 165
  male 79
Hormones
  after birth 74
  contraceptive 118–121
  estrogen 76–77, 86, 90, 99,
    101
  follicle-stimulating 88–89,
    100, 101
  gonadotropin-releasing 89,
    101
  homosexuality and 29
  luteinizing 88, 100
  menopausal 76–77
  oxytocin 21, 74
  progesterone 78, 86, 99, 101
  prolactin 101
  puberty and 89–90
  sexual desire and 86

somatotropin 88
  testosterone 77, 86, 88–89
HPV see Genital warts
HRT see Hormone replacement
  therapy
Human immunodeficiency
  virus see HIV
Human papillomavirus (HPV)
  see Genital warts
Hydrocele 150–151
Hygiene 112–114
  anal 126
  anal sex and 66
  genital 124–126
  menstrual 126
  oral sex and 65
  sex toys and 50
Hymen 97–98
Hyperarousal, male 71
Hypothalamus 21, 28
  puberty onset 89
Hysterectomy 145, 146
  bilateral salpingo-
    oophorectomy and 146
  radical 146
  sex life and 84

I

Immune system, and
  HIV/AIDS 129, 130–133
Implants, contraceptive 121
Incontinence, stress 77
Infatuation 21, 22
Infertility
  chlamydia and 136
  gonorrhea and 135
  sexually transmitted
    diseases and 126
Inhibitions
  loss with age 70, 76, 78
  reduction in 47
  sex therapy and 169–170
Intercourse see Sexual
  intercourse
Internet
  dating on the 26
Intrauterine device (IUD) 118,
  123–124
  emergency contraception
    125
  Lippes Loop 118
  menopause and 78
  pelvic inflammatory disease
    and 145
  progesterone-containing
    123–124
  side effects 123

Inverted nipples 103
Iron deficiency 141
Irregular menstruation 142
  adolescence and 90
  menopause and 76
IUD see Intrauterine device

J

Jewelry 19–20
Johnnies see Condoms

K

Kaposi's sarcoma, and AIDS
  183
Kinsey reports 31, 34, 35, 66
Kissing 42
  genital 64
  sexually transmitted
    diseases (STDs) 114
Klinefelter's syndrome
  154, 161
Kneeling Entry 58

L

Labia 96–97
  majora 96–97
  minora 97
  swelling of 40
Lactation 101, 102–103
Larynx 89
Laumann report 70, 72, 80
Legs Raised 61
Lesbianism 13, 29, 30–31
  media and 30
  monogamy 75
  political 31
LeVay & Hamer, on
  homosexuality 31
LH see Luteinizing hormone
Libido
  age and 80
  alcohol and 156, 163
  depression and 158
  long-term illness and 157
  low, female 165
  low, male 161
  medication and 81, 156, 161
  menopause and 165
  pregnancy and 70
  psychological problems
    and 73, 157–158, 161, 163,
    165
  rape and 159
  self-esteem and 158–159, 161
  sex therapy and 169–172

sexual abuse and 159, 161
stress and 70, 159
Limbic system 21, 87
see also Hypothalamus
Living together see
Cohabitation
Love 12–32
addiction 21
adult 71
advanced age and 82
course of 71
nervous system and 21–22
see also Infatuation;
Relationships
Low-level Entry 58
Luteinizing hormone (LH) 101
puberty and 88–89, 90, 101
Lying 82–83
Lymph node swelling 136, 137

M

Makeup 20
Male disorders
of the penis 151–152
of the prostate 149–150, 152
of the scrotum 153
of the testicles 149–151,
152–153
Male sex organs
penis 88–89, 91, 93,
105–110, 151, 152, 153
prostate gland 89, 90, 93,
136, 149–150
scrotum 88–89, 93, 150–151
testicles 93, 95, 150, 153
Male sexual problems 161–164
erection problems 161–163
low libido 161
premature ejaculation 39, 43,
71, 163–164
reduced sex drive 161
retarded ejaculation 164
Mammography 147
Man-on-top sexual positions
39, 52–53, 58, 62
Marriage 72–73
brokers 26
homosexual 75
parenthood and 74
reasons for 72
roles in 74
society's perception of 72
stress in 72
uncertainty in 72
Massage 42, 44–46
Mastectomy 103, 147
Masters and Johnson 104, 170

Masturbation 38–39
advanced age and 82
ejaculation and 38–39
foreplay and 39
during intercourse 39
mutual 39, 172
postcoital 39
as therapy 169, 172
Matchmaking 26
Medications
sex drive and 81, 156
Menarche 89, 90
late 90, 142
Menopause 76–77
age of 76
contraception and 78
hormones and 76
irregular periods at 76
libido and 165
male 79
premature 145
symptoms of 76–77
see also Postmenopause
Menorrhagia 141
clotting and 114
fibroids and 143
Menstrual cycle
sterilization and 121
see also Menstruation;
Premenstrual syndrome
Menstruation
blood clots during 114
cramps during 141
heavy 114, 141, 143
hygiene during 114
irregular 90, 143, 144
pain during 145
pelvic inflammatory disease
and 145
progesterone and 101
puberty and 88
sanitary protection during
112–113
see also Amenorrhea;
Menarche; Menorrhagia;
Ovulation; Premenstrual
syndrome
Midlife crises
male 76, 78–79
menopause and 76–78
Middle age 76–79
Missionary position 39, 52–53,
62
Monogamy 75
Monophasic pill 164
Morning-after pill 120
Mother/child bonding 74
Motherhood 74

Multiple orgasms 35, 107
age and 70
Multiple relationships
HIV/AIDS and 129
Mumps 150
Myometrium 99

N

Nail painting 20
Natural contraception
rhythm method 116, 124
withdrawal method 125
Nervous system 21–22
Nightwear 48
Nipples 103
areola 103
as erogenous zones 103
inverted 103
orgasm and 107
Nocturnal emissions 90
Nongonococcal urethritis
135–136
see also Chlamydia
Nonorgasmic resolution 105
Nonoxynol-9 126, 128
allergy to 126, 128
Nonpenetrative sex 42–43
pregnancy and 74
Nonspecific urethritis (NSU)
135–136
see also Chlamydia
Norepinephrine 20–21
NSU see Nonspecific urethritis
Nymphomania 36

O

Old age see Advanced age
Oophorectomy 84
Opposites, attraction of 15,
119–120
Oral contraceptive pill
amenorrhea and 142
combined pill 120
health risks and 78, 119, 120,
121
progesterone-only pill 120
Oral sex 64–65
chlamydia and 135
condoms and 128
cunnilingus 64, 82
fellatio 64–65
herpes and 65
hygiene and 65
mutual 65
Orgasms 42–43
age and 70–71, 77

duration of 105–107
female 34–35, 55, 70, 71,
105–107
frequency of 70, 71
lack of 34, 167, 168
male 35, 108, 110
male v. female 108
multiple 35
nonpenetrative sex and
42–43
prostaglandins and 94
sex toys and 50
therapy 172
vaginal contractions 106–107
vibrators 168
see also Masturbation; Sexual
intercourse
Osteoporosis 78
Ova 100–101
production of 99, 100–101
Ovarian cancer 148
combined pill protection
and 120
Ovarian cysts 144
combined pill protection
and 120
Ovaries 99
development of 100
estrogen 99
progesterone 99
see also Ova; Ovulation
Ovulation 99, 100–101
corpus luteum 101
Graafian follicle 100–101
rhythm method and 124
sterilization and 127
Oxytocin 21
after birth 74

P

Pap tests 148
cervical cancer 98, 146, 148
genital warts and 137
Parametrium 99
Parenthood
marital changes 73–74
Partnerships see Relationships
PC muscles see Pubococcygeal
muscles
PEA (phenylethylamine) 21
Pelvic inflammatory disease
(PID) 144–145
chlamydia and 136
combined pill protection
and 120
complications of 145
dysmenorrhea and 141

gonorrhea and 135
infertility and 135
symptoms of 135
treatment of 135
Penis 91–92
cancer 153
detumescence 110
foreskin 92–93
glans 92, 151–152
phimosis 152
puberty 88–89
sexual intercourse 107–110
shaft 91–93
see also Ejaculation; Erections
Perimenopause 76–77
Perineum 66
Periods see Amenorrhea;
   Dysmenorrhea;
   Menorrhagia; Menstruation
Personal hygiene 40, 112–114
Petrissage 45
Peyronie's disease 91
Phenylethylamine see PEA
Pheromones 19, 22–23, 49–50
Phimosis 152
Physiology of attraction 21–23
PID see Pelvic inflammatory
   disease
Pill see Oral contraceptive pill
Pituitary gland 89, 95, 101
PMS see Premenstrual
   syndrome
Polycystic ovaries 144
POP see Progesterone-only pill
Pornography 36–37, 47–48
Positions, sexual 52–55
Postcoital pill 58–63
Postmenopause 81
Postoperative sexual
   intercourse 84
Pregnancy
   body changes during 73
   emotional changes during
      73
   fear of 165
   fibroids and 143
   glow of 73
   libido and 73
   progesterone and 101
   sex after 73
   testing 101
Premarital sex 36
Premature ejaculation 39, 43,
   62, 71
   treating 163–164
Premenstrual syndrome (PMS)
   140–141
   treatment for 101, 140

Primary amenorrhea 90
Progesterone 100, 102
   intrauterine device and 102,
      123–124
   oral contraceptive pill and
      102, 119–121
Progesterone-only pill (POP)
   120
Progestogen 78, 86
   endometrial cancer
      prevention and 78
Prolapse 81, 145-146
Promiscuity 36, 158
Prostaglandins 94, 141
Prostate gland 93, 149
   anal sex 66
   benign prostatic hyperplasia
      149–150
   cancer of 152
   chlamydia and 136
   enlarged 149–150
   examination of 149
   gonorrhea and 135
   prostatitis and 150
Prostatitis 150
Prostitution
   HIV/AIDS and 129
Psychological problems, and
   libido 157–158
Puberty 88–90
   age of 88
   bone and muscle growth
      at 88
   boys and 88–90
   girls and 88, 90
Pubic hair
   female 86, 90
   male 86, 89
Pubic lice 138
Pubococcygeal (PC) muscles
   57, 146

R

Rear-entry sexual positions 39.
   53–54, 58, 60
Rectum 66, 115, 136
Reflex arousal 87
Refractory periods 40, 56,
   70–71, 110
Reiter's syndrome 136
Relationship counseling 172
   infidelity and 73
   marriage and 70–71
   menopause and 79
Relationships
   psychological problems in
      157–158

sexual therapy in 169–172
Religion
   dating and 26
   and psychosexual problems
      157
Remarriage
   rates 72
Resting Position 58
Retarded ejaculation 164
Retroverted uterus 99
Rhythm method 116, 124
Rubbers see Condoms

S

Safer sex 128–129
Same-sex play
   children and 27
Sanitary protection
   caps 113
   diaphragms 113
   sanitary napkins 113
   sponges 113
   tampons 113
Scent signals 19, 22, 23, 49–50
Scrotum 93
   cancer of 153
   hematocele 151
   hydrocele 150–151
   at puberty 88–89
   swollen 150–151
   varicocele 151
Sebum 23, 101
Secondary sexual
   characteristics
   female 101
   male 88
Self-mimicry, sexual 86
Semen 94, 108
   mitochondria 94
   production 93
   prostaglandins 94
   see also Ejaculation; Sperm
Seminal fluid see Semen
Seminal vesicles 93, 135
Seminiferous tubules 93
Sequential orgasms 35
Serial monogamy 75
Sex
   drive see Libido
   flush 105, 110
   reducing inhibitions about
      47, 156–157
   therapy 169–172
   toys 50–51
Sex-change operations 32
Sexual abnormalities 154
   hermaphroditism 154

Klinefelter's syndrome 154
   Turner's syndrome 154
Sexual abuse 159
Sexual fantasies 36, 51, 172
   female 37
   male 36–37
   masturbation and 38
   as therapy 172
Sexual intercourse
   advanced age and 81–84
   after birth 73
   cohabiting and 75
   disability and 43, 83–84
   ejaculation and 108–110
   fantasies and 51
   first time 36, 43, 97–98
   first date and 35
   frustration 43
   HIV/AIDS and 129, 130–133
   painful 98, 99, 166
   Pap tests and 98, 137, 146,
      148
   positions 39, 52–55,
      advanced positions 60–61
      popular variations 58–59
      pregnancy and 63
      sexual healing 62
   postoperative 84
   pregnancy and 43, 55, 73
   premarital 36
   soft-entry 57
   Tantric 56
   Taoist 56–57
   unprotected 114–115
   see also Conception;
      Contraception; Fertility;
      Sexually transmitted
      diseases
Sexual orientation 27
   Freud, Sigmund on 30
   parenting influence on 30
   see also Homosexuality
Sexual responses 104–110
   alcohol and 156
   female 70, 104–107
   long-term illness and 157
   male 70–71, 107–108
   medication and 156–157
   stages of 104
Sexual trauma 159
Sexuality see Bisexuality;
   Gender; Homosexuality;
   Lesbianism; Sexual
   responses
Sexually transmitted diseases
   (STDs) 130–139
   anal sex and 66, 114
   chancroid 136

checkups for 112
chlamydia 115, 128, 129, 135–136
clinics 115
common 138
condoms and 121–122, 128–129
counseling and 127
diagnosis of 127
foreign travel and 127
genital warts 128
gonorrhea 114, 116, 135
hepatitis 66, 139
herpes 65, 128, 138–139
HIV/AIDS 66, 129, 130–133
homosexuality and 75
infertility and 114
kissing and 114
lymphatic system and 137
mother/baby transfer of 114, 129, 135, 136
nonspecific urethritis 135–136
oral sex and 65, 114
pubic lice 138
sex toys and 50
syphilis 114, 134–135
trichomoniasis 115, 134–135
Shaft, penile 91–92
Shallow thrusting 57
Sheaths see Condoms
Side-by-side sexual positions 55, 58, 63
Singles events 25–26
Sitting sexual positions 54, 59, 61
Sixty-nine sexual position 65
Smegma 92, 114
Smoking
health and 79
Soaps, vaginal hygiene 112
Soft-entry sex 57
Somatotropin 89
Spanish fly 49
Sperm 94–95
acrosome 94
mitochondria and 94
production of 93, 94–95
types 95
see also Ejaculation; Semen
Spermarche 89, 90
Spermatids 94
Spermatocytes 94
Spermatogenesis 94
Spermicides 124
caps and 122
nonoxynol-9 124, 128
Sponges 113, 118

Spoons sexual position 55
Standing sexual positions 54, 60
Staphylococcus aureus see Toxic shock syndrome
STDs see Sexually transmitted diseases
Stepparents see Remarriage
Sterilization 126–128
Stress 159
libido and 72, 159
in long-term relationships 72
Stress incontinence 77
uterine prolapse 146
Suspended Congress 60
Sweat 45, 94, 267
Swing-Rocking 61
Syphilis 134
complications of 134
first stage of 134
history of 134
prevention of 114
second stage of 134
symptoms of 134
third stage of 135
treatment of 135

T

Tampons 113
changing 113
insertion of 113
scented 112
toxic shock syndrome and 114
Tantric sex 56–57
Tantric Tortoise 61
Tattooing 19–20
Tenting 105
Testicles 93
cancer of 152–153
cells of Leydig 93
epididymis 93, 95
loss of 95
mumps 150
orchitis 150
scrotum 93
self-examination of 153
seminiferous tubules 93
swollen 150
torsion of 150
undescended 150
vas deferens 93, 95, 148
see also Scrotum; Sperm
Testosterone 86, 88–89, 93, 95
Therapy
counseling 172

Three Feet on the Ground 60
Touching
caressing 42
cuddle chemical 21, 74
erotic 40–46
genitals see Masturbation
Toxic shock syndrome 113, 114
caps and 123
diaphragms and 123
symptoms of 114
tampons and 113
Transsexualism 32
Transvestism 32
Trichomoniasis 136–137
balanitis and 151
symptoms of 137
treatment of 137
Triphasic pill 120
Turner's syndrome 154
Twins
pheromones and 23

U

Underage sex 36
Underwear
erotic 48
hygiene and 114
Undescended testes 151
Unrequited love 22
Urethra 91, 96, 142
Uterine polyps 144
Uterine prolapse 81, 145–146
treatment for 146
Uterus 99
during arousal 106
enlargement at puberty 90
during menstruation 141
retroverted 99
structure of 99
see also Female disorders; Hysterectomy; Uterine prolapse

V

Vagina 96, 97, 98
beneficial bacteria in 112
cancer of 148
changes in advanced age 81
deodorants and 112
discharge 114, 135, 137, 143, 145, 146, 148
dryness 77, 81, 166
excitement and 104–107
hygiene 112, 114
lubrication 40, 97, 98, 144
sexual intercourse 104–107

tenting 105
see also Female disorders
Vaginismus 43, 157, 166–167
Varicocele 151
Vas deferens 93, 97
Vasectomy 127
reversal 172
Vasocongestion, during arousal 87
Vault caps 122
Venereal disease see Sexually transmitted diseases
Vestibular glands 98
Vibrators 50, 168
Vimule caps 122
Violence see Domestic violence
Virginity 36
hymen 97
see also First sexual experience
Vulval cancer 148

W

Weddings 172
see also Marriage
Wet dreams 90
Withdrawal bleed 120
Withdrawal method, natural contraception 125
see also Coitus interruptus
Woman-on-top sexual positions 39, 53, 55, 62
Womb see Uterus

Y

Yab Yum 59
Yawning Position 59
Yeast infections 143, 151–152
vaginal hygiene and 112, 114
Yohimbine 49

Acknowledgments

Additional editorial assistance
Nigel Cawthorne, Richard Dawes, Stephanie Driver, Richard Emerson, Madeleine Jennings, Joel Levy, David McCandless, Linda A. Olup, Laura Price, Jo Stanford, Deirdre Wilkins, Ian Wood
Illustrators Jane Cradock-Watson, John Geary, Tony Graham, Pond & Giles, John Temperton, Halli Verrinder, Paul Williams
Picture researcher Sandra Schneider
Makeup artists Bettina Graham, Kym Menzies
Proofreader Clare Hacking
Indexer Derek Copson
Clothing and equipment suppliers
Berlex Laboratories, Inc., Boots the Chemists Ltd., Hoechst Marion Roussel, Owen Mumford Ltd. Medical Division, Solvay Pharmaceuticals, Inc., The Upjohn Company, Wyeth Laboratories
Photograph sources American Board of Sexology 261
Archive Photos 233 (*bottom*: Reuters/Eric Gaillard)
AKG London 49 (*top*: Lessing), 257 (*second from top*)
Angela Hampton Family Life Pictures 16 (*bottom*), 263, 265 (*top*), 268, 280
Bert Torchia 257 (*third from top*)
Biophoto Associates 120 (*top*), 120 (*bottom*), 127 (*right*), 130 (*all images*)
Bridgman Art Library, London 14 (Maternity by Maurice Asselin/Galerie L'Ergastere, Paris), 70 (Johnson Album no.17 item 6, Ahmad Khan Bangash/British Library, London), 73 (prince and lady/private collection), 75 (*top*: The Orgy by Paul Cezanne/ private collection), 83 (*bottom*: dancing Shiva/Oriental Museum, Durham University), 229 (*top*: Lovers from the Poem of the Pillow by Kitagawa Utamaro/British Library, London; also page 7), 244 (portrait of Oscar Wilde/Stapleton Collection)
Bruce Coleman 180 (*bottom*: Werner Layer)
Computerized Matchmaking Online 261
Corbis-Bettmann/UPI 243 (*top*), 257 (*bottom*), 291, 296 (*bottom*)
David Murray 30 (*top*)
Digital Playground 261
Dr. R. Given-Wilson, Consultant Radiologist, St. George's Hospital NHS Trust 131 (*left*)
Eye Ubiquitous 42 (*top*)
Frank Spooner 157, 162 (*top*: Jacques Prayer), 251 (Hemssey/Liaison), 294

(Bernstein/Spooner)
Gaze 49 (*bottom*: Sunil Gupta)
Giles Duley 110
Hutchison Library 225 (*bottom*: Sarah Errington)
Image Bank 44 (*top*: Werner Bokelburg), 59 (*bottom*: David Delossy), 77 (*top*: David Delossy), 106 (Jay Freis), 109 (Real Life), 236 (Maria Taglienti), 243 (*bottom*: Marc Romanelli), 249 (Jeff Cadge)
Images Colour Library 30 (*bottom, center*), 228 (*right*)
Images of Africa 227 (David Keith Jones)
Mary Evans Picture Library 11, 13 (*bottom*), 18 (*bottom*), 31 (*right*; also page 6), 78 (*top*), 91 (*left*), 160, 162 (*bottom*), 225 (*top*), 254 (*bottom*)
Michael Marsland, Yale University 26
Mitchell Beazley 259 (James Merrell)
Mirror Syndication 260
National Cancer Institute 50 (*top*)
Niall McInerney 35 (*far right*), 35 (*third from right*), 39 (*all except main pic*), 65 (*right*)
Oxford Scientific Films 45 (*bottom right*: Gerd Pennel/Okapia)
Pictorial Press 35 (*main pic*), 39 (*main pic*), 95 (*main pic*), 95 (*third from right*)
Rex Features 13 (*top*), 17, 30 (*bottom right*), 41 (*bottom, right*), 48 (*bottom*), 54 (*top*), 57 (*bottom*), 65 (*left*), 65 (*center*), 159, 219, 223, 234, 237 (*top*), 239 (*all pics*), 245, 254 (*top*), 275, 284, 286 (*top*), 287
Science Museum/Science and Society Picture Library 161 (sponge, douche and sheep-gut condom)
Science Photo Library 43 (*top*: Alfred Pasieka), 44 (*bottom*: David Parker), 85 (Eye of Science), 93 (*right*: Prof. P. Motta/Dept. of Anatomy/University "La Sapienza," Rome), 114 (Princess Margaret Rose Orthopaedic Hospital), 119 (*top*: CNRI), 119 (*bottom*: Alain Dex, Publiphoto Diffusion), 120 (*center*: Astrid & Hans-Frieder Michler), 122 (*top*: Petit Format/CSI), 122 (*bottom*: John Walsh; also page 6 and 115), 123 (Sidney Moulds), 124 (BSIP VEM), 125 (*top*: Prof. P. Motta & E. Vizza), 125 (*center and bottom*: Astrid & Hans-Frieder), 126, 127 (*left*: Petit Format/Nestle), 127 (*bottom*: Manfred Kage), 128 (Neil Bromhall), 131 (*center and right*: King's College School of Medicine), 146 (*both images*: Biophoto Associates), 148 (*left*: Francis Leroy, Biocosmos), 148 (*right*: CNRI), 149 (J. Croyle/Custom Medical Stock Photo), 152 (*top and bottom*: James King-Holmes), 153

(*top*: Dr. Tony Brain), 155 (John Meyer/Custom Medical Stock Photo), 156 (*top left, center left* and *bottom*: Hank Morgan), 156 (*top right*: James King-Holmes), 156 (*center right*: D. Phillips), 158 (*left*: Richard Rawlins/Custom Medical Stock Photo), 158 (*right*: Hank Morgan), 163 (*top*: Sidney Moulds), 163 (*bottom left*: Alfred Pasieka), 177 (*top*: Hank Morgan), 180 (*top*: Vanessa Vick), 181 (*third from left*: Alex Bartel), 182 (NIBSC), 184 (*top*: Alfred Pasieka), 184 (*bottom left*: CNRI), 184 (*bottom right*: Jean-Loup Charmet), 187 (*bottom left*: Biology Media), 188 (E. Gray), 189 (*bottom left*: Astrid & Hans-Frieder Michler), 194 (*bottom*: Z. Binor/Custom Medical Stock Photo), 198 (*top and bottom right*), 199 (*right*), 201 (*top and bottom*), 248 (*top*: Saturn Stills), 250 (Keith/Custom Medical Stock Photo), 272 (Dr. R. Dourmashkin)
Simon & Schuster 16 (*top*: reprinted with the permission of Simon & Schuster from THE MOUNTAIN PEOPLE by Colin M. Turnbull. Copyright © 1972 by Colin M. Turnbull)
Tate Gallery, London 59 (*top*)
Telegraph Colour Library 279
The Cameron Life Collection 95 (*far right*)
The Kobal Collection 12, 57 (*top*), 233 (*top*), 255, 262 (*top*)
The Royal College of Physicians of London 257 (*top*)
The Stockmarket 3 (*right*), 15, 33, 45 (*center*), 50 (*bottom*), 91 (*bottom right*), 95 (*second from right*), 102, 211, 223, 226, 229 (*all pics surrounding main pic except penis sheath*), 231, 237 (*bottom*), 278, 290
The Wellcome Institute Library, London 161 (tortoiseshell condoms)
Thomas L. Kelly 30 (*bottom left*), 53, 176, 224
Toni & Guy Artistic Team 35 (*second from right*), 35 (*bottom*)
Tony Stone Images 3 (*left*), 32, 46, 47, 48 (*top*), 54 (*bottom*), 113, 153 (*bottom*), 169 (*bottom*), 181 (*second from left*), 215 (*top*), 229 (*bottom main pic*), 242, 248 (*bottom*), 273, 274 (also page 8), 276 (*top*), 283, 295, 296 (*top*)
Trip 24 (H. Rogers), 228 (*left*: H. Rogers), 229 (*third from right*: J. Sweeney), 238 (Dinodia), 240 (J. Stanley), 288 (B. Turner)
Tropix 20 (D. Jenkin), 29 (*bottom*: I. Sheldrick), 43 (*bottom, left*: Craig Duncan)
Werner Forman Archive (Private Collection) 29 (*top*)